THE WRITER'S LEGAL AND BUSINESS GUIDE

THE WRITER'S LEGAL AND BUSINESS GUIDE

Compiled and Edited by Norman Beil

A Presentation
of the Beverly Hills Bar Association Barristers
Committee for the Arts

ARCO PUBLISHING, INC.
NEW YORK

Published by Arco Publishing, Inc.
215 Park Avenue South, New York, N.Y. 10003

Copyright © 1984 by The Beverly Hills Bar Association Barristers
Committee for the Arts

Library of Congress Cataloging in Publication Data
Main entry under title:

The Writer's legal and business guide.
   "A presentation of the Beverly Hills Bar Association
Barristers, Committee for the Arts."
   Bibliography: p.
   Includes index.
   1. Authors and publishers—Legal status, laws, etc.—
United States. 2. Authors—Legal status, laws, etc.—
United States. 3. Authors—Taxation—Law and legislation
—United States. I. Beil, Norman. II. Beverly Hills
Bar Association Barristers. Committee for the Arts.
KF3084.Z9W74   1983   346.7304′82   83-15832
ISBN 0-668-05579-0 (Reference Text)   347.306482
ISBN 0-668-05582-0 (Paper Edition)

Printed in the United States of America

10 9 8 7 6 5 4 3 2 1

Contents

MONEY AND THE WRITER

APPENDIX

Preface

Writing is an art. Writers use their imagination and craftsmanship, talent and discipline to create ideas, shape plots, develop characters, present and resolve conflict; and to capture it all on the written page so that others may experience, enjoy, laugh and learn.

But writers do more. They also submit manuscripts, "take" meetings, sign contracts, copyright works, argue with collaborators, humor producers, hire lawyers, change agents, expose ideas, avoid lawsuits, join guilds, pay taxes, seek work, collect unemployment and plan their careers. Writing is also a business.

This book was designed to give you, the writer, a handle on the business side of your art; whether you find this side of your career fascinating or aggravating, you must deal with it. This book is an attempt to make your life a little easier, whether you write books or screenplays or write for television. It is a nuts-and-bolts survival guide to the business and the law of writing. Surrounding yourself with an entourage of agents, lawyers, accountants and managers is no substitute for being personally aware of the environment in which you pursue your career. In order to deal intelligently with and get the most out of your advisers, you must have a working knowledge of your profession. Your advisers can advise, but only you can make the decisions.

The material is presented to be understandable to the beginning writer. However, the articles are thorough and detailed, and so can be used as a valuable reference by more experienced writers, as well as by their agents, lawyers and managers.

This book is unique, I believe, in its recognition that many writers today cross over from the world of publishing to that of movies, and to television, as well. All three arenas are covered extensively. Moreover, the individual chapters are written by experts in their respective fields. These are the people who deal with these matters on a day-to-day

basis, and so are able to provide the most up-to-date information and the most practical advice.

The *Business of Writing* section provides an overview of the motion picture, television (including the new television media), and publishing industries, and an introduction to agents and the Writers Guild of America.

The *Practical Legal Guide* section covers copyright law, the protection of ideas, and liability for defamation and invasion of privacy. These are fascinating areas of the law and the articles here are quite interesting. However, the emphasis is on the practical—what to do.

This is a business of relationships, both personal and contractual. In the *Contracts* section, you will learn how the contractual process works and will be introduced to basic contract law. You will learn why you must read your contracts, and this section will help you do so with a greater understanding of what they mean and what may be negotiable. Standard contracts for motion pictures and book publishing deals are analyzed. Understanding these contracts can provide valuable insight into the inner workings of these industries.

A thorough article on the Minimum Basic Agreement of the Writers Guild explains its complex provisions in detail and with clarity. Your contractual relationship with your agent is also explained.

Money and the Writer includes an introduction to taxes (with specific tips for writers) and a helpful article on the special problems writers face in collecting unemployment benefits.

The book concludes with a directory of service organizations for writers and a bibliography.

This book was written specifically for initial distribution at the Third Annual Symposium for Writers, presented by the Beverly Hills Bar Association, Barristers Committee for the Arts. The topics for the book were selected after the editorial board had a chance to discuss the informational needs of writers with dozens of writers, agents and lawyers.

An extensive review of the current literature available to writers was made and a log was compiled at the Writers Guild of the most frequently asked questions. Specific articles were then commissioned to be written by specialists in their fields. This is truly a collaborative work, with over fifty individuals making contributions to this book in one way or another. The views expressed by the authors of the articles are not necessarily those of the Beverly Hills Bar Association, the Committee for the Arts or the editorial board.

Thanks must first go to the authors who have each spent countless hours researching, writing and rewriting their articles. No fees were paid for articles. They were contributed purely from a desire to help. I'd also like to thank the editorial board: Alan Abrams, Carol Faber, Mary Ann Gilmour, Larry Marks, Karen Green Rosin and Jackie Snyder, who helped find contributors, edited and proofread articles, and attended to the countless details that go into a work of this nature. Personal thanks must go to Mark Halloran, for setting a standard of excellence with his *Musician's Manual: A Practical Guide to Your Career*; and to Ron Nolte, for patiently and generously sharing his considerable expertise of writers' deals.

Others who helped and deserve thanks include Diane Isaacs, Marc Pariser, Bob Goodman, Victoria Hochberg, Cooder Greenfield, Melinda Benedek, Larry Rubin, Larry Blake, George Eichen, Jane Ilsa Bunkin, June Baldwin, Wheeler Coberly, Blanche Baker, Kevin Funk, Ron Dyas, Steve Linkon, Syd Field, Ken Levine, David Isaacs, Alan Thaler and Nan Waldman.

A special thanks must go to the William Morris Agency, and the law firms of Mitchell, Silberberg & Knupp; Kaplan, Livingston, Goodwin, Berkowitz & Selvin; Manatt, Phelps, Rothenberg & Tunney; Pacht, Ross, Warne, Bernhard & Sears; and Freshman, Mulvaney, Marantz, Comsky, Forst, Kahan & Deutsch for the use of their word processing and photocopying facilities. This book would not have been possible without their generous contributions in this regard.

THE
WRITER'S
LEGAL AND
BUSINESS
GUIDE

The Business of Writing

DAY/INT. HOLLYWOOD PARTY.   CUT TO Hollywood party in impressive
home. Typical, as usual we hear snatches of dialogue.

CUT TO   DON
                    Will you take a meeting with him? I'll take
                    a meeting with you if you'll take a meeting
                    with Freddie.

                                AL
                    I took a meeting with Freddie -- Freddie
                    took a meeting with Charlie -- you take a
                    meeting with him.

                                DON
                    All the good meetings are taken.

CUT TO   PHIL
                    What'd it do?

                                VIC
                    Domestically it did fifteen million --
                    abroad it did eight million.

                                PHIL
                    Twenty-three million -- what was the break-
                    even?

                                VIC
                    Thirty-four million -- so it just lost eleven
                    but I think it was the theme -- life.

CUT TO   CAROL
                    He was her gynecologist, they fell in love,
                    then he produced her record album, then he
                    produced her movie, then he directed her
                    movie, and they all lost money so now he's
                    back treating her for monilia.

CUT TO   PAUL
                    Right now it's only a notion, but I think
                    I can get money to make it into a concept
                    and then later turn it into an idea.

                                ALVY
                    Max, why didn't you tell me it was Tony
                    Lacey's party?

                                ROB
                    What's the difference?

                                ALVY
                    I think he has a thing for Annie.

Motion Pictures

David Freeman

Here in the land of famous car washes and forgotten children, there is a way of business and life called development. Until you understand the rules of this game, you will not understand what it is like to be a screenwriter.

Much has been said about the lowly place of the screenwriter in the pecking order, all of it true, particularly compared to the director and the star. Compared to the rest of the universe, however, "screenwriter" carries a big fee and temporary honor. The "temporary" is the key.

A studio feels obligated to release fifteen to twenty films a year. To do this, it commissions many, many scripts. Some production chiefs believe in what they call "casting a wide net."

At a wide-net studio, it is often said that an established writer can get his grocery list into development. The point of the wide-net school is to develop everything you can and hope for the best. Other, more cautious, organizations try to be certain that they want to make the film before they commission the script. More sensible, you say? Maybe, but there is no discernible difference in the records, financial or aesthetic, between the two schools of thought.

At any given time, your wide-net studio can have over 100 script ideas in various stages of development. This means that a first draft is being written, a set of revisions is being composed, a director or a

David Freeman is a screenwriter and a playwright who lives in Hollywood and is himself in development. This chapter is excerpted from "The Great American Screenplay Competition," which appeared in Esquire, *June 1980. Reprinted with permission. Copyright © 1980 David Freeman. All rights reserved.*

star is being sought. You get the idea. So you think, fifteen out of 100. Rough but not impossible. Wrong! First, all 100 don't stay in development for a whole year. As many as 180 might pass through development in a year. And a few of the fifteen to twenty films come not from development but as fully assembled packages—a star, a director, and a script. Some are acquired fully shot—financed by others and distributed by the studio. So the chances of a script written through development actually getting into the theaters with the studio's logo on it are in some statistical nether land.

Now what happens to the many, many losing scripts, the ones that died in development and were made into scratch pads and fertilizer? Did the screenwriters have to give back the money they were paid? Did they have to apologize and hang their heads in shame? No, yes, and maybe. What happens to these scripts, these unplucked flowers, is nothing. Nothing happens to them. Oh, there are a lot of phone calls and desperate attempts to revive these projects. But, mostly, nothing happens. Except, of course, the writer doesn't have to give the money back. In fact, he or she can raise the price of the next unproduced script.

Thus it is that a subculture has sprung up in Hollywood, this city of forgotten promises and famous parking lot attendants: people who make a lot of money and who never, or rarely, have their scripts made into films. They are in great demand. Oh, there's an emotional price to be paid, but the bucks just keep going up, from one deserted project to the next. Now the money part (what you've all been waiting for, brutish, vulgar lot that you are): We are not talking David Rockefeller here, but we are speaking of jokers who make between $100,000 and $150,000 a year, and that's conservative, with minimally visible film results. Granted, there are not thousands of such people, but there are, I would guess, over 100. There were over 18,000 scripts and "literary properties" registered with the Writers Guild in 1979 and over 35,000 guild contracts—that is where money, real money, changed hands. Now this includes television, but, then, what doesn't? Studios often spend $10 million a year on development. From 1980 to 1981, one major studio is rumored to be spending $20 million on all phases of development. The vast majority of what is developed will not be filmed.

Every producer and every studio has a director of development, or some such title. Screenwriter Steve Gordon calls these people "developists." Many developists want to be screenwriters so they can later want to be directors or producers. Their job is to get ideas into development. They are, collectively, doing a hell of a job.

Most scripts that succeed are in an observable tradition—a romance, a comedy, a mystery. This means the story will sound like a movie to begin with, but not too much so. Alfred Hitchcock always said, "Oh, no, that's how they do it in the movies. Let's do it the way it is in life." Of course, then Sir Alfred did it as in the movies, only better. So your arena and primary relationship should be fresh, funny, touching, or whatever, and original but not so original that it's baffling to someone who controls millions of dollars. Millions-of-dollars controllers tend to be conservative. If you want to write *El Topo*, don't do it in Burbank.

There have been a number of books written about scriptwriting—sort of guidebooks in the do-it-yourself tradition. They all seem to have titles such as *Write That Script!* or *Let's Go!—Hollywood on 200 Thou a Year*. There are even, I'm told, such places as movie colleges, where one can take an advanced degree in it all. One of the script books, *Screenplay*, by Syd Field, a well-known story editor, recently passed through my hands. The volume, written in something purporting to be English, is—surprise, surprise—not bad. It's full of common sense, an uncommon commodity, and you can learn a thing or two from it.

I will tell you how I learned the rudiments of scriptwriting, when I decided to do it myself. I wangled copies of professional screenplays. A lot of them. (Remember, hustling is fun. Shameful, sinful,

but fun.) And from them I learned the form. The rest is equal parts common sense (no to a story about cavemen set in the Himalayas, yes to a passionate love story between a boy and a girl set in modern San Francisco. Get it?) and mystery (the ability to duplicate speech and create character; to tell a lot, using few words; to create images that at once mystify and explain, that tell a complex story and seem to be simple). You're on your own there, but it's possible to do. It's not a high calling, but it has its rewards.

Jerome Coopersmith, a screenwriter of skill, has written a booklet on screenplay and teleplay form. It tells you all you need to know about spacing, margins, and the like. I think he wrote it because he got tired of people endlessly asking him how a screenplay looks. It's available from the Writers Guild East, 555 West 57th Street, New York. It's $2.50, and it's a bargain.

There are four major categories of screenplays: originals, assigned material, adaptations, and revisions and rewrites. These categories slide into one another, and each is bound up with politics and money.

An *original* can be done speculatively or on assignment. On spec, it's just you and your idea off somewhere, plugging away. When you're done, you put it on the market hoping for the best. If you sell it, you can make a killing and probably a movie. Scripts acquired complete, even from novices, frequently sell for what the columns like to call "six figures" and for what the rest of us call a pile of money. Of course, most don't sell at all. If possible, make a deal before you write. You'll get less, but you'll be assured of getting something, and often it will still be quite a lot.

Now, to get an *assignment* to write a script of your choice is no small achievement. You have to persuade a producer or a studio that your idea, your private dream of a movie, is in the producer's or the studio's aesthetic and mercantile interest. This is called pitching. You go to an office or a restaurant and you tell your story the best you can. Mel Brooks is famous for pitching. He's been known to jump on desks, upset furniture, and kiss vice-presidents. When you're Mel Brooks, give it a shot. In the meantime, Paul Schrader, a man who has pitched with some success, says, "Have a strong early scene, preferably the opening, a clear but simple spine to the story, one or two killer scenes, and a clear sense of the evolution of the main character or central relationship. And an ending. Any more gets in the way."

Now, if you've been able to persuade the producer or the studio and strike a deal, you must be ready to give up some rights. You now have a partner, and you're accepting his checks, so compromises are in order. Cooking up a script means endless choices and decisions. No two people will agree on everything, unless one of them isn't listening. Sometimes the ideas are imposed on you, sometimes they are mutually agreed upon. Often they seem petty, and they may come from the producer's maid, mistress, gunsel, or just from malice. You must field everyone. It's a collaborative medium. If you don't have any political or diplomatic instincts and don't feel able to develop them, go into another line of work.

An *adaptation* usually means writing from a literary source of identifiable origin—a novel, a play, a short story. A producer or a studio acquires a worst seller and hires a bandit to write a screenplay. Movies frequently used to be dramatized novels, and many of the films you love best began as something else, as in "It's okay, but the book was much better." Does an adaptation of this sort make the screenwriter more of a technician than anything else? Maybe, but the transformation of a book into a film script is often a re-creation of the source with all the attendant agonies of the original creation. In recent years, a prime source of material for the movies has been magazine articles. *Saturday Night Fever* came from a magazine piece. A recent *Esquire* article by Jean Vallely about Aspen ski bums is being turned into a script by William Goldman, one of the most celebrated of screenwriters.

There are scripts that fall somewhere between an adaptation and assigned material, which usually means that the idea and some research have already been started by the producer. A newspaper article, for example, about a political situation such as the immigration problems at the Texas–Mexico border, may have triggered additional research, providing a tantalizing arena. The screenwriter would then add the plot and the characters. Each of the situations (with assigned material) is a little different.

Revisions and *rewrites*: After you've done your script—your first draft (or the collection of pages and indecisions you're calling a first draft)—you're ready to face the battle. If you're being sensible, your script will contain no major surprises for your auditors that are not in the spirit of the plans the two or three of you made. That is, if you agreed upon the Texas–Mexico border, don't bring it back set in Sweden. Your work and, as you see it, your future and your integrity are on the line. His money and, as he sees it, his effectiveness are on the line. Where you draw the line between compromise and cracking under pressure is your business.

Most contracts call for a set of revisions. The substance of these revisions is to be agreed upon by all the principals. Revisions are usually the product of a lot of wrangling and the studios shoving the changes they want down your overcrowded throat.

A *rewrite* usually means that the previous writer is no longer available or, in the eyes of the boss, is incapable of further improving the script. Another writer is brought in to straighten it out. To do it, you have to be part critic, part diplomat, and part shark. When it's done to you, you need a thick skin and a few days in Palm Springs.

A *step deal* is a situation in which you are paid a certain amount to write a script in stages—a treatment, a first draft, a second draft, and so on. In a step deal, the producer or the studio has the right to end the arrangement unilaterally after each of the steps. It's not an ideal situation, but it does keep you on your toes, and it's usually the only thing open to a novice.

When you're fired after one of the steps in a step deal, you are said to be *cut off*, and indeed you are. It's a miserable feeling, and there's no solace for the cut-offee except another deal.

When your script is finished and "turned in" to the studio (a lot of school jargon in the movie business), it's either ignored, quickly made into a minor motion picture or put into *turnaround*. That means the studio doesn't want it, and the producer and, maybe, the writer are free to take it elsewhere, to turn it around. It's a time of great hope.

Everyone knows that the studios have story departments. Few people seem to know what the story department does. Story analysts, as their union calls them, or readers, as they call themselves, make up the story department. They read scripts, books, magazine articles, matchbook covers—whatever someone thinks will make a film—and they do it all the livelong day. As they read, they write a summary of the story line and give an opinion as to the commercial and aesthetic prospects for whatever it is they are covering.

Like the screenwriter who wants to be something else, most of the readers want to be something else. Fast. Producers or directors or executives or even, yes, screenwriters. The readers tend to be very smart and very unhappy. The studios treat them as if they were opinion machines.

There's a persistent rumor that studio executives themselves never read anything. Wrong! They read all the time. They read till their eyes are blurry. It's a point of honor among them. They boast (privately) about how many scripts they plowed through over the weekend. But they don't like to read "cold"— that is, without a summary in front of them (so they can skim if they want to) and without an educated opinion in front of them (so they can react rather than act in forming their own opinions). So on a typical Hollywood weekend, every studio executive takes a stack of scripts and matchbooks home, along with the accompanying coverage. Now this is not necessarily bad. It is kind of funny but not bad. Funny because all the executives tend to have similar stacks, and the coverage, from studio to studio, tends to be similar. But that's how it works.

Now everyone submitting a script or a matchbook wants to be special. They want to get around coverage and get their matchbooks directly to a vice-president. Avoiding coverage is seen by these dreamers as a worthy goal. But, short of standing over the vice-president from the time he or she is handed the damn thing until it's read and returned, attaining this goal is unlikely. You see, the coverage is the studio's way of tracking material. They assign it a number and log it in so the studio can check to see if they've passed on the thing a week before under a different title. It's a clerical necessity as well as a decision-making aid. You can override disastrous coverage and get another reading—sometimes, if you have some muscle. But usually bad coverage from a trusted reader stops your matchbook cold. No one but insiders is meant ever to see the coverage, so a sort of shorthand develops. The readers can be scathing. I remember the following comments about various scripts:

"This thing is to screenwriting what Oblath's [a restaurant adjacent to the Paramount studio lot] is to La Tour d'Argent."

"The writer of this script has the attention span of an eighteen-year-old speed freak."

"This is trying to be *Tammy and the Bachelor*. It should be so lucky."

Now, the readers are not always right. One reader's coverage of *Jaws*, which now hangs framed on a studio vice-president's wall, says: ". . . by definition is uncommercial. . . . It's bad pulp."

To get a little perspective on this, you should know that a major studio gets as many as 2,400 submissions a year from reputable agents. This makes for a lot of coverage, and since the scripts are frequently semi-readable, a lot of sarcasm.

HOW I DID IT: A CAUTIONARY TALE

How does it work? How does a poor lad with mammaries and mammon in his eyes come to this place and make a killing and remain so persistently obscure? How? How? Hmmm.

Suppose our lad is me, and when we meet me, I'm in my late twenties, come to Nueva York after going endlessly to graduate school. Soon, artiste that I am, I'm writing plays for theaters you've never heard of, on streets you've never walked. And I fancy myself a journalist and even, yes, an A * U * T * H * O * R.

I manage to wangle an interview with a Very Famous Producer (VFP) with white, wavy hair. So I cook up an earnest story to sell to the VFP. I outline a movie, make a few notes, and go in to tell it and sell it. This is called, as we now all know, pitching. But back then, I didn't know that. I just thought it was a story. On the day of the appointment with the VFP—oh, callow youth, a meeting, I was taking my first meeting, and I called it an appointment—I bopped into his office, which had no discernible desk, only sofas and chairs. Sort of like the faculty lounge. We sat opposite each other, sofa to sofa, and the VFP said: "Tell me a story." Some primal, tribal instinct told me to put aside my notes and strut a bit. Give the man a show. And I did. Cranking up my little yarn, a simple story of journalists, radicals with bombs (the Sixties were a fresher memory), and romance. I paced about the room, gesturing and approximating creative heat as if all this were just rolling out of me, apparently inspired by the presence of the VFP and his sofas. The VFP listened and nodded and cheered the young shaman (that's me) on. And when my tale was fully unfolded, the VFP reached out his arms and announced, "You have talent! I . . . I . . . bow down to talent." He fell to his knees and crawled across the floor, collapsing at my feet, clutching my ankles, and dropping his silvery brow to the carpet, muttering and stammering (the VFP was known to stammer in heat), "I bow down to talent."

Now what I didn't know then but will tell you now, saving you several years of confusion, is that this means no deal. If the boss gets excited in front of you, he wants to make another deal. Some material of his choosing. If he wants to make a deal for the story you're pitching, he won't allow so much excitement, lest you try to raise the price. And sure enough, the next day the VFP called and said no to the journalists and the bomb throwers but offered me the opportunity to rewrite another script. That is, take some dog-eared nonsense and try to make it less so.

And with that, there was no looking back. Just one glorious deal after another. One day small sums, next day lots of zeroes and the next day, no sums, only zeroes. An adequate living was gained, and it's a long way from East Fourth Street.

Television

Harvey Harrison, Jordan Kerner, Stuart Sheslow, and Marc Sheffler

For the novice writer to understand network television, it's important to identify those key individuals involved directly with a project from its creation through its development and hopefully on to the air.

The process begins with the writer's imagination—(a key ingredient, but not necessarily essential in television today). An idea, drawn from some life experience, and channeled through the

Harvey Harrison received his B.A. in philosophy from Yale University, and his J.D. from Stanford. Previously with the law firm of Dern, Mason, Swerdlow & Floum, Mr. Harrison now works in motion picture and television packaging for the Sy Fischer Agency.

Jordan Kerner received his A.B. in communications and film from Stanford University, a M.B.A. from the University of California at Berkeley and a J.D. from the University of California San Francisco. He is currently Director, Dramatic Series for ABC Entertainment. Previously, he was Director of Program Development for QM Productions and before that held the same title at Universal Studios, was a Talent and Program Negotiator at CBS, and was with the law firm of Ball, Hunt, Hart, Brown & Baerwitz.

Stuart Sheslow received his B.A. from Ithaca College and his M.A. from New York University. He is currently an independent producer. He is a past Vice President of Drama Development at NBC. He also held the position of Vice President of Current Comedy and Director of Comedy Development at NBC, as well as Manager of Comedy-Variety at ABC.

Marc Sheffler is a comedy writer.

required format. Once the writer is happy with the idea, the process of selling begins. This process may begin with a cab driver, the writer's father, who passes the script on to his passenger, a noteworthy series writer/producer. It may also begin in a more orthodox manner.

Two categories of persons can assist the writer at this stage: the *producer*, by providing direct employment, or more typically, the *agent*, who, after helping to develop the new writer, solicits employment. Whatever route the writer chooses, it's best to have a writing sample—whatever the writer considers to be most representative of the work he or she is capable of doing.

One manner in which a writer might further his or her career in television writing is to choose an established show and write what is called a "spec" (speculative) episode. This will demonstrate the writer's craft at capturing the essence of existing characters and placing them in novel contexts. This is especially helpful if a writer meets a producer first. That particular script may not sell, but the writer will now have a producer who knows him, and when script assignments come out again, he may find himself with a job.

AGENTS

The agent should perform a variety of functions for the writer, and it's the agent who may be the first of many to evaluate the writer's idea and its potential success as a television program. It's the agent's responsibility to know the constantly changing demands of the television marketplace and to let his clients know them before they begin creating the format for an idea.

The writer must remember that agents love to see material that excites them; something that they think is unusual, interesting or compelling because *that* makes it more salable. Also, having the services of an agent is necessary because many producers refuse even to open material unless it's submitted by an agent, since the producer is all too frequently inundated with similar material from a variety of sources. When one is selected and the other rejected, claims by the rejected writer against the producer for the alleged use of the material are commonplace. Because the agent is known within the television community and understands that producers receive similar ideas, he can explain these circumstances to his client to prevent any poorly founded claims.

PRODUCERS

When the writer and the agent both feel that an idea is ready to be shown, they may take the idea to a producer or, depending upon the writer's credibility, directly to a network or other buyer, circumventing the producer (at least initially).

One such buyer is the *syndicator*. A syndicator is a company which produces or buys previously produced programs for broadcast on independent stations domestically or groups of foreign stations. In addition to syndicators, there are individual sponsors, such as Hallmark or Procter & Gamble which, through their advertising agencies, develop and commission the production of television programs as well.

If a writer goes alone to a network and the network decides to develop the idea, the writer will then be put together with a production company acceptable to that network. Networks do this to ensure that the creative and business reins of production down the line will be in skilled hands.

The term "producer" can mean many things, but all producers are in the business of finding properties and developing them into successful television programs.

"Producer" sometimes means "Major" studio, such as Twentieth Century-Fox, Columbia, etc. The

Majors, because of their size and resources, have pools of talent in every area of development, production and distribution. This sometimes offers a network a more reliable and salable package. Although not opposed to outside submissions, most Majors have writers on the lot hired specifically to create and develop properties—these are usually old reliable writers or young "hotshots." One way a new writer may break in is to have a Major option or buy the rights to a story for a series from the writer, and then have one of its own writers do the script. The novice writer's agent should seek some continuing role in the series, if ordered, based on his client's original story. In prime-time television, the Writers Guild of America requires that any producer, including a Major, pay a per-episode "royalty" (a payment which is due the creators every time an episode is broadcast) to the writer of the original idea.

Next, there is the independent production company, or "Indie." An Indie is usually a smaller corporation than a Major, with its own financing. It typically has many of the same characteristics as a Major, excepting ownership of a studio lot and a broad distribution arm. It may consist of a few individuals who receive office space and expenses from a Major or larger Indie in connection with certain projects. In this case, the Major or larger Indie assumes liability for production deficits (i.e., that portion of the budget or a program which is in excess of the amount that the network has agreed to pay) in exchange for the smaller Indie's exclusivity in development, production, distribution and syndication of programs.

The most recent type of producer to emerge is the "Mini-Majors," who have almost all the characteristics of a Major except the actual studio lot. These are the large distribution/syndication companies like Lorimar or MTM.

The last category of producer is the "Individual Producer." He or she is an individual with experience in producing and, in many cases, writing television programs. Individuals with this dual ability or teams with this composite ability are often attractive to a network.

It is the producer's perceptiveness of the market and experience with networks that can change the writer's vision into a television series. It's important for the writer, guided by his or her agent, to select a producer established in the genre in which the writer seeks to develop projects. Also, the writer should bear in mind that the producers are clearinghouses for ideas, but that they all have their own interpretation of the networks' needs. Remember, unlike the networks, which number only three, there are hundreds of producers, and failure by one or even several producers to accept an idea does not mean that the idea is bad or not salable.

THE DEVELOPMENT DEAL

To begin with, we assume that a writer has taken an idea to an independent producer and together they plan to approach the network. To protect all concerned, the deal between the writer and the producer is usually structured before the network meeting. This usually happens while the writer and the producer are meeting creatively to plan their pitch to the network. Deals vary with the writer's strength and credibility, but basically, they will be structured something like this: the producer requires an option for a certain period to develop the idea and to take it to the networks or other buyers. Sometimes this option is referred to informally as a "hold" on the idea, or the right to shop the idea. Many times this is for no money, since the period of time is short. The deal between the writer and the producer may provide that the writer will write the first draft if the network approves the story, but that the producer may engage another writer, after the first writer has taken his shot, to write the final teleplay. This is called a "first draft cutoff." (In writing for episodes of existing series, the cutoff is generally after the story.) Occasionally the producer's commitment to the writer is on a "pay-or-play" basis, essentially—whether or not the producer requires the writer to write the script (for example, if the network abandons the project after the story stage), the producer is obligated to pay the writer as if a script had been written. Other points of the deal between the writer and producer, such as credit and residuals, are thoroughly covered by the Writers Guild Minimum Basic Agreement (discussed in a later chapter). A good deal should have the writer sharing a percentage of the producer's profits.

Before making any deal with any producer, the new or unrepresented writer should check with the Writers Guild of America. They will let you know what the minimum compensation should be and whether the producer is a guild signatory. Once the deal is set, you are ready to go to the network.

ON TO THE NETWORK

A meeting is set, then postponed and reset. The heavier the writer/producer package, the heavier the network programming department executive attending, but usually it's like this: the meeting takes place in the network executive's office with the writer, the producer, a network vice-president, and/or a network director and, possibly, one or two other network development executives. Many network vice-presidents have the power to "order a script" right in the meeting. However, the executive may choose to discuss the matter with his department, getting back to the producer in a few days. (Don't call us—we'll call you: it happens on all levels). If the idea is "passed" (rejected), the writer and producer should first go to other networks, then other buyers, syndicates, etc. If, however, the network buys the idea, the writer gets a chance to do the first draft. Once the order for script is given, everyone agrees on a delivery date, usually varying from four to six weeks from the day the pilot story is approved. Don't hand the script in too soon. Networks get nervous when material is handed in too soon.

A FIRST DRAFT IS BORN

Once the writer and producer are happy with the draft, it goes to the network. The network executives take about one or two weeks to make their notes. Then they call another meeting and usually open it up by saying they love it. Then, in a matter of fifteen or twenty minutes, they tell you how they want you to change it, make revisions, add something, delete something, make something larger, make something smaller, make it brighter here, make it lighter there, but overall "it's just what we want." The writer then will have another two weeks or so to turn in a revised teleplay to the producer, and subsequently to the network. This process of revision is where writers can significantly develop their craft.

Once the network orders a script, the network executive issues an order to the business affairs department of the network, which, in turn, negotiates a deal with the producer, also known as a development deal. Under the terms of the network development deal, the network agrees to reimburse the producer for all or part of the costs of his development deal with the writer. Once the writer has prepared the material ordered in connection with the development deal, and after that material has been revised and modified, the network has a period (which differs according to the kind of program) in which to elect to require the producer to produce a pilot or other television program based upon the material written by the writer. This determination by the network is made by the programming department.

If the programming department accepts the project for series production, the producer negotiates, once again, with the business affairs department in order to set the "license fee" (which can range from $350,000 to in excess of $1 million). This is the amount that the network will pay the producer in connection with the pilot. For this sum of money, the network receives the right to broadcast (usually two or three times) the program to be produced. Typically, the license fee is the source of funds which the producer uses, in whole or in part, to produce the television program. If the producer spends in excess of the license fee, it is said to have deficit-financed the pilot. If the network decides not to require the producer to produce a television program, then the producer and writer may take the literary material prepared in connection with the development deal (once released by the network for which it was prepared) to another network or buyer. The development deal structured with the first network typically provides that the first network is repaid the money it had invested in the development of the project, if a second network or other buyer agrees to produce a program based upon the material. It is in this manner that a project already developed to the script stage may be submitted to a number of different buyers by a producer and a writer.

Finally, if the writer's idea progresses beyond the pilot program stage and becomes a television series, the writer may find himself offered a creative position in connection with the series. This position affords the writer an opportunity to write a number of scripts during the first season of the series. In the event that the network renews the series for a second season, the writer might find himself in the position of editing and supervising scripts of others, as well as writing his own. This story editor position, as mentioned above, is the position which may lead the writer into developing the production skills necessary to become a key pilot writer/producer and, ultimately, to control both the words and the look of the program which he helped to create. After a period of time and exposure to the networks, he may be in a position to meet a novice writer and read his script which was handed to him by the writer's father in his cab while driving to a distant location. . . .

The New Media

Allen Rucker and
Ted L. Steinberg

Ideally, the new video technologies—what TV expert Les Brown calls "Television II"—will become the entry point, the farm system, for new writers breaking into the big leagues of film/TV. Pay cable, basic cable, subscription television (STV), direct-by-satellite (DBS), multipoint distribution service (MDS), low-power broadcasting, video discs, video cassettes and so on—it sounds like a world of opportunity for the talented, aggressive, uncredited writer.

We're not there yet. Right now, these technologies are merely new ways to bring video product into the home and, for the most part, the product being delivered—movies, sports, news, concerts and "filler" programming—has not created much additional work for writers.

So far, "new and innovative" programming in the new media is little more than a pipe dream promulgated largely by an industry trying to sell more cable subscriptions and cassette players. There is some original programming on pay cable television (like Home Box Office, Playboy Channel, Showtime and Spotlight), the advertiser-supported basic cable

services (like Cinemax, Cable Health Network, Cable News Network, ESPN, Hearst/ABC ARTS Channel, MTV and USA Network) and on STV services (like Home Entertainment Network, ON-TV, Select-TV and Wometco). But original programming opportunities in these areas are limited, tentative and underfinanced. The irony is that most of the writing work in well-financed original programming is going to seasoned Hollywood/New York professionals, or at least *through* these established talents. It is certainly not a field day for writers with fresh ideas and raw talent. But don't be discouraged. Read on.

All of this will probably have changed by the time you read this. The new media is a very volatile ball game. Huge entertainment corporations are still jockeying for position, meaning that whole marketplaces come and go with the pronouncements of a few corporate moguls. CBS Cable recently has folded and the Disney Channel recently lost its Group W partner. ESPN is about to make major programming changes to expand its viewer base, but at the same time, it will be cutting back in staff and production. At last count, there were twenty-one basic cable programming services and fourteen pay services ready to fight it out. Many could be gone in a year. For a new writer, it's like playing hopscotch in the sand. Just as you get a few moves down, the tide rushes in and destroys the playing field.

APPENDIX B OF THE WRITERS GUILD 1981 MBA

What won't change, at least until February 28, 1985, is the bitterly-fought-for Appendix B of the Writers Guild of America 1981 Theatrical and Tele-

Allen Rucker is a TV writer/producer currently with Universal Television. He co-founded the experimental video group TVTV and helped create the NBC series, SCTV, among other credits. He holds an M.A. in communication from Stanford University.

Ted L. Steinberg received his A.B. in English and his J.D. from the University of North Carolina (Chapel Hill). He is currently a partner in the law firm of Steinberg & Demoff and is counsel to the firm of Finley, Kumble, Wagner, Heine, Underberg & Manley. Mr. Steinberg is the entertainment law editor of the California Trial Lawyers Association Forum.

vision Basic Agreement (MBA) pertaining to minimum compensation. Appendix B is heady reading. It took more than a year for the parties involved to codify in writing exactly what they had agreed on, and it might take you a year of night school in labor law to understand it in detail. Here, in brief, are some of its salient features:

Programming Excluded From Coverage. Sporting events, cartoons, industrial and religious programs, other informational programs not covered by the MBA, commercials, advertising shorts, trailers and travelogues. Educational and instructional programs are excluded, except when produced for the home video disc/video cassette market, and such programs are excluded when written and performed by the same person.

Compensation. The minimum initial compensation is the same as in Article 13.B. of the MBA, which provides for minimums in commercial television. Where the program is of a type generally produced for other than prime-time network television, the rate for such other type program shall be applicable. This initial compensation represents payment for use of the product in the first "window" (pay television and video disc/video cassette market) until the producing company's receipts exceed certain "break amounts." The formula for break amounts can be found in Appendix B.

Additional Compensation (Residuals)
1. *Pay Television and Video Discs/Video Cassettes.* In addition to the initial compensation, for uses of a covered program in the pay television and/or video disc/video cassette markets, the producing company must pay residuals to the credited writer(s) in an aggregate amount equal to two percent of the producing company's gross income from such sources which exceeds the applicable break amount.
2. *Free Television.* If a covered program is broadcast on free television, the producing company must pay the credited writer(s) for the first such broadcast the applicable second run fee under Article 15.B. of the MBA for such broadcast, and any subsequent broadcasts of such program shall be governed by that re-run formula.
3. *Theatrical Exhibition.* If a covered program is released in theatrical exhibition, the producing company shall be obligated to pay to the cred-

ited writer(s) the applicable minimum compensation set forth in Article 13.A. of the MBA.
4. *Basic Cable.* If a covered program is licensed for exhibition on domestic basic cable (other than as part of domestic free television licensing), the producing company must pay the credited writer(s) two percent of the company's accountable receipts in accordance with Article 51.3 of the MBA.
5. *Supplemental Markets.* If a program produced under these provisions is licensed for exhibition in other supplemental markets (such as "in flight"), the producing company shall pay the credited writer(s) in accordance with Article 51 of the MBA.

Many people in the industry think the writers undersold themselves in this new marketplace and indulged in an expensive, thirteen-week strike to do it. That may be so. Nevertheless, writers are getting work in the new media under the terms of the MBA while guild directors, because of the oppressive terms of the new Directors Guild of America agreement, are having a hard time. Budgets for original cable shows are simply too small to accommodate the demands of the DGA, or so goes the argument from producers and programming services. The minimum compensation for writers doesn't seem to be that much of a problem. Of course, network deals usually involve larger staffs and larger over-minimum paychecks. But at least there is now a workable framework for writers and the new media to meet and negotiate.

BREAKING INTO THE NEW MEDIA

Knowing the MBA is one thing—finding work is another. The unsolicited treatment or manuscript sent by an unknown writer to the head of programming at one of the new programming services probably won't get you too far, just like in mainstream TV. Many of the executives at the cable companies have less development money than do commercial networks, and, in some cases, are less experienced at programming and less likely to take chances than more secure network types with larger development budgets. Most programmers are more comfortable when there are some heavy credentials in the room, and if you don't have them, it is unlikely that you will be able to sell a project unless you hook up with someone who does.

In TV, including TV II, it's best for new writers to attach themselves to experienced producers or production companies. There's a term currently in vogue in the TV business called "auspices." As in, "I love the idea, Charlie, and I thought the kid from UCLA who dreamed it up was great, but the project's got no auspices. I gotta pass. . . ." "Auspices" means the people who can execute the idea as a pilot or special will stay with it in series and can be "depended on" to make sure the product that was sold actually gets delivered. These are people with names and reputations, so the programming executives will pay attention when they're in the room. Additionally, they probably know how to take your ideas or jokes and explain them, shape them, budget them, negotiate them, produce them and promote them onto television. In some cases, of course, they also know how to rip them off.

If you are totally at bay in the world of the new media, operating without a knowledgeable agent, lawyer or associate in the business, you can easily succumb to some of the producer-types who say they're "well connected" in cable or discs or STV. It's easy to say, since there are a lot of levels to the new media and very few people know much about it, including most professionals in Hollywood. You might strike gold out there in the netherworld of non-pro TV—a number of public-access shows in Los Angeles, like *New Wave Theater*, have gone on to new marketplaces—but it is very risky if you're not working with knowledgeable allies. You could be just spinning your wheels dealing with people on the fringes.

Access to those who are more established— agents, lawyers, producers, development people at production companies and studios—is obviously tough going for neophytes. Ultimately, your best calling card is finished, polished material, whether it is in script or sketch form. An untested writer trying to sell a project based merely on an idea or treatment is like someone trying to win a beauty contest in a shroud.

MARKETS AND GENRES TO EXPLORE

Right now, variety programming (sketch comedy, light information shows and music specials) offers most of the work for writers in the new media. This is good for seasoned variety producers/writers, since it's hard to find much variety television on the networks nowadays. It's also good for the novice, since most variety/comedy is written in groups and there's often a spot for a bright rookie among the old pros. (Some of these old pros aren't so old; it is not uncommon to find twenty-five-year-olds who are experienced sketch-comedy writers.) You won't find an opening on a made-for-pay movie, but you might on a Gallagher special if you have an inspired idea for Gallagher and can get to the right people. It's recommended that you watch as much original cable programming as you can simply to see what they buy and how you might fit in. Some original cable programming is thoroughly offbeat, if not original, and didn't come from network pros. If you watch Showtime for instance, you probably have seen *Aerobicize*, a classy mix of aerobic exercise and soft-porn photography. This is not network fare.

Other forms that are prevalent in the new media, and which might grow in quality and volume, are original theater productions, dramatizations of well-known public domain material and new video program forms like music promotional films and how-to video discs. Hearst/ABC ARTS Channel is one of the few services to tap into the ripe market of original theater productions and, in fact, has hooked up with the Center Theater Group of the Mark Taper Forum to further develop such material. The Entertainment Channel has created a similar arrangement with the Nederlander organization. The advantage to the new playwright is that he or she might get a small (perhaps equity waiver) production off the ground with minimal costs to an investor, as well as maintaining subsidiary rights (such as film and television). Such a production would serve as a forum for those programmers looking for a "tested" product. It provides them with even more than a script; it's almost like an audition/pilot.

As an example of public domain sources, Showtime is offering *Faerytale Theater*, an anthology of videotaped fairy tales using noted talent like Robin Williams and Jean Stapleton, produced by Shelley Duvall and Lion's Gate Productions. Otherwise-unproven writers might find that they have a head start by dramatizing such public domain material and trying to sell this adapted material. It affords the writer with familiar (and therefore tested) material and a key to a sale.

Musical promotional tapes and films are also adaptations of another sort. Short one- or two-song music videos, as they are called, are used constantly on TV II as interlude programming. One cable service, MTV (Music Television), runs them continually. Longer music videos can involve whole albums and much visual and theatrical dazzle. The promotional film for Olivia Newton-John's *Physical* album was presented as an ABC network special. Although there is not much "writing" work on these programs, there is certainly a need for creative conceptual and story-telling input. Much of the work, again, goes to tested producers and directors, but there may be an opening here for a writer to get his or her concepts onto the screen—if the writer has access to the artist or the artist's representative.

Original programming for video discs is just getting off the ground, especially in the interactive mode. An interactive disc program allows the viewer to participate in a demonstration or learning exercise with the use of a remote control device. A "learn pro football" disc, for instance, can lead you through the basic rules of the game, then give you a game situation and let you coach. It's much different thinking and writing than normal passive TV and could become a real marketplace for innovative ideas if enough disc machines are sold to build a market that will support new programming. Much like the *John Gnagy* and *Winky Dink and You* shows which encouraged children's

at-home participation in the early days of TV, disc programs like MCA Videodisc's *First National Kidisc* could make TV a lively learning tool again.

Original sitcoms on pay TV are coming. So are dramatic series. It is hoped that they are coming in more innovative packages than typical network offerings. An indication of how much the pay people want network quality series is shown in two recent examples: HBO fought to get *Taxi* after ABC dropped it, and Showtime recently picked up *Paper Chase*, a series already tried in commercial and public TV. Made-for-pay TV movies are coming too, which sounds perfect for the low-budget-minded, independent filmmaker or writer. But until there is more of a buying and programming pattern for these forms, it's hard to be encouraging. It's just too soon to tell.

There's an old show-biz saying: "You can die of encouragement in Hollywood." For new writers, the new media is, by and large, another form of encouragement, perhaps as hollow as the rest. It *is* another access route, and it is enough on the fringe to afford some experimentation and chance-taking. There is simply no other marketplace for a series like *Faerytale Theater*; perhaps, after its exposure on cable TV, there will be. Cable TV and the other new media are not going to change the way Hollywood does business overnight. But given the calcified nature of network TV, they provide a small, perhaps growing, ray of hope.

Book Publishing

Bob Oskam

Almost everyone feels he or she has something to say to the world, but relatively few either have something truly original to say or can approach an old idea or subject in such a way as to bring new life to it. Similarly, many people feel they want to be writers, but relatively few have the talent or discipline to write well. Those two facts confront many would-be authors in their first efforts to have a book published.

It's not simply a matter of the many unqualified automatically falling by the wayside as publishers filter out what is good from what is bad. It's also that publishers are so routinely presented with such masses of material, the bulk of it substandard in quality, that good material is frequently overlooked. This is at times a publisher's fault. But it is at least as often because a potentially desirable author presents writing in an awkward or careless fashion. At first glance, the impression given is that this is not a capable writer. Because of the pressures of submission and workload at almost any publishing house, a brief first glance is all that many manuscripts ever get.

Bob Oskam was previously senior editor at Hawthorn Books and Elsevier-Dutton Publishing Company. He is currently a freelance editor, writer and literary representative. His writing credits include The Winning Negotiator *(a monthly business consultants' newsletter);* Search: A Handbook for Adoptees and Birthparents *(with Jayne Askin);* The Negotiator's Problem-Solving Handbook *(with Henry H. Calero). His article "Negotiating a Publishing Contract" appears in the revised edition of* Editors on Editing.

SHOWCASE YOUR WRITING ABILITY

A writer who wants a publisher's attention in order to maximize chances for landing a publishing contract has to be able to set him- or herself apart from the crowd. That means, first of all, having the ability to communicate well with the written word. And that ability should be evident in your first communication. After all, whether you want to propose a cookbook or the next great American novel, it is essential that you be able to express yourself in such fashion that others pick up on what you are saying.

Good grammar isn't the only ingredient here. You need also to develop a pleasing style. That, of course, depends on subjective criteria you can't wholly control, "pleasing" being substantially in the eye of the reviewer. What pleases one editor doesn't necessarily please another. More than one author has had the experience of multiple rejections before winning a contract for a book that subsequently made the best-seller list.

Nevertheless, there are objective criteria you should strive to meet. A publisher does want to feel he's dealing with a literate person. Although you can at times get by with less-than-perfect spelling if your sense of word usage is well developed, poor spelling almost always counts against you. Unwitting use of bad grammar will certainly count against you. And inability to organize your material so that sentences and paragraphs develop a logical flow will just as certainly lead to rejection of your submission. Primary to being seen as a writer is the presentation of evidence that you've mastered your craft.

Certainly there are exceptions. A person with a specialized skill of great potential interest to the public, or a person with a strongly established reputation for abilities or achievements unrelated to writing may get by even with poor writing. A professional can always be called in to polish it up. But *if you want to be seen as a writer, then show you can write.*

FORM COUNTS

In addition to demonstration of writing ability, there are further objective criteria to meet in the submission of material. All manuscript material should be neatly typed, double-spaced, on one side only of standard-sized (8½" × 11") typing paper. Avoid erasable paper. It may be convenient for your correction of typing errors, but it's hell to edit on. Occasional typos will be overlooked as long as the manuscript is otherwise easy to read.

Be sure whatever you submit is presented so that a prospective editor can easily follow its organization. This is particularly important with nonfiction submissions. A good table of contents can go a long way toward convincing an editor that you have considered your subject from all the relevant angles. But even a novel should have chapter breaks clearly indicated on a separate contents page.

Number each page of manuscript sequentially from beginning to end. At one corner on the top of each page, type either the title or a key-word identification. That serves as your protection against the disorganization of the average editor's office. Be sure your name and address are on the title page. And to protect yourself further, be sure to keep a copy of your material at home. That way you won't lose all your hours of hard work if either the publisher or the post office loses what you've sent.

CHOOSE THE RIGHT PUBLISHER

Naturally, eliciting a publisher's interest goes beyond the simple presentation of a reasonably well-written and correctly prepared manuscript. You must also somehow signal that what you've written fits into the publisher's list and that it has the kind of sales potential the publisher is looking for. That usually takes a little research on your part.

There are dozens and dozens of publishers. Virtually all are listed in R. R. Bowker's annually issued *Literary Market Place* (*LMP*). There you will find address references, a list of the officers and professionals working within each company, and an indication of the type of books issued by each. However, publishers are often vague in listing or slow to update in LMP the types of books they are currently acquiring. Therefore it's generally advisable to double-check at a bookstore who is presently issuing titles in a genre or subject area you've taken on. (Check the copyright date to be sure you have a current book.)

Don't assume only the major, name publishers are worth your attention. Houses like Doubleday and Random House, because of their size and visibility, receive enormous numbers of manuscripts and proposals. The screening process can therefore take quite a bit of time and yet may still be fairly cursory. And it's not only the big publishers who can build books into best-sellers. Look at the record and you'll find publishers like Schocken Books (*When Bad Things Happen to Good People*) and M. Evans (*The Ninja*) making a contribution to the best-seller lists as well.

In addition, all publishers have something of a character of their own. Even a house like Doubleday, publishing hundreds of titles a year over a wide range of subjects, will look with more favor on certain types of projects than on others. Sometimes it's just a matter of knowing or sensing that while one publisher is comparatively conservative, another will go for more offbeat or controversial material. For example, all other things being equal (which they rarely are), you're likely to find a novel with a gay theme easier to present to St. Martin's Press than to Doubleday, even though Doubleday's listing in *LMP* includes the same subject areas indicated for St. Martin's.

Remember the Publisher's Profit Motive

Always keep in mind that a commercial publisher is in business to make money on books. Profit is a prime consideration, whether the publisher markets his product through trade bookstores, by mail order or for adoption as school textbooks. Are you thinking about undertaking a textbook for university students? Well, besides any academic merits you can cite, you'll have to provide the appropriate publisher evidence that your textbook can more than recoup the investment necessary to see it into print. Are you proposing a novel? The publisher has to be convinced that this kind of novel stands a good chance of making him money. Even university presses, which have traditionally been subsidized by the academic community, are finding they need to pay more attention to sales potential, i.e., income considerations.

Home in on a Person

If you simply identify a likely publisher and then send your material as a blind submission (addressed just to the house and not to anyone in particular there), the material may well be returned to you without anyone having reviewed it. The flood of blind submissions is of such proportions at many houses, and the percentage of worthwhile submissions so limited—not more than one percent or so—that it's generally not considered worthwhile going through the bother of review.

Identify an editor at a house, and chances are your manuscript will get at least a once-over. But even then your best chances lie in identifying an editor with an interest in the kind of material you're submitting. Some writers have the inventiveness, the determination, the connections, and/or the good fortune to accomplish this on their own. Others find the services of an intermediary necessary, so they try to work through a literary agent.

AN AGENT CAN MAKE A DIFFERENCE

The advantage of working through a literary agent is that you turn over the task of polling publishers and editors to a professional who has a clearer idea than you can have of who's most likely to be receptive. He or she has an overview of the industry that you don't have, routing material to people you don't know and have no ready access to. The advantage of that should be obvious.

What do you pay an agent? The conventional arrangement for years has been that the agent serves in exchange for a ten percent commission on *all* income from the book. However, a number of agents have recently raised the charge of their service to fifteen percent. Some have a variable scale, depending on how involved they get in actual preparation of a proposal or project for submission.

An agent does more than make presentations to publishers. He or she also acts as your representative when it comes to negotiating the actual publishing contract. This is an equally important part of the service provided. The agent's knowledge of what is usual practice in the industry, what exceptional circumstances may affect the viability of a particular project at a given house, and what fine-print inclusions or omissions in a contract to be alert to can work to advance and protect your interests substantially. The agent also acts as your intermediary with the publisher throughout the life of your book whenever business questions are raised.

The great and increasing difficulty for unproven writers is that it's every bit as hard to tie in with an agent as it is to locate a publisher. You will find a listing for almost all well-established literary agents in *LMP*, but many of those have closed the roster of writers they represent. The clients they already have provide them enough business. They haven't the time or inclination to wade through a mountain of manuscript material from a whole array of would-be authors, most of whose work they won't be able to sell. It's the same problem as with the publishers themselves.

A few agents deal with this problem by imposing an evaluation fee for review of material from authors not already on their list. That fee can run as high as $350, although from $50 to $150 is more usual. The evaluation will not necessarily include a detailed critique of the sort you might be willing to pay for.

Locating an agent who will agree to review your material and consider representing you—and with whom you feel comfortable—requires the same inventiveness, determination, etc., you'd need to put into locating a publisher. There are actually fewer solidly established literary agents than there are publishers, so you can imagine what the odds against you are if you can't somehow get an inside track to an agent. There are a fair number of individuals with a background in publishing, notably ex-editors, who do some agenting work. But because they are only occasionally listed in *LMP* or other publishing reference resources, they are as difficult for the average writer to link up with as a long-established agent.

YOU HAVE A SELLING JOB

Whether you're represented by an agent or acting on your own, *you are the person who has to take the initiative* in providing both the material for consideration and the rationale for its publication. This is accomplished with a book proposal. Even if you have a complete manuscript ready to send off, it's often more expeditious to make your first approach through a proposal, especially for nonfiction projects. With fiction, the publisher may from the very outset want to monitor your ability to sustain a plot successfully through to conclusion.

The following directives on how to prepare a book proposal were developed by the editors at Hawthorn Books to aid authors in making solid presentations to the house.

HOW TO PREPARE A BOOK PROPOSAL

The most essential element of any book proposal is its ability to sell your ideas to a publisher. Nevertheless, it is important you present a realistic evaluation of yourself and your book. It is to no one's advantage for you to make impractical claims or promises you will not be able to keep. Your proposal—which is essentially your first introduction to the publisher—will set the stage for your eventual relationship with your editor. Furthermore, you should bear in mind that the tone and writing style of your proposal should reflect those of the book you plan to write.

Your book proposal should include the following:

—*A chapter-by-chapter outline of the text.* Include a 100-word description of each chapter. Explain the content and depth of each chapter. *Note:* If you are submitting a completed manuscript, you should still prepare a chapter-by-chapter outline/summation of your book.

—*Sample text.* Include your Introduction if you plan to have one in the book, along with one or two sample chapters. The text you include in the proposal should be indicative of the style that will be employed in the rest of the book.

—*Author's biography.* This needn't be lengthy, but it should inform the publisher of your education, your background, and your professional experience as it relates to the subject of your book, and your special qualifications for dealing with the subject. In addition, you should inform the publisher of any publicity programs (television and radio appearances, lecture tours, etc.) with which you have been involved.

—*Additional published material.* Include copies of articles you have written as well as a list of previ-

ously published books. In the case of the latter, include information on financial successes and failures, book club sales, and reprint rights sold.

—*Cover letter.* In addition to any other information that you think will be of use to the publisher, your cover letter should offer the following:

1. A description of the market for your book, which may include statistics on general interest and trends in your topic; membership statistics for clubs and societies that exist within the field; and a description of similar books in the area which could very well support interest in your own book. (Give sales figures on these when possible.) Also, as best as you can, try to offer some insights into the review attention that your book might receive. What magazines are aimed at the audience you plan to reach? Does your topic lend itself especially well to a specific branch of the media (radio as opposed to feature article, for instance)? Does your subject appear particularly often in news stories?

2. A list of the competition. Consult bookstores and libraries as well as the *Subject Guide to Books in Print.* Explain briefly how your book will differ from those already available.

3. Potential markets. Describe whatever thoughts you might have on how your book might fare in terms of retail bookstores, institutional (library) sales, book clubs, foreign sales, and mass market paperback reprint rights.

4. The importance of your book. Does it offer a unique point of view or new information in the field? What are the special needs your book will fill?

5. The package. The projected length of the manuscript; the number and type (color or black-and-white) of photographs and drawings; the type of illustrations of any kind (charts, maps, graphs, etc.). Explain how you plan to obtain these. Include also information on whatever back matter (e.g., appendixes) your book would include.

6. The delivery date of the completed manuscript.

7. Your methods of research and resources. Tell whether you have obtained or plan to enlist the cooperation of special groups or individuals.

You will observe that these instructions imply submission of a nonfiction project. Obviously a novelist can't be expected to fulfill all the requirements indicated above. However, even an aspiring novelist should make the effort to provide as much of the information above as is applicable or would be helpful to the publisher in evaluating the submitted novel's potential.

Some writers, in an understandable effort to minimize the delay that results from submitting material to one potential publisher at a time, submit to several publishers simultaneously. Although there is no great harm in this as a rule, you should advise each publisher that you have submitted to one or more others.

Send an original cover letter to each publisher in a simultaneous submission. Never send a photocopied form letter as cover for your submission. That almost inevitably turns the recipient editor off completely. The assumption will be that you've submitted more or less at random, without going to even minimal trouble to check that the house is a logical candidate to publish your work. More often than not, a photocopied form-letter submission results in the submission being treated as junk mail.

Avoid an overblown hard-sell approach in your cover letter. It is the mark of the rankest amateur to open a letter to a publisher or editor with words such as "Now at last you have my best-seller . . ." or to project immediately minimum sales figures in the hundreds of thousands or millions if only the publisher will send out a publishing contract and undertake adequate promotion for the book eventually issued. This approach betrays such a lack of awareness of how publishing works, and so little sense of realism in general, that the recipient will not take it, or you, seriously.

Avoid as well a statement of credentials along the line of "All my friends have urged me to submit my material for publication," or "My children love this story." *Your submission has to make its own impact on the reader or editor reviewing it.* If it is to be accepted for publication, it must be on merits evident to professionals with experience in evaluating writing and potential book markets. These professionals are still fallible, of course. Nevertheless, your chance for success depends on ultimately impressing one of them. You will impress none of them with an amateur's hard sell or endorsements from friends, family or neighbors who otherwise have no connection with the publishing world or professional credentials meaningful in that world.

Following Through on a Contract Offer

Assume that you've actually done everything right and had your manuscript or proposal accepted. The next step is negotiation of the contract for publication. If you have an agent, he or she will handle that for you. If you haven't, then you negotiate directly with the publisher—more specifically,

with the acquiring editor or a house contracts manager. You can have a lawyer negotiate for you, but that's ill-advised if the lawyer is not familiar with publishing considerations and practice. A lawyer without that familiarity more often than not unnecessarily complicates things.

Do note one thing: It's usually not difficult to get an agent to represent you at this point, even if you haven't previously been able to find one. Many agents will agree to represent you if they know you've already located a publisher—they know there's a payoff for the time to be invested. And it may still pay off for you to cede the ten-percent commission. A watchful, experienced agent knows where to ask for royalty, rights or other concessions that you may not be aware are possible. The income difference to you can more than offset the commission payable on the agent's service. Simply having someone undertake the job of negotiating can be worth the commission in some cases, since it's commonly an unexpectedly extended process that can be very wearing on the uninitiated. As in working with any professional you employ, come to a clear understanding of what service will be provided and on what explicit terms.

A lot of authors do negotiate their own contracts. If you decide on this for yourself, be sure you educate yourself thoroughly as to what to expect and what to be alert for. (For details on contract specifics you will have to deal with, see the chapter "Your Hardcover Publishing Agreement" in this book.)

THE EDITOR TAKES OVER

Once your manuscript is accepted in final form by the publisher, you must realize that it's not just your book anymore—it's also *their* book. And it is at the editing stage that *they* take control. That is accomplished through the agency of the editor.

An editor has three major roles: (1) acquiring book properties for the publisher, (2) overseeing the preparation of manuscript material into final book form and (3) acting as spokesman for the book and author to the rest of the house. It is a position that requires multiple talents, and some editors handle one role better than another. From your perspective, you want to feel secure that your editor will oversee your project capably and act effectively as your spokesman to others in the company who also play their part in its production and marketing. But recognize that there are editors whose primary value to a house lies in their acquisitions ability. Such editors may turn over actual editing to an assistant or other editor who then serves as overseer of the manuscript through the stages of production.

Except where that task is delegated, the acquiring editor takes on the first processing task: overall review of the material and line editing. The manuscript's organization is checked, and if it benefits the presentation, adjustments are made. The text is read line for line. The editor works to smooth the flow of language as necessary, to delete redundancies, to question points that are not clear, to suggest supplementations at points where material that would seem logical for inclusion is not included, to see that the discussion or plot does not get lost in digressions.

At least this is ideally what the editor does. Because the editor's job is a labor-intensive one on each front, you may find that your editor will not or cannot undertake as close an editing review as might be desirable. Because of bureaucratic pressures within the company, because management may require an editor to focus primary energies on acquisitions without separately providing for a line editor or possibly because of other priorities on the list of books handled by your editor, it can happen that your manuscript will routinely pass to the stage of copy editing without being polished into the best possible shape. If you've been painstaking in your work, this may not compromise your presentation. If, however, you've been counting on the editor's contribution to pull your material into better shape, you may find yourself disappointed.

When you submit your final manuscript, speak to your editor about any areas you feel need review or about uncertainties you have about the presentation. You will likely assure that attention is directed at least to those points.

But if you have serious problems pulling the final manuscript together, don't wait until the last moment to ask for your editor's input. Mention to him/her the difficulty you're having as it arises. Assuming the difficulty isn't essentially that in taking on the book project you've bitten off far more than you can chew, your editor should be able to provide advice and insight on how to resolve whatever problem you have.

Copy Editing and Design

After the editor has completed his or her review, the manuscript is passed on to a copy editor (almost always a freelancer) for copy editing. This involves going over the text in careful detail to assure correct spelling and word usage, that rules of grammar have been adhered to and that all material (text, footnotes, captions, bibliography, etc.) is styled according to publishing convention and the specific needs of the book. In addition, a good copy editor is alert to factual discrepancies or inconsistencies in the text that the editor may have missed. Because a good many editors either can't or don't take the time to line edit as carefully as they might, a really good copy editor can make a significant contribution to a book that may have been submitted in less than perfect shape.

Usually, once the manuscript has gone through copy editing, it is turned over to the editor and then to you for review. The object of this is to have you respond to any questions that may have been raised in the editing-copy editing process and to make sure that the substance of your presentation hasn't been altered to its detriment.

Occasionally an author finds it difficult to accept being "corrected" by either editor or copy editor and sets to work erasing the editor's or copy editor's mark-up of the manuscript. The end result is negation of professional work that usually follows a clear rationale. The better alternative to follow if you have a question or objection to editing or copy editing work is to note it on a separate sheet for the editor's consideration. If you have a compelling reason for wanting something done your way, your editor will probably go along with you.

The reviewed, copy edited manuscript next enters the first production stages. If a duplicate manuscript hasn't already been marked for design, this happens now. A book designer specifies typeface, type size and text and illustrations layout. Then the copy edited manuscript goes to a compositor to be set into type.

From Proofs to Bound Book

The book returns from the compositor in galley form. One set of galleys will be read by a proofreader (again usually a professional freelancer) who checks for errors made in the setting process. Another set is sent off to you for your review. You, too, are being asked to double-check for setting errors—and to make any *necessary* last-minute corrections in text.

Often a writer who sees his or her book in type for the first time experiences the urge to revise material substantially. Enough time has passed since the actual writing and the previous review of the copy edited manuscript so that something of a fresh look is possible. But once a manuscript has been set, any change involves resetting. Even if only a comma is inserted into a line, the entire line has to be reset. Inserting or deleting words can require the resetting of an entire paragraph, depending on the tightness of the setting and the change requested. The compositor may charge as much as $2 for each line that is marked for resetting due to a request for revision. (There's no charge for correction of printer's errors.)

Because all publishers recognize the desirability of necessary changes even in proof stages, you will be allowed to indicate "author's alterations." But almost all publishers will charge *you* the cost for author's alterations beyond ten percent or so of the expense of setting the whole book the first time. That's why it's important that you make every effort to satisfy yourself with the shape of the book text in the editing stage.

You may or may not get to work on the book again once you've seen the initial galley proofs. Unless it's a book with a complicated layout that you should review in mechanical stage (when the book is fully laid out with all elements in place), chances are you won't see it again before publication.

The galleys, marked for necessary correction and/or revision, go back to the compositor, who does whatever resetting is required. They are then made into page proofs, which, once they have been approved, push through a final page layout stage to be reproduced as book blueprints and then as the actual printed book itself. That is then bound and jacketed and shipped from the bindery to the publisher's warehouse for distribution. Within a few days the publisher starts shipping the book to accounts that have preordered it. Official publication is generally announced several weeks thereafter—the delay is to allow time for the book to be stocked in bookstores around the country for immediate availability to the public once publication is announced.

The entire process from submitting a finished manuscript to publication takes, on the average, at least nine months. A complicated book may take twice that long. A rush book can be crashed through in less than a month if necessary, but this is only rarely done.

You must accept that *in most cases the publishing process is controlled by the publisher.* Except for those few authors with the clout to insist in their contracts on some element of control, the publisher makes the final decision on book format, jacket or cover design, pricing, publication date (although many contracts are now stipulating a minimum period within which a manuscript, once accepted, must be published), final length and initial print run. You can try to negotiate for some voice in these decisions, but as a rule you will find the publisher resistant to compromise on the question of control over the actual publishing program.

SUBSIDIARY RIGHTS

As soon as a manuscript comes in to the publisher, there will be attention paid to its subsidiary rights potential. "Subsidiary rights" refers to the licensing of secondary publication/presentation rights such as to book clubs, paperback reprinters, newspaper syndicates, magazines or TV and film producers. A very "hot" book may be licensed to one or several of these while still in manuscript form. Otherwise, subsidiary rights interest is solicited at the galley stage and also once finished copies of the book are available. Although you will read of multimillion-dollar deals for licensing rights, most books do not earn more than $10,000 from a sale of these; many earn no money at all here. In fact, around half of all books published never earn out the monies that have been advanced to the author before publication.

SELLING THE BOOK

The sales success of a book is often determined before the first copy of the book has even arrived in the bookstore. This is because the publisher's sales representatives are out soliciting orders for the book prior to publication. And the advance order is what determines the number of books that will be available to the public in bookstores upon publication. If the sales force experiences difficulty selling your book to the bookstores, the book may never win the opportunity to develop the momentum needed to assure reorders. For this reason, it's important that you provide as much backup detail as possible if you feel your book has a particular market potential, and you should provide that months *before* publication.

Many an author is bitterly disappointed to find after publication that the publisher is prepared to undertake only minimal advertising and promotional activity on the book's behalf. This grows out of the reality that advertising and other promotional activities entail considerable expense. The profit margin on books is too low as a rule to support more than a few major promotional campaigns. Naturally the publisher reserves such campaigns for titles the publisher feels have the greatest potential.

Ironically, the better received a book is before any promotion has been undertaken, the more likely it is to be backed with promotion monies. If advance sales have been poor, it is more likely that an advertising budget will be cut than that it will be increased. After all, if the book isn't out in the stores in quantity, the public won't find it even if it is advertised. The point of advertising is not primarily to move books into the bookstores—except for pre-publication ads in trade publications like *Publishers Weekly* and in the *New York Times Book Review*—but to move books out of the stores.

Be alert to the reality that advertising space in national consumer magazines and the daily press is very costly. Books tailored to a specific market, however, can often be advertised in publications aimed at that same market for but a fraction of the cost of space in a mass circulation publication. If you know of a publication or other forum for publicizing your book that doesn't require major expense but does stand likely to prompt sales in a specific market, suggest advertising there. You'll obtain a more sympathetic hearing from your publisher with this kind of suggestion than if you keep pushing for a page in the *Times Book Review*. The cost for that now runs in excess of $7,000 per page *plus* the cost of producing the ad.

Whatever the actual advertising budget, you can expect that your publisher will at least send out review copies to newspapers, magazines, special interest publications and to appropriate radio and television spokesmen. These copies, it is hoped, will result in reviews, feature articles and/or interviews that can have much of the same effect as advertising. If you can contribute the name of influential individuals positioned and amenable to publicizing your book, be sure to submit these as far in advance as possible to the publisher's publicity department. To the extent that activities you undertake or contacts that you have can push book sales, stress these from the very outset of your contact with the publisher. They may help prompt the publisher to take on your project, because they give the publisher a better sense of how sales can be pursued once the book is published. Don't ever hesitate to provide your publisher specific sales leads to individuals or organizations able and willing to take or move the book.

Selling books to the public is increasingly in the hands of a few major chains whose buying responses more and more affect decisions publishers make on what to publish. Books are sold to bookstores on consignment. Until the book is declared out of print, the bookstore has the right to return unsold copies virtually at any time for full credit.* In today's high-volume sales operation, this means a shelf life of only months for the average title. If the store has ordered the book in quantity and finds it moves quickly, the book will be reordered. If the store has ordered only a few copies, even if these sell out, the total volume registered will often not be sufficient to prompt reorders. Here again the pre-publication stock-up of orders plays a crucial role. Where the bookseller finds disappointing response to a title that is in stock, he is likely to ship excess stock back to the publisher for credit. Some booksellers make the decision to return the stock as early as within two months of receipt.

ROYALTIES

Publishers present their accounting of sales to the author in semi-annual or, less frequently, annual royalty reports. Until the royalties and your share of subsidiary rights income exceed the amount of the advance monies paid you, you will receive nothing. However, if your book fails ever to earn out its advance, you will not be expected to pay back the difference.

In the first one or two accounting periods you may find your royalty statement indicates a "reserve against returns." What the publisher is doing is withholding a percentage of the funds that comprise your royalty—generally around fifteen percent—against the possible eventuality that books sold to the bookstores on consignment will be returned in quantity.

---

*One publisher, Harcourt Brace Jovanovich, in the fall of 1980 announced a policy of "no returns" on trade books delivered to bookstores. By early 1982 that policy was reversed, as other publishers did not join to create a general trend, and bookstores were less inclined to order HBJ's books in quantity directly from HBJ.

The publisher's sales figures, upon which your royalty statement is based, are primarily a record of sales to the bookstores or other middlemen, not to the public. If copies of your book are returned unsold, the royalty due you drops accordingly. The reserve protects the publisher somewhat against the commonly realized possibility that a subsequent royalty period may show *net returns* (an excess of books returned over the number of new orders fulfilled). The publisher—naturally, from his point of view—wants some protection against paying out monies for books that ultimately wind up unsold in his warehouse. Holding a royalty reserve serves that purpose. If, on the other hand, the book continues to build in sales, the royalty reserve is properly "reversed," i.e., paid to the author, after two or three royalty periods.

Royalty reserves can form a bone of contention between publishers and authors—there's frequently an understandable difference in perspective on the subject. Whatever the publisher's practice in this area is, it is something that should be spelled out in advance in the contract for the book.

WHY DOES A BOOK FAIL?

A lot of factors go into why a book does or does not sell. If it does not, the *timing may have been off* for a book of its type; the *competition may have been too stiff*; the *market may have been more limited than anticipated*; the book may have won *little review attention*; the book may have been *badly executed either in text or packaging*; the *publisher may have failed to pursue sales potential*, etc. There's such a multiplicity of factors that it's common to find disappointed authors and publishers at odds on what the problem may have been.

One fact to recognize is that the United States is not a book-consuming society as a whole. It's estimated that less than five percent of the public visits a bookstore more than once a year. And to the extent the public does buy books, the orientation is very much toward best sellers and media tie-ins. Consequently, the average trade book in the United States, a country with a population of roughly 220 million, does not sell that much more than an average book in the Netherlands, with a population of around 14 million.

GOING OUT OF PRINT

Once a publisher finds that sales activity on a book has pretty much ceased—for whatever reason—he usually declares the book out of print. This means no further copies of the book will be printed, no further orders accepted and no further returns accepted after a specified date. You should be notified of the decision to declare your book out of print, but often publishers are careless on this point. It's best to be alert to the likelihood that your book will be declared out of print once sales slow down to near nothing. If copies remain in stock in the warehouse, you should have a first crack at buying these leftovers at a much-reduced "remainder" price before the stock is sold off to a remainder house (the source for those $2.98 hardcovers that originally sold for $12.95) or otherwise disposed of.

At this time you may decide you want the publishing rights to your book back—you may still see some potential for exploiting the book your publisher missed. If that is the case, direct a letter to the publisher (or have your agent do so) asking for formal reversion of rights. Most publishers will routinely acquiesce to this request, with the proviso that any outstanding licensing agreements growing out of a previous sale of subsidiary rights be allowed to run their course. Ask for a listing of what those are. Then you can decide whether to resell publication rights, either immediately or some time later when the market seems open again for a reissued edition of your book. This is not often easily accomplished, but it does happen regularly.

YOU NEED TO BE INFORMED

Book publishing is a complex business, and one that contains many an opportunity for frustration and surprise on the part of writers. This summary overview will help you orient yourself to much of what goes on in the business. However, there is much more that merits your attention and consideration. For a more in-depth view of the book publishing world, there are several reference works available describing the industry. One I'd recommend in particular is Richard Balkin's *A Writer's Guide to Book Publishing* (revised edition, Hawthorn/Dutton, 1981), because it is specifically presented from a writer's perspective. Other books for further reference are listed in the bibliography of this book and elsewhere.

If you are serious about breaking into book publishing as an author, do make a concentrated effort to be informed. That can spell out the difference between a successful effort and a frustrating series of abortive attempts. If you have a talent for writing, it's worth making the effort; there is a place for you in publishing.

Karen Green Rosin and
Jane Sindell

This chapter is intended to answer the questions of a writer just starting a career. Although the beginning writer may not yet have heard all the nasty stories about agents that veteran writers like to swap, this chapter does not contain any such tales. To assuage those who might want equal time, however, the editors have allowed the inclusion of the following quote:

> You can take all the sincerity in Hollywood and stick it in the navel of a flea and still have room for two caraway seeds and the heart of an agent. . .
> —Fred Allen

Why do I need an agent?

While it is possible for a writer to sell material or find work without an agent, the established "system" in the entertainment/publishing industries recognizes the agent as the salesperson for the writer's literary property. The "buyers" in the literary marketplace (e.g., producers, publishers, studios, networks) depend on agents to deliver material or writers to suit their needs, and agents are a part of the "weeding out" process involved in choosing the best writer for a project.

Karen Green Rosin is a writer who became a lawyer. (She is the daughter of a writer, the sister of a writer and is married to a writer.) She received a B.A. in threatre arts and a law degree from the University of California at Los Angeles. She currently practices entertainment law at the firm of Loeb and Loeb in Los Angeles.

Jane Sindell is a literary agent in the motion picture division at International Creative Management. Upon graduation from Stanford University, she spent five years at the William Morris Agency, where she represented writers in both television and motion picture activities. She is a native of Los Angeles.

The pool of potential writers is enormous, but being represented by an agent gives the unknown writer some immediate *credibility*; the buyer knows the agent's livelihood depends upon representing writers whose work will *sell*. If the buyer has been satisfied with previous clients of the agent, or if the agent or agency has a good reputation, the unproven writer's credibility is all the more enhanced. But even a less well-known agent can provide credibility by showing that *someone* believes the writer will generate a return on the investment of that agent's time.

Indeed, time is itself one of the important reasons for using an agent; just as the producer or publisher cannot spend all of his or her time reading material in search of a writer, a writer's time is better spent *writing* material than trying to sell it. It takes time to develop fruitful "contacts," relationships with the people who can authorize purchases or make offers of employment to writers. Moreover, an agent can save time by calling on past experience to avoid submissions to people or companies that are unlikely to be interested in a given property, and to pursue the avenues with the highest potential for sale at the outset.

In addition, as will be discussed in greater depth below, an agent can provide other valuable services, including, for example, "packaging," i.e., finding a director, star and/or a producer to offer to a studio or network along with a given script as a "package deal." Agents are familiar with the payment schedules and going rates for writers' services, while writers, particularly the inexperienced, may not be; negotiating skills may at times earn the agent's commission. An added benefit of using an agent is that business records are regularly kept (or should be) of all submissions and meetings involving the writer, thus providing a greater degree of protection in case a dispute should arise.

For the writer just starting a career, an agent may make the difference between getting one's material read and remaining anonymous. As the writer's reputation grows, the value of the agent may derive more from the other services such as adept negotiating. For the experienced writer who is constantly sought after, the agent may serve to screen out offers made by producers—an envied state of affairs. This latter stage, a dream for most writers, will never materialize until the writer takes the first step and finds his or her first agent.

How do I go about finding an agent?

Before outlining some suggested steps in finding an agent, a few basic points need to be mentioned. The purpose of the following discussion is to make it a little easier for the beginning writer to understand how he or she will be perceived by agents generally. Many writers find the process of obtaining an agent a demoralizing and disappointing experience, because they do not understand why phone calls are not returned and manuscripts are not read. The following should explain why these events need not be taken personally, and will suggest some strategies in agent-searching.

First, it is fair to say that an agent only wants clients who can make money—not necessarily immediately, but definitely over the long term. This does not mean a writer must be "commercial" to get an agent. It does mean that the writer must be a *professional*—or have the capacity to become one. Professionalism comes with experience, of course —it is not an innate quality—but the inexperienced writer who appears to have the potential to become a professional, with the least amount of effort and time, is way ahead of the game.

The beginning writer who has no professional experience to speak of, or very little, ought to expect rejection from a number of agents for that reason— lack of experience—alone, no matter how talented that writer may be. It is a rare career that takes off full speed ahead from the outset, and therefore agents have to work without compensation at first when they "develop" new writers. Many agents don't have the time, or the interest, to do so. Some new writers resent the belief apparently held by some agents that a writer is more likely to "sell" in the future if that writer has "sold" in the past. It must be remembered, however, that a person who

has been paid for writing has already received approval beyond his or her immediate family and friends, who naturally offer praise and support regardless of merit. The experienced writer achieves a degree of legitimacy in the agent's eyes because some third persons have invested money in that writer—just as the writer attains credibility in a producer's or publisher's eyes due to the agent's investment of time.

In approaching the search for an agent, remember that an agent who has never heard of you has no way to distinguish you from the great masses of people with little or no talent who are also trying to be perceived as writers. Thus, you must make yourself stand out from the crowd, at least long enough for the agent to assess your potential by reading your work.

Where can I find out which agents might be interested in me?

For screen or television writers, a good starting point is to obtain a list of approved agents from the Writers Guild of America. The list notes which agents accept unsolicited material and which, as a general policy, do not. Some agents may refuse unsolicited material because they do not want to take on any more clients, or at least any "new" writers. These agents should be distinguished from those who refuse unsolicited material merely to avoid receiving a lot of junk from people who cannot write complete sentences, let alone salable material. The latter type of agent may be willing to take on new clients, but may prefer to draw upon those referred by someone they know. (Remember, it takes time to read material and time is a valuable commodity to an agent.)

A list of literary agents who deal in the publishing world is contained in a reference volume called *Literary Market Place*, which may be found in most public libraries. In addition, the Society of Authors' Representatives (New York) publishes a list of its members.

Try to find out as much information as you can about all the agents that you can, from every source available—the "trades," and everyone and anyone you know—to determine whether you should try to approach certain agents or whether it would be a waste of your time, for any number of reasons: Do they deal in the field you want to work in, i.e., episodic television, feature films, publishing, etc.? Do they *ever* take on inexperienced writers?

Are they well-respected agents or are they regarded as somewhat sleazy?

Next, poll everyone you know to find out if any of them personally know any agents. Even if an agent is willing to accept unsolicited material, you can bet that it is more likely to be read when it is received through a referral. If you do find that some people you know (or are related to) also know (or are related to) agents, before becoming overly optimistic you should assess the strength of the connection between you and the agent. The best type of person to provide a referral to the agent is someone who is "in the business," whose opinion the agent respects, and who thinks highly of your work. If the person is not someone whose professional opinion the agent respects, or someone whom the agent personally likes or owes a favor, that person's value as a contact becomes more dubious. For example, you may not want to use your landlady's niece's roommate whose boyfriend is the agent's pool man as a referral except as a last resort. If you do have some good contacts who can readily introduce you or your material to an agent, the searching process may be relatively easy. If not, you may just have to use a little more effort.

What should I do to attract the attention of agents?

Start off with a broad attack; i.e., rather than approach agents one at a time until each accepts or rejects your overtures, start off with about twenty initial "targets," or as many as your research has indicated will be worth a shot. You want the agent who is best suited to work with you, not necessarily the first one to express interest.

It is better to establish some initial communication before you actually send a sample of your writing to an agent. It is discouraging to have scripts returned unread, and you may save a lot of money in photocopying alone if you hold onto your scripts and call or write first. The following is one suggested approach for getting your foot in the door with agents you have never met.

First, send a letter which will arouse the agent's interest in you. It should *not* be a form letter, and should be well written, even clever, if possible (stand out from the crowd), and of course, neat (be professional). You may want to include a resume of your prior credits, experience, educational background. If you are trying to sell a particular script or book, you may want to describe briefly the project

(e.g., a medium-budget science fiction thriller with two strong male leads, or whatever). Mention that you will follow up the letter with a phone call if you do not hear from the agent within, say, a week or ten days. The object of the call is to introduce yourself to the agent and ask him or her to read your work. Hopefully, when you call, your name will ring a bell with the agent, who remembered your letter, or who is expecting your call because of a contact's referral.

You may have some trouble catching the agent at a free moment, but if you are nice to the secretary, he or she might give you some tips on the best time to call. (Tip: find out what time the agent usually arrives in the morning and try to be the first caller.) Some more aggressive souls, who want to make their first impression in person, simply show up at agents' offices on the chance it's a slow day, but this can become very time consuming.

It is not recommended to make excessive calls or to camp out on the agent's doorstep. (Be professional.) If you annoy or irritate the agent your chances of success are minimized. Keep seeking out other agents—there are a lot out there. On the other hand, if your calls, letters and contacts are all to no avail, you may want to use your ingenuity and try a more unusual approach. (Stand out from the crowd.) Put yourself in the agent's shoes and try to think of a method that would get *your* attention, if positions were reversed.

Once you get your foot into an agent's door, i.e., get the agent to acknowledge your existence and perhaps to agree to look at your work, you are ready to submit your material. (Of course, as noted, you may send the material at any time but your risk of the loss of a copy is greater if you send it "cold.")

What material should I give to agents for their first exposure to me as a writer?

Some agents will be looking at the sample only as something they can or cannot sell, in which case certain criteria will be used to evaluate it: if it is a screenplay, can it be produced for a feasible amount of money? Can it be cast easily? Will it need extensive revisions to be workable? Alternatively, even if the particular script is unlikely to be made for whatever reason, an agent with more long-term interests will be assessing the work's value as a "calling card"—something to give to people in the industry to introduce you as a writer and show off your skills.

The material you send should be the best sample of your writing *in the form the agent works in*. If the agent deals only in feature films, send a full-length screenplay, *not* a one-act play or a thirty-minute sitcom script. Agents who work primarily with one form are used to reading material in that form. A different format might seem foreign, or less professional, even if it is well done for the type of writing it is. It is also simply easier to read what one is used to reading, as myopic as that might sound.

(You should already be aware of what form(s) the agent deals in from your initial investigation or at least from your phone conversation. You may find out simply by calling the agency switchboard or receptionist, at the Writers Guild or from other writers.)

Send only your *best* sample, not a collection of different material (unless the agent so requests, of course). If the sample is appealing, the agent can always ask you for more, but being faced with a stack of material all from one writer may discourage starting in on it in the first place. Also, the sample should be something you wrote by yourself, not with a partner—unless you are only seeking representation as a team.

The sample should be in proper form, cleanly copied, and professionally typed. As to the form, there is a relatively standardized form for screenplays, for example, which includes certain conventions for margins, treatment of shot set-ups, camera angles, sound effects, etc. Also, find out the standard limits on length and stick to them—e.g., 54 pages for a sixty-minute TV episode, 90–120 pages for a feature film. If you are trying to sell a book, it is not necessary to submit a complete manuscript. It is sufficient to submit the first few chapters (three or so, roughly 50–100 pages), along with an outline or summary of the rest of the story.

Finally, be sure the sample has a strong opening. It is often said that if a screenplay does not catch and hold the reader's attention within the first twenty pages, the next hundred pages could be magnificent but they'll never be read. No doubt a masterpiece *could* start more slowly—but perhaps that masterpiece is not the best sample to send to an agent.

What if the agent likes my material?

If the agent is sufficiently impressed, he or she will want to meet with you. Some agents place a lot of weight on the way a writer "comes off" in person. One reason for this is that the agent may desire a personal rapport with the client as the basis of the working relationship. Others do not care about establishing a "friendly" as opposed to "business" relationship, but may want to be confident that, when the writer is introduced to potential buyers/employers, the writer will make a good impression.

With this in mind, it is wise to give some attention to personal appearance and grooming, as corny as it sounds, when you prepare to meet the agent. Besides the physical preparation, psych yourself up to appear confident in yourself and your ability.

At the meeting, the agent should ask your goals, what direction you'd like your career to take. In turn, you should use the meeting to assess not only the agent's ability to find you the kind of work you want, but also the likelihood of maintaining a mutually satisfying relationship. For example, if you are going to expect a lot of hand-holding and a shoulder to cry on, an agent who is "strictly business" may not be for you.

It is hard to tell all that much from a single meeting, but if there are no blatant signs that you and the agent are a mismatch, you both may want to enter into a relationship on an informal basis. You may wait to sign a contract until after a trial period of perhaps three to six months, or until the agent gets you your first deal.

(If for some reason the agent does not want to represent you, try to find out why. Don't be discouraged, whatever the reason. The next time you reach this meeting stage in the agent-search process, you will at least have some experience with which to compare it.)

What if I already have a deal?

Some new writers are fortunate enough to make a sale without an agent's aid. In such a case, the writer can offer more than past experience as an indicator of future earnings—there is the commission on the present deal to offer as well. It is surprisingly easy to get through to agents when one has a contract in hand.

Remember, however, that you do not want just any agent to represent you; you want one suited to your needs and goals. For this reason, do not feel pressured, by the time demands of the sale in question, to sign a contract with just any agent, or an agent about whom you have doubts. In fact, if it is a relatively simple deal that will require little or no negotiating, a lawyer who will sufficiently protect your interests may cost you less at an hourly rate than the percentage an agent would receive.

Nevertheless, if you have made a sale you should certainly try to take advantage of such an opportunity to get an agent. The producer or publisher of the project may provide some fruitful referrals, and those agents are likely to be very interested in you. Investigate by asking others in the business about these agents, in order to make an informed decision. Look beyond this particular deal to assess what the agent can offer you in the future.

What, specifically, will my agent do for me?

Sell a particular property of yours.

If the writer has a property that has the potential for sale, the agent will figure out a game plan by which to present it to the buyers in the marketplace. The agent will determine, for example, which studios or production companies might be interested in the project, perhaps by sending out feelers to contacts at these places, or from requests already received. The agent and writer may discuss whether a "shotgun" approach should be used, putting the script up for auction at all the studios, or whether they want to be more selective and limit submissions to one or two buyers at first. Along these lines, the agent will be considering which people already know and like the writer, which have expressed desires for the particular type of project and which are most likely to be able to get the project moving.

Similar tactics are used for the sale of a book, but the targeted buyers will be editors at publishing companies. Since it can take much longer to write a book than a screenplay, book contracts are often entered into based upon the first three chapters plus an outline, so that the writer can receive an advance to subsidize the writing.

Package television and motion picture projects.

"Packaging" is important today because the motion picture studios have changed from the self-contained, complete production facilities they once were, with their own in-house staff of producers, directors, writers and actors. Now the studios' emphasis is on financing and distribution, and as such they are more interested in as complete an offer as can be made; a script as finished and polished as possible (as opposed to rights to a story that must first be developed or adapted to screenplay form), a production company ready to produce the film, a director and actors with some drawing power committed to the project on at least an informal basis.

Thus, the literary agent tries to find one or more of these other elements to offer to the studio—or to the network, if applicable—along with the literary property, as a "package deal."

Packaging is more often and more easily accomplished by the larger, multidepartmental agencies than by smaller agencies or independent agents. The larger agencies have access to the different elements because they represent all types of talent, as well as producers. Nevertheless, if there is no one within the agency who is right for the particular package, the agent should look beyond the home-base agency's clients. In the same way, the smaller agencies and independents can put together packages by using their contacts in the industry (this is one reason you want your agent to have good relations with other agents as well as with buyers).

Get you development deals for movies and TV.

While the agent pursues the agreed-upon game plan for a completed property, the writer will want to begin other projects. The agents can offer advice as to which of several ideas might be most easily salable, based on what certain buyers (or actors, or directors) are currently looking for. The agent may try to get the writer a development deal for an idea the writer has. This would involve finding a production company or studio to "back" the writer in developing a screenplay (or TV movie, pilot, etc.) in stages, with the ability to "cut off" the writer after delivery of each stage of development (i.e., story treatment, first draft, etc.). This could be done either through a purchase of the rights to the story, in which case the purchaser would own the rights after the writer is cut off, or through an option to purchase the rights at a later time. In that case the writer would retain the rights if the option is not exercised. This would allow the writer to offer the property to a new buyer, although less money is paid for an option than for an outright purchase of rights.

Obtain television employment for you.

The agent can also try to find the writer employment in episodic television, if the writer so desires. The agent who keeps abreast of the needs of various shows will know whether there are any openings for staff positions, or whether there are episodic assignments available for freelance writers. If an agent does not have the necessary contacts, it will be nearly impossible to "break into" an established series, for many reasons. The road from the germ of an idea through the developmental process—story, script, revisions, casting, filming the pilot, etc.—to the ultimate order for an initial seven or perhaps thirteen episodes is so difficult that producers understandably want to work only with people they already know and can trust to "deliver."

Most shows are staff-written, but quite a few do have at least a small number of episodes open to assign out to trusted or proven writers. An agent with the right contacts and good timing, however, can get even a new writer in to pitch an idea for a story to the story editor (probably after submission of a writing sample). Here, as in many situations including the development deal mentioned above, writers' personal and verbal talents are almost as important as their writing skills. The agent will set up the meeting, but the writer must convey the story effectively, and convince the prospective buyer/employer that the idea will come across effectively on the screen.

Secure other forms of employment for you.

The agent may also seek out other forms of employment, as where the writer works from existing material. Two examples are adaptations of books into screenplay form, and rewrites of films or TV movies that have gone through one or more drafts but still need work.

Negotiate fees.

Agents are responsible for negotiating the fee for their clients, who often rely heavily on the agent's advice. In general, the agent will consider the going rates, the buyer's financing situation, and what the market will bear, and will try to get at least as much or more than the writer has received in the past for a given type of work. The agent should keep the client apprised of the progress of the negotiations, reporting in when an offer is made and a counteroffer returned. Sometimes the writer will set a floor limit on the amount, and most writers want the agent to try to get as high a price as possible without "blowing the deal."

The agent will advise the writer as to whether an offer is reasonable, whether it's probably the best they'll get or whether the buyer is likely to go higher. It is when the writer really does not need (or want) a project too badly that the agent can make the most demands. When the primary objective is to get the deal made and the work produced (which is most of the time), the writer may have to make concessions. Sometimes deals fall through because the agent and writer rightfully refuse an offer that is too low for a given property. Unless the work is so topical that it will soon be outdated and/or worth-

less, or unless the writer needs a sale right away, the correct choice may be to wait for a better offer rather than settle for a quick deal.

An inexperienced writer can expect to be offered no more than the Writers Guild minimum rate of compensation at first, because the buyer will want to risk as little as possible on an unproven commodity. When the writer becomes much more in demand, the agent can use more leverage and negotiate not only higher flat fees but also perhaps a percentage of the net profits derived from exploiting the literary material. Another possible arrangement is for the writer to receive a lower amount up front, but to then receive additional monies as the project proceeds, in deferred payments. For example, the writer might get a bonus at the start of principal photography and at the close of photography or on the date of the first general release of a film project. (This is a good way to lessen the risk on a newer writer—if the project doesn't go forward, the writer won't get the bonuses; if it does go forward, the compensation is due.) With some deals the agent may also try to include a provision for percentages of the profits from supplemental markets, cable and cassettes (see the chapter on Contracts).

Give you career guidance and exposure.

In addition to obtaining employment or selling properties, the agent should be trying to guide the writer's career in various ways. For example, for the more advanced writer, it is important to know when to turn down a job for strategic reasons—when the project will not reflect well on the writer's reputation, or when the writer wants to focus exclusively on one medium such as film, or when a writer's "unavailability" will serve to increase the demand and interest in that writer.

For the new writer, however, the agent will want to provide exposure, putting out the word to the buyers in the marketplace that new talent has arrived on the scene. In addition to actually talking to people about the writer, the agent will distribute the writer's material (the sample, the "calling card") and set up meetings to introduce the writer to people in the industry. Sometimes when a writer is needed, the buyer remembers meeting and liking one writer in particular and calls the agent to check on availability. The more people out there who know you, the more likely this will happen to you. Thus, your agent should be arranging meetings just to introduce you to people who may be able to hire you in the future, if not today. If you are a recluse and abhor such socialization, you do not have to pursue this route; if you can do it, however, you will be helping your agent to help you.

Criticize your work.

Agents vary as to the degree of editorial advice or criticism they want to offer, and this is a matter to be worked out between the agent and client. What happens, however, if the agent hates a script or manuscript the writer wants to be sold? The agent has an obligation to at least test the market, to get some other opinions—the agent could be wrong. Some agents go by the motto, "Sell it, don't smell it"—and will push the property to the hilt regardless of their personal opinion of it. Others will not be able to manufacture the false enthusiasm and support necessary for the project; in that case an agreement can be reached whereby the writer can either try to sell that project alone or can take it to another agent (who would get the entire commission).

Review your contracts.

The larger entertainment agencies have staffs of lawyers who review and negotiate contracts on behalf of the agency's clients. Although regulations do not permit them to provide legal advice, on many deals a client can save substantial legal fees by having the contracts handled by the agency's business affairs department (whose services are rendered at no extra charge) rather than by the client's own lawyer. For certain deals, a client may feel more comfortable having both his own lawyer and the agency's lawyer work together on the contract.

Provide accounting services.

Larger agencies also have accounting departments which, in connection with the client's professional income, perform bookkeeping and collection services. Agents in the smaller agencies have to call the writer's employers to chase down the checks that haven't been received (or sent), and this takes time. At the larger agency, the accounting department can take care of such matters and free the agent to concentrate on sales.

What other differences are there between large and small agencies?

In smaller operations, as with independents, the agents cover the entire field of buyers in attempting to cultivate contacts for their clients, whom they alone represent. Sometimes such agents also deal in more than one form or medium, and so instead of concentrating solely on sitcom story editors, for example, they also try to establish relationships with many different buyers at studios, production companies and perhaps even publishing houses.

While in practice the agents at larger agencies may work this way also, the larger agency may be set up with a very different underlying plan or structure. The William Morris Agency, for example, separates its agents by department, and within a department each agent is supposed to cover a certain segment of the market. Thus, an agent in the motion picture department is theoretically responsible for only two or three studios and a number of independent producers. The agent tries to stay abreast of the needs of all its assigned buyers, and each agent has access to all the writers' material represented by the agency. International Creative Management (ICM), another very large agency, is structured somewhat differently in that the coverage of the market by each agent is not so restricted. ICM agents have their own clients, independently of the other agents, although in practice they too are often in close contact with their fellow agents regarding filling the buyer's demands.

One benefit the large agency can offer is its name. Even if buyers haven't heard of a particular agent, they have heard of ICM or William Morris. Such names carry prestige and open doors even if the individual agent's might not. On the other hand, there are also quite a few small agencies or independents that are highly respected, perhaps even more than the largest agencies, by those who do know of them.

For the beginning writer, the most important attributes of an agent are the willingness and ability to take the time to nurture the new writer's career, to develop the necessary contacts and find a sponsor to get the writer started. Although new writers are often advised to start off with smaller agencies, the question is not whether the agency is big or small, but whether the agent will provide the new writer with the amount of attention a fledgling career demands. And that answer will vary with each agent, even within one agency, regardless of its size.

How can I develop a good relationship with my agent?

It is in both your agent's and your own best interests for your agent to represent you as well as possible. Moreover, your agent has a duty to be fair and above board with you regarding all dealings made on your behalf (see the chapter on Agency Agreements). For these reasons, you should try to start off by giving your agent the benefit of the doubt that he/she is doing his/her best. Both agent and client should try to develop a relationship of mutual trust and understanding, which naturally requires meaningful communication.

The agent and writer should discuss at the outset any ground rules for their joint efforts. For example, the agent should inform the writer about all submissions of material, and the writer should not embarrass the agent by independently giving an exclusive option to a third party on work that the agent has already submitted to others. Similarly, while the agent should inform the writer regarding the progress of negotiations, the writer should not compromise the agent's ability to negotiate (for example, by contradicting earlier representations made by the agent with the writer's approval).

Unless you have a very unusual relationship, your agent probably will not appreciate frequent calls to see what's happening. If something is happening, the agent should call you. Once you and the agent have agreed to a game plan in trying to sell a project, for example, you should only be calling if you have new thoughts or suggestions about it. This way, your agent will know that all calls from you are important and must be returned. If you want to talk to your agent every day, or twice a week—"no matter what"—then this is the kind of thing you should work out as soon as possible, to avoid hurt feelings or mistrust on either side before it develops.

How will I know when to leave my agent?

It is recognized as the nature of the business that, when clients reach a certain level of success, they move on to greener pastures, i.e., new agents. Frequently such a writer will be approached, sought after by other agents and may be lured by hopes of better contracts and bigger fees. (When the belief in

better results is well grounded, it is quite a legitimate reason for changing agents.)

Sometimes the agent/client relationship simply is no longer productive or satisfying (if it ever was), for any number of reasons: a lot of little irritations have been tolerated for a long time; the agent's contacts are not in sync with the writer's style; or the agent just isn't working hard enough for the writer. The writer has to focus on his or her career rather than on the personal relationship, although the decision to move on can be very difficult if the agent has become a friend.

If there are some particular complaints prompting you to want a different agent, it is both fair and prudent to sit down with your agent and talk about your dissatisfaction. The agent may have no idea that you are unhappy—or at least unhappy enough to leave. Especially with agents who are not too set in their ways, such feedback can help to make them better agents, if not more attentive to your needs. Give the agent a chance to improve, perhaps set an agreed-upon time limit, such as thirty to sixty days or so. If there are no signs of change, a move would probably be advisable. (The chapter on Agency Agreements outlines the proper procedure to terminate such relationships and explains the obligations involved.) By that point, it is hoped, you will have made enough contacts to find an agent more easily than you did the first time!

Armed with the information contained herein, the writer with marketable skills should be able to find an agent, and should know what to expect in return for that ten percent commission. Although as a group they are the butt of many jokes, most agents are hard-working, sincere, knowledgeable and even creative people who provide a valuable and necessary service for their clients and for the industry as a whole.

The authors would like to thank Lew Weitzman, whose excellent article, "The Literary Agent," from The Movie Business *(edited by A. William Bluem and Jason E. Squire), provided valuable information for this chapter.*

THE WRITERS GUILD OF AMERICA— WHAT IT IS AND WHAT IT DOES

Molly Wilson

The Writers Guild of America (WGA) is a labor union. Its primary function is to represent writers for the purpose of collective bargaining in the motion picture, television and radio industries. The primary current collective bargaining agreement is the WGA 1981 Theatrical and Television Minimum Basic Agreement, which has been signed by the major motion picture studios, independent production companies and other employers of writers in the industry. This agreement is discussed in a later chapter. The WGA also has collective bargaining agreements with the three networks, public broadcasting stations and radio producers.

The Guild does not obtain employment for writers, or help writers find agents, or offer writing instructions or advice. It does not accept or handle literary material for submission to production companies.

The combined membership of the WGA is now more than 8,500.

A BRIEF HISTORY

The Writers Guild of America is an outgrowth of the Authors Guild, which was organized in 1912 as a protective association for writers of books, short stories, articles and so forth. The Authors Guild

Molly (Margaret) Wilson joined the WGAw as Associate Resident Counsel in May 1979. She has also practiced labor law at the firm of Silber, Benezra & Taslitz. Ms. Wilson is a graduate of the UCLA School of Law and received her undergraduate degree in Russian Studies and Language from the University of California at Riverside.

later became a branch of the Authors League, whose other branches include the Dramatists Guild, the Screenwriters Guild (SWG) and the Radio Writers Guild. The first collective bargaining agreement with the industry was signed in 1942 by the SWG. In 1954 these branches combined to form the Writers Guild of America, consisting of the Writers Guild of America, West (WGAw) and the Writers Guild of America, East (WGAe).

WGA MEMBERSHIP

There are four classes of membership in WGA: Associate, Current, Non-current and Withdrawn. The minimum requirement for Associate membership in the Guild is that the writer have had employment as a writer for screen, television or radio, or have sold original material to one of those media.

Membership in the other classes depends upon the amount of employment or sale of work during the last two or three years.

The Guild is a union shop, which means that any writer employed by a signatory company must become a member of the Guild not later than thirty days after first employment, and must remain a member in good standing during employment.

A member in good standing who intends to suspend writing in all fields under WGA jurisdiction may upon request be placed on Withdrawn status.

The initiation fee for new members is $1,500. Basic dues for Associate, Current and Non-current members are $25 per quarter. In addition to basic dues, members must pay an amount equal to one percent of the gross income from the sale or licensing of unexploited literary material and earnings from motion picture and television employment. The percentage dues are credited against the basic dues per quarter.

WORKING RULES AND DISCIPLINE

The Guild has working rules governing the working relationship of members with employers, agents and others with whom writers have professional dealings. Their basic rationale is to protect writer-members as well as the Guild.

Perhaps the most important is Working Rule 8, which prohibits a member from accepting employment with, or selling literary material to, any person, firm or corporation that is not a signatory to the applicable Minimum Basic Agreement (MBA). A writer cannot rely upon the statement of his or her agent or any other third party, but must personally verify that the employer is a signatory by telephoning the WGA Signatories Department.

VIOLATIONS

Compliance with Working Rule 8 is crucial. Any violation or evasion poses a serious threat to the Guild as a whole, as it threatens the integrity of the collective agreement. Thus, violations of Working Rule 8 are vigorously prosecuted against the writer, with penalties ranging from $500 up to the full amount received from the non-signatory.

Another key rule is Working Rule 6, which prohibits members from making any agreement to write for less than minimum compensation. A related rule, Working Rule 14, places a prohibition upon speculative writing. (Writing "on spec" is explained in detail in the chapter on the MBA.)

Working Rules 3 and 4 are particularly important from a legal standpoint, since they require that all agreements for writing services between writers and producers must be in writing, and that a writer may not work without a contract.

As will be seen from the discussion below, it is very much in the writer's interest to comply with the Code of Working Rules. An alarming number of the claims handled by the Guild's legal department have come about because a writer wrote on speculation, agreed to write for less than minimum compensation, began to perform writing services before obtaining a written contract or worked for a non-signatory producer.

REGISTRATION SERVICE

As discussed more fully in the chapter on Copyright, the Guild maintains a registration service, with which writers can register literary material that is intended for theatrical motion pictures, television and radio. The Guild charges $5 for each registration to Guild members, and $10 to non-Guild applicants. The registration process provides the writer with Guild-backed proof that a certain work was registered by a certain time and date, and then officially sealed and filed in the Guild's locked warehouse. It is a good practice to register any property before submitting it to a third party.

DETERMINATION OF WRITING CREDITS

The career of a writer is substantially dependent upon his accumulation of writing credits. For this reason, the Guild probably devotes greater attention to the subject of writing credits than it does to any other single matter. The forms of credit, the adjudication of those credits, the appearance of credits on screen and in advertising and publicity receive constant scrutiny in the day-to-day operations of the Guild.

In pre-Guild days, the producers had sole authority for determining writing credits on films. This power was often exercised in an arbitrary, nepotistic and discriminatory manner. A basic objective of the Guild in negotiating its first industry-wide collective bargaining agreement was to give the Guild the sole authority to adjudicate writing credits. Such protections were achieved in the first contract and the Guild's system of credit arbitration and the MBA provisions regarding forms of credit and their appearance in paid advertising, in publicity and on screen have been developed in great detail with the passage of time.

In general there is nothing in the MBA that prohibits a writer from negotiating for better terms and conditions than the minimum terms provided for in the MBA. There is one exception; the Guild requirements with respect to writing credit constitute both a maximum and a minimum. Since the Guild has final authority to determine who shall receive writing credit and in what form, the contract between the individual writer and producing company can only provide for writing credits in accordance with the MBA.

Procedure for Determining Credits

Upon completion of principal photography of a television or theatrical film, the producer (referred to as "company" in the Minimum Basic Agreement and throughout the rest of this chapter) is required to file with the Guild a Notice of Tentative Writing Credits, with a copy to every writer who has participated in the development of the material. That notice indicates the company's proposal for the final writing credits. If any participating writer in the project does not agree with the company's determination, he may file a protest in which event a credit arbitration is conducted.

In conducting a credit arbitration, all written material relating to a given film is submitted to the Guild and is sent to three Guild members who have volunteered their time to conduct credit arbitrations. They read all of the material and make a final determination of writing credit in accordance with guidelines laid down in the Guild's credits manuals. Their names are not revealed to one another nor to the participating writers involved in a given arbitration. Once a majority decision is reached by the three arbiters, the company and all participants are notified, and the result is binding on all parties.

Enforcement of Credit Requirements

Since 1973, the MBA has contained provisions whereby violations of the credits provisions may be submitted to an expedited arbitration wherein the arbitrator has the power to grant injunctive relief, to award damages and to order correction of prints and of advertising and publicity material. This machinery has been strenuously utilized by the Guild since 1973 in enforcing compliance with the Guild's credits requirements.

Credits Manuals and Working Procedures

The Guild disseminates to its members television and motion picture credits manuals, which explain the credit determination procedure and the writer's responsibilities in that process. All writer-members should thoroughly familiarize themselves with these manuals, and contact the Guild for any necessary clarification.

There are several steps that the writer should take to protect his or her potential credits. First, the writer must ascertain the names of all other writers currently assigned to the literary material at the commencement of employment. The writer must then notify such writers of the fact that he or she has been assigned to the material.

The writer must also file a copy of his or her employment contract with the Guild office no later than one week after receipt of the contract. Finally, and very importantly, it is imperative that the writer keep copies of all written work done. The work should be dated. Notes should also be made of suggestions in story conferences that do not appear as the writer's work in the final script. See the chapter on the Minimum Basic Agreement for a discussion of the forms of credit.

ENFORCEMENT OF COLLECTIVE BARGAINING AGREEMENTS

The Guild maintains a legal staff which will represent individual members (and the Guild) in connection with certain claims.

The main categories of claims covered include:

1. Claims for unpaid compensation under the writer's individual employment contract, up to a limit of $75,000 for television employment and $150,000 for theatrical (motion picture) employment.
2. Violation of the writing credits provisions of the MBA.
3. Claims involving alleged violations of any of the terms or provisions of the MBA.
4. Disputes between the Guild and the company concerning the interpretation, application and effect of the terms of the MBA.

Except for the foregoing types of claims, the Guild is not in a position to provide legal representation to writers. Accordingly, it is not a function of the Guild to give advice to writers in the areas of copyright, defamation, plagiarism and so forth. Nor can the Guild legal staff provide representation in the negotiation of individual deals. (However, in certain cases where a member's agent also represents the producer, the Guild will provide a Guild negotiator—see the chapter on Writer-Agency Agreements.)

OTHER FUNCTIONS

Other important services of the Guild include collection and distribution of residuals payable under the collective bargaining agreements; legislative and judicial participation in legal matters concerning writers, including First Amendment matters, defamation, etc. (such participation includes lobbying activities and filing of *amicus curiae* briefs); checking of individual writers' contracts for violations of the MBA; enforcement of working rules; distribution of "unfair" lists and strike lists; maintaining a pension plan and health fund; affiliation and cooperation with other guilds and various industry associations; public relations; maintaining a credit union; providing a group insurance plan; maintaining a film society, and numerous other functions.

The Guild also negotiates an agreement with talent agents, governing the minimum terms between writers and their agents. The substantive provisions of that agreement are discussed in the chapter on Writer-Agency Agreements.

A PSYCHOLOGICAL PRIMER FOR THE YOUNG HOLLYWOOD WRITER

Charles Rosin

Like most Hollywood-based writers, I seem to spend a lot of time waiting for various powers (networks, studios, agents) to pass judgment on various projects (outlines, story treatments, screenplays) that lie waiting in various stages of development. While I wait I am neither optimistic nor pessimistic, neither anxious nor depressed. I'm not comatose either—just aware after six (oh-my-God-has-it-really-been-six) years of writing for film and television that the whole process can be compared to the sensation dust feels when it's settling. After all, like most writers, dust has no control over the elements that are determining its fate. Moreover, dust tends to expend an inordinate amount of energy swirling around the periphery, trying desperately to gravitate to some glossy surface, knowing from the outset that in all probability it will either be swept into the dumper or just blown away.

As fond as I am of my writer/dust metaphor, the analogy is basically inaccurate because there has never been a speck of dust that has seriously questioned its sanity.

Theoretically, most of the information contained in this book should give you a better perspective on how writers function, or are supposed to function, within the framework of this industry. The agents, lawyers, producers and representatives of the Writers Guild who have contributed to this manual are all well-versed on the rules and protocol of show business. They know it is a crazy business. You know it's a crazy business. And if you don't, let

me be the first to tell you—it's a crazy business. A business of subjectivity, timing, whim and luck. A business where patience is a must, and talent helps, too.

To my mind the most pressing problem facing the young (or novice) writer has little to do with finding a good agent, or receiving a "fair read" or even getting a foot through the door—the real problem is learning how to cope with the craziness. It's loony tunes out there, and it's contagious.

To this end, the ultimate creative struggle isn't between you and your typewriter, or you and a given producer, but between you and that frenzied inner voice that keeps asking, "Why are you willfully subjecting yourself to all this abuse?" I can't answer that one, but I can offer a few therapeutic observations—battle scars, if you will—culled from experience that may help your psyche from going down for the count.

ON RISING EXPECTATIONS

Guard against them at all costs. Keep your perspective. Compliments are nice, story conferences with VIPs are exciting, optioned properties and development deals pay the rent, but unless the work is produced and distributed, it's all speculation and conjecture. The higher your expectations, the longer the drop. Protect yourself. Anticipate the worst and be pleasantly surprised if anything else occurs. Whatever happens, never stop believing in yourself and in miracles.

Charles Rosin, a native of Los Angeles, was groomed to be a lawyer.

ON REJECTION

It's all pervasive and quite debilitating. Even a skin of leather can't lessen the sting of the darts that are constantly trying to puncture your spirits. Try to remember that when a reader or a producer does not respond favorably to your work, it is just one person's opinion and not necessarily a reflection on you, your talent or the words on the page. It may be that a company has a similar project in development, or they are not interested in the genre, or maybe, just maybe, your script was not up to snuff—a painful conclusion to be sure, but one that can save you a lot of frustration and sleepless nights. Always assess the quality of the feedback. If the suggestions make sense, make changes. If the comments are nebulous and you feel the reader missed the point, don't waste your energy trying to persuade that person to like your script. Find another reader. Or another project. Do anything, but don't dwell in self-pity. Not only are literary lamentations extremely boring, they are ultimately destructive.

One other thought on rejection. An executive story editor for a major production apparatus once told me in confidence that most scripts get rejected because "it is safer for an executive to be negative. Otherwise the studio mogul will have to take responsibility for a project that might fail and cost him his job."

ON PRESSURE

Writers, especially novice writers, tend to be their own worst enemy. We have trouble accepting the fact that unfulfilled promises, unreturned phone calls and unemployment are basic byproducts of this industry. We can't adjust to the long lulls, the cancelled meetings and the anonymity, so we become defensive, cynical and insecure . . . and then we wonder why our behavior seems to be alienating old friends and potential allies. Moreover, we resent those sensible, uncreative kids from college who opted for conventionality and are now successful lawyers, doctors and MBAs. You know who I'm talking about . . . the ones your parents use as a point for comparison . . . the ones who seemingly will never suffer the indignity of poverty or the malaise of self-doubt. What can I tell you? You have

chosen a hard way of life, but you will only make it harder by imposing an artificial set of pressures on yourself.

There is no pat formula for success. More importantly, there is no time frame under which you are expected to succeed. If you are lucky (and I mean LUCKY), you'll score in six months, but more likely it will take years before your talent is respected and your services are in demand. You, your parents and your loved ones must realize that a career spans a lifetime, and that most of the top-name writers in this town are survivors who paid dues and somehow managed to endure the ignominity and the pressure. So, in the interim, develop your craft, keep your emotions in check and strive to attain a reputation over what could be a long, long haul.

ON RAGE

When scorned or emotionally abused by a particularly nasty producer or executive type, your first impulse will be to settle the score. To get even. To release your anger and pain in the form of a sarcastic note, or a sharp phone call. Better yet, a hostile tête-a-tête. You'll probably feel vindicated for a moment or two, but for the sake of your career, be adult. Just walk away. Take up TM. Take a cold shower. Do whatever is necessary to transcend the trauma, but don't burn your bridges. Hollywood is a small town that seems to be getting smaller all the time. Alliances are constantly shifting. Yesterday's arch nemesis is tomorrow's meal ticket. A paycheck down the line is its own retribution.

ON ENVY

As a diversion, a friend of mine who had worked production on documentaries decided to write a script. To my knowledge, he had never written a declarative sentence before, let alone a full-blown screenplay, but he pounded the thing out in three weeks and two days later it was optioned by a major producer for a lot of money. Needless to say, my friend's good fortune caused me to become clinically depressed. I avoided him for months. When I finally found the courage to call, I learned that the producer had decided to shelve my friend's script.

In retrospect, I was temporarily afflicted with the "why him and not me" syndrome which is endemic to all Hollywood parvenus foolish enough to evaluate their intrinsic worth in terms of someone else's progress. This regressive and petty mind-set is common among insecure, obsessive types who have yet to learn that writers aren't competitors but peers. To avoid this dreaded affliction, remember that you are not in a race with anyone—especially yourself.

ON DOING BUSINESS WITH FRIENDS

Rather than dwell on my producer friend who brought in a stranger to punch up my dialogue without giving me the opportunity to fix my own non sequiturs, or on my director buddy who toasted to our 50-50 partnership, only to dissolve the union when he decided that his consultant's role merited a larger percentage of the profits neither of us would ever receive, let me just echo the central theme of this symposium: preserve your friendships—get professional advice, and then get it in writing. It may seem like too formal a modus operandi for ex-college roomies, but nothing can shatter the heart more quickly than the realization that that special friendship you thought was built on years of trust and confidence was actually being supported by a foundation of expedience and mush.

ON NEPOTISM AND CONTACTS

Given the sorry state of our contemporary value system, probably many of you are resigned to the popular school of cynical thought which maintains that it's not what you do, it's who you know. Obviously nepotism exists in the "Hollywood Family"— and anyone fortunate enough to be in a position to take advantage of a blood connection is probably out on location somewhere taking full advantage of it—but someone's lineage does not prevent the rest of us from writing exceptional scripts. Admittedly, however, a socially adept writer can further his or her career by finagling invitations to, and making valuable connections at, Hollywood's "A," "B," and even "C-plus" parties. But if you are an unconnected recent arrival/weekend TV watcher with an open calendar, take heart. I know a writer who has never been invited to a glitzy Hollywood extrava-

ganza, who has never sold a shred of material to anyone who agreed to see him out of a social obligation to his family, and has only been hired by producers *after* they read his material. I don't bring this up out of any sense of self-righteousness, but because I want to make it clear that my wonderful wife and I are available for parties and screenings on weekends and most weeknights.

ON THEFT

Converting someone else's idea into cash and credit is not a figment of some bitter writer's imagination. Horror stories abound—and for good reason. Theft is a recurring, unconscionable problem that seems to be getting worse and not better.

A lawyer can give you sound advice on how to protect yourself and what recourse is available once a transgression has occurred. I can share a few thoughts and a painful memory.

Three years ago I was ripped off. The thief wasn't a beleaguered story editor from a long-running series lifting a subplot from a rejected manuscript. It wasn't a schlock-house producer of dubious repute pilfering a generic idea for the B-movie circuit. The man who violated my right of creation was an executive for a major television production company—a signatory of the WGA agreement, no less. Not only was I assigned to develop a "concept" without payment, but once I delivered my material I was abruptly terminated because the company did not want to jeopardize its chance for a network sale by attaching a then unknown and "unapproved" writer to its package.

Why did they take advantage of me? Because they knew they could exploit a young writer. What did I do in retaliation? Nothing. I rolled over and played dead. Why? Because I listened to the advice of a well-intentioned professional who told me that if I lodged a formal protest with the WGA I would become known as a "troublemaker." To this day I regret that I didn't take those pikers to the cleaners.

The fear of being labeled "difficult" should never deter you from exercising your rights as a professional writer. If you feel you have a *legitimate* grievance, don't be afraid to stand up and fight because you perceive yourself as a nonentity with no credibility and no chance to triumph over a powerful corporation. And don't feel intimidated by ludicrous threats that some kind of evil conspiracy will deprive you of a career for the next decade or two. This is not to say the Blacklist era is something any writer in Hollywood can afford to forget, but it is doubtful that any single person in this town has the clout to keep a quality writer out of the market-place.

One note of caution, however. Paranoia is a crippling way for a writer to conduct his or her affairs. If you believe that every story editor who listens to your oral pitches is a potential thief, or every producer an unscrupulous entrepreneur, you will never be happy writing for film and television. The keystone of this business is trust—you trusting the professional reputation of a producer; the producer, in turn, trusting your creative instincts.

ON WRITING ON SPEC

To clarify, writing on spec means working for others for no compensation. Don't do it . . . and not only because you will be violating the central tenet of the WGA agreement, but because as a writer all you have to offer is your talent and your time—and your talent merits remuneration, and your time can be better applied developing your own, unencumbered ideas. Besides, any independent producer who cannot afford to pay for your services probably doesn't have the wherewithal to get the project off the ground in the first place.

ON WRITING IN HOLLYWOOD

While novelists, dramatists and, to a lesser extent, screenwriters can enjoy the luxury of living and working in any locale they choose, any writer who wants to be in the business of prime-time television must live where ninety percent of all network fare originates. So say "Good-bye, Peoria," and "Hello, Hollywood." Living in this city of the fallen angels is a culture shock at best. You'll be an immigrant in a town full of immigrants. Like any new arrival there will be times you'll feel lonely, disconnected and therefore susceptible . . . and I don't mean susceptible to unscrupulous producers. There are a lot of diversions out here in Hollywood. Lots of cheap thrills. So take care of yourself. Who knows? You may even like living in Los Angeles—as opposed to Hollywood, which is little more than a state of mind anyway.

ON WRITING

Before I became a Hollywood-based writer, I believe I was a reasonably healthy human specimen. Now, I would have to classify myself as a certifiable schizophrenic with two distinct parts, each with its own approach to the business.

The first part, the jaded part, wants to warn the "mommas" of the world not to let their babies grow up to be writers. This part considers writers to be the hookers of Hollywood, because, as they say, nine out of ten times we are on the bottom "getting screwed" by people who take us for granted. Moreover, this jaded part compares writing in Hollywood to a crap-shoot with a loaded pair of dice, and defines a Hollywood intellectual as anyone who buys a hardback book.

Then there is the other part, the idealistic part, the part that wants to reach out and hug you and remind you that you possess a rare gift with which very few are blessed and cursed. This part urges you to stop trying to second-guess what some honcho will consider commercial and begin to write with the passion, clarity and humor that can only be found in the deeper layers of your soul.

Needless to say, the two parts have very little in common and are constantly bickering with each other. In fact, the only thing that keeps them together is a mutual respect for a fundamental, albeit oft-forgotten concept—writers write, and that alone is what makes them special.

A Practical Legal Guide

COHEN & O'BRIEN
900 Wilshire Boulevard, Suite 123
Beverly Hills, California 90212
Telephone: (213) 999-9999

Attorneys for Plaintiff

IN THE UNITED STATES DISTRICT COURT

FOR THE CENTRAL DISTRICT OF CALIFORNIA

RONA RITER,
 	
        Plaintiff,
 	
    vs.
 	
MARAMOUNT PICTURES CORPORA-
TION, WYZ PRODUCTIONS,
 	
        Defendants.
	)))))))))))))))	NO. _____
		
		COMPLAINT FOR COPYRIGHT
		INFRINGEMENT, UNFAIR
		COMPETITION, EXEMPLARY
		AND PUNITIVE DAMAGES,
		MISAPPROPRIATION AND
		CONVERSION OF INTELLEC-
		TUAL PROPERTY, FALSE
		DESIGNATION OF ORIGIN,
		BREACH OF IMPLIED CONTRACT,
		UNJUST ENRICHMENT, AND
		BREACH OF CONFIDENTIAL
		RELATIONSHIP

NOW COMES RONA RITER, AS AND FOR HER CLAIMS FOR RELIEF

AGAINST DEFENDANTS, EACH AND ALL OF THEM, AND DEMANDING TRIAL BY

JURY, ALLEGES, AVERS AND COMPLAINS AS FOLLOWS:

1. Plaintiff Rona Riter (hereinafter "Riter"), a citizen

of the United States and a resident of Los Angeles, California.

2. Defendant Maramount Pictures Corporation (hereinafter

"Maramount") is a corporation duly organized and existing under and

by virtue of the laws of the State of California.

The Role of an Attorney in Representing Motion Picture and Television Writers

Joseph D. Peckerman, Esq.

The role that an entertainment attorney plays in representing a writer in the motion picture and television industries is largely a function of three things: the writer's own needs and desires, the services provided by the client's other advisers (agent, personal manager and/or business manager) and the personality and interests of the attorney himself.

Next only to the writer's own needs and perceptions, the most important of these factors customarily is the agent. The threshold question then becomes whether a writer should have an agent. As a lawyer, I believe that it is very important for a writer to be represented by an agent who is qualified and aggressive, who has a strong creative sense of the client's strengths (and weaknesses) and who has a clear vision of what the writer's potential and therefore his future can be.

The agent's job is to know what projects and what deals are being made at every company in the industry, and the agent can be expected to know that information better than any of the writer's other advisers, including the lawyer. Thus, the agent is in the best position to sell ideas and scripts and secure jobs for the writer, and to make the richest deal for the writer in the process. While it is true that some writers do not have agents, they are clearly the exception. Indeed, of all the persons whose services are "above the line," writers tend, and for good reason, to be the most heavily represented by agents.

Assuming that the writer is represented by an agent and that the agent is the primary force in at least the business side of the writer's professional life, the role that the attorney will perform will largely be shaped by what the agent does and what he chooses not to do. The functions of the agent do vary—from agency to agency and from one agent to another. Hence, it is the *writer's* responsibility to insure that the agent and the attorney, both of whom are working for him or her have a clear sense of what each expects the other to do.

DEAL POINTS

Obviously, the writer will expect his agent to "make the deal." What does that mean? Essentially two things: matching the writer with the buyer of his services or of his already-written idea or script, and then negotiating the basic terms of the deal. This can be as simple as the following hypothetical figures for the commissioning of an original screenplay:

$25,000 for a first draft and set of revisions, an option in the producer for a second set of revisions for $10,000, all against $75,000 for sole screenplay credit or a $10,000 bonus for shared screenplay credit, plus 5% to 100% of net profits for sole

Joseph D. Peckerman is a partner in the law firm of Haldeman and Peckerman. He is a graduate of Yale Law School and Johns Hopkins University. His specialty is entertainment law, focusing on theatrical motion pictures, television and print publishing.

screenplay credit or 2½ to 100% for shared screenplay credit.

Such an outline covers many major points and, frankly, for a writer these are probably the most significant business terms of the deal, since many other points, such as credit, are rather well taken care of in the Writers Guild Minimum Agreement.

SECOND-TIER POINTS

The above outline, however, leaves out many very important terms of the deal, and the Minimum Basic Agreement (MBA) is exactly that—a minimum, which can be bettered. For example, will the writer of the original story retain print publishing rights? Will he have any reversion or turnaround rights if the producer or other financier doesn't produce the project? Will he receive any bonus or profit participation if the project is rewritten and he receives "story-by" credit but not screenplay credit? Will he be paid additional amounts in excess of any applicable Writers Guild minimum if a sequel or remake is produced? Will he have any right to render writing services on the sequel? These points, while not essential terms of the deal, can clearly be very important. Points of this nature fall in the category of what I call "second-tier points"—points that may not be, at least in all cases, economically significant enough to be worth blowing the deal over, but points which can nevertheless be very important in financial and in some cases (print publishing, for example) career terms. Some agents choose to deal with these second-tier points, others leave them for the attorney. However, as subsidiary rights (publishing, sequels, remakes, video discs, soundtrack albums, etc.) become economically more important, these second-tier points become more critical, and often must be negotiated "up front" (at the same time the basic deal is made) in order to preserve the writer's leverage and ability to realize these benefits. What this means is that, in many cases, it is in the best interest of the client to have the agent and lawyer backing each other up and making the deal, including *both* deal points and second-tier points together. And, in this connection, it is well worth noting that, ultimately, it is the *writer's* willingness to back up both of his representatives, by refusing to start work until these points are closed and money changes hands, that will determine how successful the agent and attorney will be.

LEGAL POINTS

In addition to this second level of issues, the hiring of the services of a writer or the sale of an idea or screenplay involves a contract. These rights acquisition or employment contracts, like any other legal agreements involving substantial sums of money, include numerous "legal" or "language" points. While some agents do have the time and inclination to get into these points, my experience is that most agents feel that it is far more important for them and for their writer clients to concentrate their persuasive and sales abilities on the essential deal terms, and not to squander either their leverage or their time on these matters.

What are these so-called legal points? The most important of them, of course, is the assurance that the contract is accurate, that it correctly memorializes the deal. On this, the attorney's legal training can be invaluable.

Secondly, if the writer has a deferment or net profit participation or some other participation in the contingent receipts of the picture (e.g., an adjusted gross after artificial break-even participation), the terms by which the contingent compensation is defined and computed and accounted for and paid all must be worked out. This can involve some fairly substantial business and accounting negotiations, which can deal with such questions as: Will development costs on other projects of the same producer be included in the negative cost of the project on which the writer is working, thereby deferring break-even and reducing the amount ultimately payable? Will the profits of the writer's picture be cross-collateralized with the profits of any other picture? Is the contingent compensation to be in addition to any residual or supplemental markets payments under the Writers Guild Basic Agreement or are the WGA payments to constitute a credit against the contingent compensation, or vice versa? Will the studio include in gross receipts for purposes of the writer's participation the revenues from the exploitation of ancillary rights, such as music publishing, soundtrack album and merchandising? Will the distribution fees that the studio will deduct in computing the writer's share of net profits be the same distribution fees as are being charged to the producer, or will they be higher? And on and on and on.

Finally, the most intensive negotiations generally involved in rights and writing agreements involve questions regarding the warranties that the writer is expected to make and the indemnification (agreement to cover the other party's costs and expenses) that he is required to give to cover violations of the warranties. Producers customarily ask that the writer warrant that the project is original and that it does not violate or infringe the rights of others. However, this apparently simple request can bring with it a multitude of problems, since producers further ask that the writer be responsible under the indemnity for claims brought by third parties that the writer's material does not comply with the warranties the writer has made—whether or not the claims are even correct! These issues and those of rights acquisitions and title clearances are the traditional province of lawyers.

COMPLEX DEALS

These three tiers of points—deal points, second tier points and "legal" issues—will be involved in any agreement affecting a writer's career. Some agreements will be even more complicated. For example, the producer may demand an option on the services of the writer for a second screenplay. Or the writer may wish to reserve print publishing or dramatic stage rights and exploit these rights directly. Many writers, having been burned by the loss of control which is the result of someone else producing the film, attempt to move into producing or directing. These deals are in general more complicated than most basic rights and services agreements that writers are involved in, and on which they do receive the protections of the MBA.

TAXES AND OTHER MATTERS

Finally, the entertainment attorney's services to the client are not limited to assistance in the negotiation of deals. As a writer's income increases, it becomes more advantageous to consider planning strategies to reduce income taxes. One very common method of doing this is to set up a loan-out corporation, which will employ the writer and loan out his or her services. This device, if properly used, can permit the writer to set up pension and profit sharing plans that may result in the deferment of

substantial amounts of taxes. In conjunction with the writer's business manager and/or accountant, the attorney will form the corporation and endeavor to insure that it complies with all legal and tax requirements. Similarly, the attorney can be of great assistance in negotiating the writer's contracts with his other representatives, including the agent.

Of course, the attorney's general services may be useful to the writer in such matters as real estate deals, banking relationships, trusts, wills and general business and personal planning.

On the most general level, the lawyer, as another of the writer's advisers, can play a role in general career guidance, helping the writer to decide whether to take a particular project, advising on whether a particular deal is especially advantageous at a given time, and in giving advice on how the writer can shape his career so that he can satisfy other goals, such as producing and directing.

On the same note, the very presence of the lawyer in the writer's life can offer both the writer and his other advisers an opportunity to discuss the financial, business and creative needs of the client with someone who is not only knowledgeable about the industry and the client, but who retains an independence and a dispassionate perspective on whatever issue is at hand.

THE OVERALL ROLE OF THE LAWYER

Almost every writer should have an agent. Assuming that a writer's agent is aggressive and does his job well, the lawyer's primary role is not to make money per se for the client, but rather to work within the parameters of the deal set by the agent to extract every cent possible and to minimize the business and legal risks. In other words, involving a lawyer is somewhat like buying an insurance policy—an attempt to insure that all of the possible financial benefits of a deal are realized by the writer. Further, the lawyer provides a second insurance-like service. The lawyer is attuned to confronting possible problems in advance and devising solutions that will best protect the client if they materialize. These include problems that often neither the client nor his other advisers feel comfortable dealing with, such as the possibility of the writer being replaced by another writer to do a re-write, by the agreement's being suspended for a force majeure event, such as a strike, and for claims by third parties which may or may not involve ma-terial that the writer has written. Indeed, it is pre-cisely these kinds of issues which make up what are referred to as "legal" points.

Establishing a Relationship with a Lawyer

Mark E. Halloran, Esq.

WHEN TO GET A LAWYER

Timely retention of a lawyer can be a crucial step in your career. The cardinal rule in seeking legal representation is: See a lawyer *before you sign.* In essence, when you sign a contract, you are setting up your own law (with the other party) that will govern your relationship with that party. Even though a lawyer may not be able to negotiate more favorable contract terms for you, at the very least he or she can explain the agreement so that you know what you are getting into. More likely, however, the lawyer can help by negotiating terms more favorable to you. An additional warning: Don't sign a contract assuming you can get out.

FINDING AN ATTORNEY

You should see a number of different lawyers before retaining one. Lawyers have various personalities, legal skills, experience and contacts. Do not be afraid to "interview" a lawyer. Be prepared to ask pointed questions as to the lawyer's industry experience. It is best to talk to successful writers and agents who can recommend lawyers who have done good work for them.

Mark E. Halloran practices law with Orion Pictures Corporation in Los Angeles. He is co-author of Musician's Guide to Copyright, *to be published by Charles Scribner's Sons in 1983, and editor and co-author of* The Musician's Manual *(Hawthorn/Dutton).*

© *1980, 1982 Mark E. Halloran*
All Rights Reserved

In recent years many lawyer referral services have been established in California. The usual procedure is for a prospective client in need of legal assistance to call a central referral office. The referral person discusses the caller's problem, and then the caller is typically referred to an attorney on the lawyer referral panel. The panel attorney then interviews the referred client for a moderate fee. After the first interview, however, the fee arrangement, and the legal services to be rendered, are left up to the lawyer and client. Often the panel attorney will pay the lawyer referral service a percentage of the fee collected from the client.

These referral panels, however, only provide you with the name of an attorney who has registered with it and who claims to have some experience in your area of concern. The panels do not rate lawyers; thus, you cannot be guaranteed that the panel attorney will have the skills and experience you need. It should also be noted that the "heavyweights" typically are not on these panels.

FEES

Financial arrangements between the writer and the attorney are negotiable. These arrangements typically fall into four categories: (1) a percentage arrangement, which is essentially similar to that which governs the writer/agent relationship; (2) a straight hourly fee arrangement based on the lawyer's current rate (ranging from $50 per hour to as high as $250 per hour); (3) a "reasonable" fee basis in which the attorney adjusts the hourly fee, either upward or downward, depending on the results (or lack of results) which the attorney is able to achieve for the client; or (4) a "fixed fee," that is, a specified sum of money such as $500. Which of these arrangements is preferable will depend on the client. One thing that should be noted by a writer who is considering a percentage arrangement is that certain kinds of services, such as tax planning, wills and trusts, and litigation, are customarily excluded, so that when work is requested in these areas, the hourly (or reasonable) meter will start to run. However, the percentage typically does include corporate work, real estate problems and general business matters.

Lawyers also typically ask reimbursement for their out-of-pocket costs, which include long-distance telephone calls, photocopying, word processing, postage, messenger service, etc. These typically are *not* considered part of the hourly fee, which is for the lawyer's *services*.

The quickest way to sour your attorney-client relationship is not to pay your bill. Most lawyers will render a monthly statement that sets out the services rendered, the costs and the total bill. If you *can't* pay the bill, you should at least call to say you can't pay it, and arrange some payment schedule.

Many lawyers require an initial payment, or "retainer." Most retainers are credited against your bill. Thus, usually if you retain an attorney and give him a $500 check, that $500 will be credited to your account. Up until your lawyer renders legal services sufficient to justify his right to the money, he holds these funds "in trust" for you. In theory, at least, he can't take these funds until he is entitled to do so by doing sufficient work for you. For example, in the first month your attorney negotiates and drafts a publishing contract, and spends six hours at $100 an hour doing it. He or she will send you a bill showing $500 received, $600 in charges, and $100 due for services rendered. Thus, you owe $100 at that point. Some attorneys also will require that you keep replenishing the retainer. In the foregoing example, they would bill you $600 so the retainer would be brought back up to $500. A reminder: keep a record of all legal bills so you can try to deduct them as a business expense. You should also keep copies of all documents and correspondence.

Although many lawyers do not require that the fee agreement be put in writing, this is a good idea, as it helps to prevent future misunderstanding or dispute. However, a fee arrangement need not be in writing in order to be enforceable.

Your relationship with your lawyer is subject to both contract law and ethical restraints on the lawyer. There are legal restrictions on how much a lawyer can charge. The fee cannot be exorbitant or disproportionate to the services rendered. An attorney may be disciplined for charging or attempting to collect an exorbitant fee, although this sort of discipline is unusual.

Feel free to consult another attorney concerning your fee arrangement to see that it is fair. Also, an attorney who enters an exorbitant fee arrangement will not be able to enforce the fee arrangement in court if you discharge (fire) the lawyer, as after discharge you are bound only to pay the attorney the reasonable value of the attorney's services, even if the fee arrangement was for a higher amount.

CHANGING LAWYERS

Although many attorney-client relationships are long-lasting, you may well find that you want to change attorneys. If you do, you should inform both your new and old attorneys. Your new lawyer cannot represent you simultaneously in a matter that is being handled by another lawyer.

The technical description is that you "discharge" your lawyer. Under California law, a client has an absolute right to discharge his attorney at any time. This does *not* mean, however, that you don't have to *pay* the discharged lawyer for the reasonable value of the services already provided to you. As an initial step, you new lawyer will want to have your previous files turned over to him. Your old lawyer has a legal duty to let the successor counsel inspect and copy the documents in the file. Because much of the information in the files is confidential, you must authorize that the files be copied. The fact you may owe your old lawyer money is irrelevant as far as turning over the files is concerned. Your previous lawyer still owes you a duty to represent your best interests (and this includes turning over the files), and he or she also has a duty to cooperate with your new lawyer.

CONCLUSION

1. Developing an effective attorney-client relationship can be a valuable step in your career.

Your decision in selecting an attorney is crucial—it should be an *informed* decision.

2. Remember, your lawyer's time is money. If you are organized in your legal and business affairs, it makes a lawyer's job easier, and therefore cheaper to you. Be prepared with specific questions before phoning. Better yet, put your questions in writing.

3. Pay your bills on time.

4. Keep your lawyer informed, so he or she can *prevent* difficulties. The old adage that an ounce of prevention is worth a pound of cure is appropriate in legal affairs.

5. Don't sign anything (except autographs) until your lawyer has reviewed it.

Copyrights in Literary Properties

Mark E. Halloran, Esq., and Harris E. Tulchin, Esq.

As an author of a literary property you have various legal rights in the literary property you create. The following discussion will concentrate on what is termed "copyright law," that is, the federally enforceable rights you have in your literary property. Our discussion will examine the questions you are most likely to ask and give you some guidance in enforcing your federal copyright protection in your literary works, and in avoiding infringing on the works of other authors.

Mark E. Halloran practices law with Orion Pictures Corporation in Los Angeles. He is co-author of Musician's Guide to Copyright, *published by Charles Scribner's Sons, and editor and co-author of the* Musician's Manual *(Hawthorn/Dutton).*

Harris E. Tulchin practices entertainment law in Los Angeles, with United Artists. He is a graduate of Cornell University and Hastings College of Law, where he served as Editor-in-Chief of the Journal of Communications and Entertainment Law (COMM/ENT). He was also a contributor to The Musician's Manual *(Hawthorn/Dutton).*

What is a copyright?

A copyright is a form of protection given by the laws of the United States* to authors of literary material and other original works of authorship. The United States Constitution authorizes Congress to enact laws protecting such creators. There are a variety of these privileges ("exclusive rights") and they vary depending on the type of creation ("work"). From the novelist's perspective two very important privileges are the exclusive monopoly to make and sell copies of your work, and to distribute the copies to the public. Generally, these rights are collectively referred to as "publication rights." From the screenwriter's viewpoint, a very important exclusive right is the right to make a derivative

*Countries other than the United States have copyright laws, too, but a discussion of foreign copyrights is beyond the scope of this chapter. Generally, the United States has entered into treaties with many countries which give reciprocal protection to the works copyrighted in each country. However, despite claims such as "International Copyright Secured" there is no such thing as an "international copyright" nor a unitary "international copyright law."

work* of the property by using it as the basis for a motion picture or television program, and the right to publicly perform the motion picture based on the screenplay. In general, these rights are collectively known as "motion picture rights." The writer makes a living by creating copyrighted works for his employer, or by selling or licensing these exclusive rights embodied in copyrighted works.

What exclusive rights do I have in my copyright?

Copyright owners have the exclusive rights to do and to authorize others to do the following:

1. to *reproduce* a work in copies
2. to prepare *derivative* works such as screenplays and motion pictures or television programs
3. to *distribute copies* to the public by sale or other transfer of ownership, or by rental, lease or lending
4. to *perform* works publicly
5. to *display* works publicly

Since a copyright includes more rights than just the right to *copy* a work, commentators often refer to the above rights as the "bundle of rights" which comprise a copyright.

What can be copyrighted?

Two prerequisites have to be met before a novel or screenplay can be protected by copyright. The work has to be: (1) *original* to the author; and (2) *fixed in a tangible medium of expression.* "Original" means only that you yourself created the work. "Fixed" in a tangible medium of expression means you put your literary work on paper or on tape, or in any other medium from which it can be perceived. Having an idea for a book or screenplay is not enough—you must make it tangible. Thus, if you discussed your idea for a story with a development executive at a motion picture studio (before

*A derivative work is a work based upon a preexisting work. Thus, a screenplay derived from a novel is a derivative work, and a motion picture derived from a screenplay is also a derivative work. In both cases the permission of the copyright owner of the preexisting work must be obtained by the person preparing the derivative work.

you wrote it down) there was no fixation. At that point the story is not yet sufficiently "fixed" for you to have a copyright in it, although you may have rights under contract law (see "Protecting Your Ideas"). Once you put your story on paper you have a copyright in the story. Copyright law terms you the "author" of the literary work (story).

What cannot be copyrighted?

Literary works not fixed. As we discussed, unless you put your literary work on paper, or otherwise record it, the work is not protected by copyright. You may have been pitching your idea for your next screenplay to a studio development executive (which idea, it turns out, was very similar to *Fame* by Christopher Moss, a year before he wrote it), but unless you put that story on paper or tape, you cannot claim the copyrighted original screenplay *Fame* (or the movie of that title) invaded your rights. You *may* have what are termed "common law" rights (those enforced by the states) at this point, but federal copyright law requires the work be *fixed*. Additionally, you may disclose your idea in such a way as to give rise to an implied contract with the studio by which the studio is obligated to compensate you for their exploitation of the idea (see "Protecting Your Ideas"). However, your remedies against the studio would not be under federal copyright law, but rather under state law.

Probably the most famous case regarding literary property rights in conversations concerns Ernest Hemingway. Before his death, Hemingway had a lengthy set of conversations with A. E. Hotchner, a writer companion of Hemingway, who subsequently wrote a best-selling book based on these conversations titled *Papa Hemingway.* Hemingway's estate sued Hotchner, claiming proprietary rights in the book. The New York courts rejected the suit, and determined that Hemingway's estate could not enforce any literary property rights in the conversations chronicled in the book (*Estate of Hemingway v. Random House* 296 N.Y.S.2d 771 [1968]). Although it is an overstatement to say that *no* proprietary rights can exist in conversations, it is usually a good idea to write down or record your conversations if you wish to guard the expression of your ideas.

Ideas and facts. Because the copyright law is designed to encourage the interchange of ideas,

ideas are not copyrightable. George Lucas could not write *Star Wars* and then forbid writers to write space adventure screenplays. What you cannot take is the *expression* of the idea, that is, what the previous author has put on paper or tape. Thus, you cannot make *copies* of the *Star Wars* screenplay and sell them, or produce a movie that substantially copies *Star Wars*, but you are free to write a space adventure (which is an idea) screenplay that is original and different from the *Star Wars* screenplay. (Indeed, the fine line between ideas and their expression is being tested in a pending lawsuit between the owners of the rights to *Star Wars*, 20th Century-Fox Film Corporation and Lucasfilm Corporation, and Universal Studios, which produced the television series *Battlestar Galactica*.)

A recent copyright infringement lawsuit highlighted the fundamental concept that ideas and historical facts are not copyrightable. This case involved a copyright infringement lawsuit brought by A. A. Hoehling, the author of *Who Destroyed the Universe?* Hoehling sued the writer of a subsequent book titled *The Hindenburg,* and also Universal City Studios, the owners of motion picture rights to the book *The Hindenburg.* Hoehling contended that the author and Universal had copied the plot of his account of the 1937 disaster involving a German dirigible (Hoehling's theory was that a crew member had sabotaged the ship), as well as research facts and certain phrases and scenes in *Who Destroyed the Universe?* The court rejected Hoehling's claim, pointing out that only very limited copyright protection is extended to historical works, and determined that Hoehling's interpretation of a historical event was not copyrightable. The factual material appearing in Hoehling's book also was not copyrightable since such material is in the public domain (discussed on page 55). The court further stated that copyright protection may not preclude an author from "saving time and effort by referring to and relying upon prior published material." Finally, the use of certain "stock" or standard literary devices (*scene à faire*) such as a scene in a German beer hall (which appeared in the Hoehling book, the subsequent book and the Universal film) also were determined to be noncopyrightable. Thus, when you do research for your story, you are free to consult and use ideas and historical facts from previously written materials. Yet, you still cannot use substantial portions of the previously published materials word for word.

In the *Hindenburg* case the court cautioned, however, that while denying protection to noncopyrightable elements, the court should not overlook any "wholesale usurpation" or "verbatim reproduction" of a prior author's expression. The court further noted that one of the purposes of copyright law—encouraging creativity in contributions to historical knowledge—would best be furthered by allowing a "second author to make significant use of a prior work, so long as he does not bodily appropriate the expression of another." It should be noted you may be able to use limited parts of previously written books under the doctrine of "fair use,"which is discussed below.

Titles, names, short phrases and slogans. To be copyrightable, a work must contain a certain minimum amount of authorship in the form of original literary, musical or graphic expression. Names, titles and other short phrases do not meet these requirements.

Titles are not copyrightable, as they do not possess sufficient expressive content. Even if you were the first to write a book titled "Love" you could not use copyright law to prevent others from using this title. However, this does not mean you could write a new screenplay totally unlike *Star Wars* and title it *Star Wars* with total impunity. The owners of *Star Wars* might have legal recourse, but this recourse would be under unfair competition law rather than copyright law.

Titles *may* become legally protected if they are recognized by the general public as being associated with a particular product, service or company and so take on what the law terms a "secondary meaning." It is likely that *Star Wars* has a secondary meaning at this time.

Although names, short phrases and slogans may not be copyrightable, legal protection may be invoked by copyrighting a *design* incorporating the slogan. Using copyright law you may be able to stop others from copying the design, but you cannot stop them from using the name, short phrase or slogan if they do not copy the design.

There are companies that can provide a title report indicating the previous uses of a certain specific title or similar titles. Also, the Motion Picture Association of America (MPAA) maintains a registration service regarding titles for those film financiers/distributors who agree to be bound by the terms of the registration agreement. The registration procedure permits members to "reserve" a specific title and prevent its use by fellow signatories who might otherwise legitimately use the title without fear of a claim for unfair competition.

What is the public domain?

Not all literary works are copyrighted. Works that are not protected by copyright, e.g., works intentionally published without copyright notice, works whose copyright term has expired, and works published by the government, fall into what is called the "public domain"; they are owned by the public. For example, the Copyright Office forms included in this book are public domain material—permission was not sought from the Copyright Office to reproduce the forms. Works whose copyright has expired fall into the public domain. You are free to use a work in the public domain in any way you choose even if you take it word for word. But you cannot *create* a copyright in public domain materials merely by incorporating them into your own work—remember, to create a copyright the work must be *original*. If you add original material to a work in the public domain (such as preparing a screenplay from a Shakespeare play), the copyright law will protect only your original contribution. Thus, if you prepare a screenplay from *Twelfth Night*, others are still free to prepare their own screenplay versions of this play so long as they do not appropriate your original elements.

How do I secure a copyright?

You do not send off to the Copyright Office in Washington, D.C., to get a "copyright"—you get one as soon as you create the work—but for a certificate of copyright *registration*, a very valuable piece of paper that makes a public record of the facts of your copyright. In general, failure to register does not invalidate the copyright. However, your copyright *may* be invalidated if you fail to take corrective measures to cure this failure.

How do I obtain copyright registration forms?

The Copyright Office provides forms to use when registering a copyright. Copyright registration forms can be ordered by writing the Copyright Office, Library of Congress, Washington, D.C. 20559, or by calling the Copyright Office at (202) 287-9100. The forms are free. Allow at least two weeks for de-

livery. This time does vary, however, so you are well advised when calling to ask the person at the Copyright Office how long you will have to wait. The Copyright Office is also very helpful with any questions you have regarding registration. Sample forms are attached at the end of this article. Please note the forms (as filled out) are merely illustrative and should not be followed blindly. Also, the Copyright Office does *not* accept photocopies of the forms—you must submit *originals*, as these originals are of archival quality and are kept as a public record.

Can the Copyright Office render legal advice or opinions?

No. Although the Copyright Office is glad to furnish information about the provisions in the copyright law and the procedures for making registration, and to report on facts found in the public records of the Office, federal law prohibits Copyright Office employees from offering legal advice or opinions. The Copyright Office cannot do any of the following: (1) comment upon the merits, copyright status or ownership of particular works, or upon the extent of protection afforded to particular works by the copyright law; (2) compare for similarities copies of works deposited for registration or give opinions on the validity of claims; (3) advise on questions of possible copyright infringement or prosecution of copyright violations; (4) draft or interpret contract terms; (5) enforce contracts or recover manuscripts; (6) recommend particular publishers, agents, lawyers or registration services; and (7) help in getting a work published, recorded or performed.

What do I submit to the Copyright Office?

To register a copyright, you must submit the following three things: (1) properly completed application form; (2) $10 fee for each application; (3) deposit of the work being registered. The appropriate forms for registering screenplays and novels are Form PA and Form TX, respectively, copies of which are at the end of this chapter.

Form PA (Performing Arts) includes works prepared for the purpose of being performed, including "dramatic" works such as a screenplay. Form TX is the appropriate application for non-dramatic literary works, such as novels.

What are the advantages of registration with the Copyright Office?

In general, copyright registration is a legal formality which places on public record the basic facts of a particular copyright. While registration is generally not a requirement for copyright protection, the copyright law provides several advantages to encourage copyright owners to make registration. Among these advantages are the following: (1) registration establishes a public record of a copyright claim; (2) registration is ordinarily necessary before any infringement suit may be filed in court; (3) if the registration is made before or within five years of publication (distribution of copies to the public), the registration will establish *prima facie* evidence in court of the validity of the copyright and of the facts stated in the registration certificate; and (4) if registration is made prior to an infringement of the work, or if registration is made within three months after publication of the work, the copyright owner will qualify in court for an award of statutory damages and attorneys' fees. Otherwise, only an award of actual damages and profits is available to the copyright owner. Because damages and profits are frequently hard to prove, and the infringer faces an additional award of attorneys' fees, timely copyright registration is a definite advantage to the copyright owner.

Are there alternatives to registering with the Copyright Office?

Because of the cost of copyright registration, misunderstandings as to the method and purpose of federal copyright registration and the desire for confidentiality (registered works become public records, open for perusal to anyone)*, alternative forms of "registration" have arisen. The theory underlying these alternative methods is that they offer proof from a disinterested third party of the date of creation (fixation) of a work, which is crucial in determining who originated the work. Unfortunately, *no* alternative means of registration will protect your work to the extent of protection that formal registration with the Copyright Office provides. Al-

ternative registration methods are listed below.

Poor Man's Copyright consists of sending a copy of your script by registered mail to yourself, and not opening the envelope. The idea is that the postmark serves as proof as to the date of creation of the work. This method is not recommended because proof of creation offered by a person other than the creator is generally perceived to be more reliable. Also, it is impossible to prove no one has "stuffed" the envelope after the postmark date. Some variations on the "Poor Man's Copyright" include having a notary public stamp a work with a signature and date, placing a work in a safe deposit box, and having people read the work so that they may testify that the work had been created as of a certain date.

The *Writer's Guild of America (West)* maintains a Registration Service to assist writers in establishing the completion date and the identity of their literary works written for theatrical motion pictures, television and radio. Although registration with the Guild does not confer any statutory protection, it does provide evidence of the writer's prior claim to authorship of the literary work and its completion date. Just as the law of copyright does not protect titles, neither does registration of the work with the Guild. The Writers Guild Registration instruction sheet follows this article.

What is publication?

A work is *published* when it is distributed to the public by means of a sale or some other means of transferring ownership or by rental, lease or lending. Publication was more crucial under pre-1978 copyright law, as federal copyright protection was not invoked until a work was either published with notice or registered in an unpublished form. Under the new law, however, federal copyright protection is invoked upon creation.

Is it a publication of your screenplay if your agent sends it to twenty producers? Probably not, as there is no intent to transfer ownership, and the distribution is to a limited group. To be safe, however, some writers include the proper copyright notice (discussed below) on all copies. Other writers prefer not to put a copyright notice on screenplays as this "dates" the material.

What is the proper notice for literary works?

All published copies should contain notice of claim to copyright.

---

*It should be noted that the Copyright Office keeps records of persons who inspect deposit copies, and the inspection is supervised by Copyright Office employees, who do not allow the deposit copies to be photocopied. Thus, the fear about registration as inviting "stealing" may be exaggerated.

A proper copyright notice for a literary work must include three elements: the © symbol, or the word "copyright," or the abbreviation "Copr."; the year the work was created; and the name of the author. It should look something like this:

© 1982 Sam Screenwriter
All Rights Reserved.

Notices that vary from this form are widespread. Popular notices include Copyright © 1982 Sam Screenwriter, and © Copyright Sam Screenwriter 1982. All the law requires is that the three elements appear together, and that they "give reasonable notice of the claim of copyright."

The words "All Rights Reserved" are *not* required by United States copyright law, but they are recommended because they provide additional copyright protection in certain foreign countries.

What if I omit the notice?

Under the pre-1978 copyright law, omission of a copyright notice in published copies was fatal to a claim of copyright. This is not necessarily true under the new law, which allows certain corrective actions. These curative provisions may be invoked when the notice has been omitted from a small number of copies, when the work is registered within five years of publication and a reasonable effort is made to add the notice to copies already distributed to the public or if the notice has been omitted in violation of a written requirement that published copies bear the required notice.* There are also curative provisions if your work is published with inaccurate information (e.g., the wrong publication date). The proper form to file to make corrections is Copyright Office Form CA.

What if I want to write a screenplay from a copyrighted book?

The copyright law gives the owner of a copyrighted book the exclusive right to make or allow others to create "derivative" works from the composition. Thus, the copyright owner in the book must give *permission* for the writing of the screenplay and subsequent creation of a motion picture as both the screenplay and motion picture are "derivative works." Typically the arrangement for the

---

*The omission of a proper copyright notice in published copies may require you to register the work within five years of publication. This is the only instance in which registration is a prerequisite to the claim to copyright.

grant of motion picture rights is made prior to screenplay development.

Of course, as discussed above, if the book is in the public domain, you are free to take from it, even word for word. You can check to see if a book is in the public domain by hiring a copyright search service, or by having the Copyright Office do a record search, which it does for an hourly fee. You can avoid the creation of a derivative work by making sure your work is different from any previous works you rely on by avoiding wholesale usurpation or verbatim reproduction, and adding your own original creativity. Remember, you are free to take the *ideas* from the book, but not the *expression*. This is especially true if you are basing your screenplay on non-fiction works, such as historical works (see discussion of the *Hindenburg* case earlier in this chapter).

However, if you are going to prepare a "derivative" work (i.e., a work based on the expression contained in a prior work) based on a copyrighted work, you must obtain permission from the copyright holder. The search of the Copyright Office records will reveal the last copyright holder of record, as well as previous copyright holders. Lawyers representing a producer in connection with literary purchase agreements will usually obtain a "copyright report" on the property at the outset of negotiations. The copyright report is analogous, in purpose and content, to the preliminary title report normally obtained by the buyer of real property prior to consummation of the sale. The firm supplying the report will undertake a research of the records of the Copyright Office to determine if a copyright registration has been filed with respect to the property. In addition, the report will include any registered assignments of rights in or prior publications of the property unearthed by the research. Finally, the report may include pertinent notices which have appeared in entertainment trade publications (e.g., *Variety, Hollywood Reporter*, etc.) regarding purported acquisitions of or productions in development based upon the property. The report will usually conclude with an opinion of the firm as to the present owner of and status of the protection available under the copyright in the property and any problems in this connection which the research has revealed. You, or preferably your lawyer, should contact the copyright owner to work out the deal. Essentially, you will purchase from the copyright owner the rights to create a screenplay (and concomitantly to create a motion picture based on

the screenplay) for a fee and perhaps for a participation in receipts from the motion picture (see "Literary Purchase/Option Agreements" for further
discussion).

How long do copyrights last?

The new copyright law has given authors extra
protection by extending the lifetime of copyrights.
Under the pre-1978 law, a copyright began at the
date of *publication*, and lasted for an initial period
of twenty-eight years, with a twenty-eight-year renewal period for a maximum of fifty-six years.

Under the new law, however, copyright protection originates from the date of *creation* (i.e., fixation in a tangible medium of expression) and, in
most cases, lasts for the lifetime of the author plus
fifty years. Thus, if you wrote a novel in 1982 and
died in the year 2000, the copyright would last until
2050. Under the old law, if the novel had been published in 1982, the copyright would have expired in
2010 (twenty-eight-year initial term) if not renewed,
and 2038 (twenty-eight-year renewal term) if it had
been renewed.

For works "made for hire" (discussed on pages 60
and 61), and for anonymous works, the term is
seventy-five years from the date of publication, or
one hundred years from the date of creation (fixation), whichever is shorter.

Can copyright ownership be transferred?

The ownership of a copyright, or of one, several
or a subdivision of any of the exclusive rights noted
above, may be transferred by a sales instrument, by
will or by the applicable laws of intestate succession
(a statutory procedure for distributing the property
of a person who has died without a will). Typically,
literary property agreements include both a "grant
of rights" and a provision for "rights reserved."
These provisions can be complex, and legal advice
should be sought before you transfer any rights to
your literary property. You should also consider
that unanticipated uses may be made of your work,
especially in the age of exploding video technology.
You should insist on a clause that states: "All rights
not specifically granted are reserved to the writer."

However, ownership of a copyright or of any of
the exclusive rights under a copyright is clearly dis-
tinguishable from ownership in any material object
in which the work is embodied. For example, the
sale of a book does not of itself convey any rights in
the copyrighted work embodied in the pages of the
book. Thus, if you buy a copy of a book, you cannot
claim to own the copyright in it. The copyright remains with the author or publisher. Conversely, the
transfer of ownership of a copyright or of any exclusive rights under a copyright does not effect a
conveyance of property rights or ownership in any
material object such as a copy of a book. Thus, once
you have purchased a copy of a book you own your
physical copy of the book outright. The subsequent
transfer of the right to make copies of the book to a
new publisher does not affect your ownership in
your copy of the book.

Generally, a transfer of copyright ownership is
not valid without a written instrument typically
called an "assignment" signed by the owner of the
rights tranferred or by his authorized agent. Two
form assignments are at the end of this article.
Thus, a novelist (who has, among other rights, the
exclusive right to make derivative works such as a
motion picture from his novel), may transfer the
right to create and exploit a screenplay and a motion picture to a studio. This is commonly referred
to as the sale of "motion picture rights." Also, separate agreements are often made with publishers for
hardcover and paperback exploitation of a novel.
Both hardcover and paperback rights are part of
the author's exclusive rights to reproduce and distribute the copyrighted work, but these rights can
be subdivided into hardcover rights and paperback
rights. In addition, publication rights may be further
subdivided by territory. For example, you could
have different domestic and foreign publishers of
your novel.

Must a transfer of copyright be recorded with the Copyright Office?

If you transfer your copyright (or any part of it),
the transfer of ownership must be written, must
specifically identify the title of the work and its
copyright registration number, must be signed by
the copyright owner, and must be recorded in the
Copyright Office. The fee for recording a transfer
generally is $10. Unlike copyright *registration*
forms, there is no Copyright Office assignment recordation form. Upon receipt of the recordation fee
and the written transfer, the Register of Copyrights
will record the transfer and return a Certificate of
Recordation. Recording is important to the person
to whom the copyright is transferred, because it is a

prerequisite for bringing a copyright infringement suit. Also, conflicts may emerge between persons who each claim they purchased rights in the same work. In such a case, generally the first to record the transfer will prevail in a lawsuit arising from a dispute over copyright ownership. Failure to record the assignment does not invalidate the transfer agreement, but exposes the person to whom the rights are transferred to having his rights defeated by a previous recorded assignment.

Can I get my copyright back after transferring it?

Because a newly created work is hard to value, the copyright law formerly provided that after the initial twenty-eight-year term, despite assignment of the copyright to others, the renewal copyright would revert to the author or the author's heirs if the author had died.

The new law, however, does not provide for a renewal period. Instead, it provides that the author or author's heirs may get the copyright back between the thirty-fifth and fortieth years after transferring the copyright (the termination period) by serving a written notice of termination of the transfer on the person who then currently holds the copyright. However, if the transfer conveys the right to *publish* the work, the termination period begins at the end of thirty-five years from the date of publication of the transferred work, or at the end of forty years from the date of execution of the transfer, whichever term ends earlier. The notice must be served not less than two years nor more than ten years prior to the effective date of the termination. The author or his heirs then regains ownership of the copyright for the remainder of its duration. Thus, if you wrote a book and transferred the right to publish the paperback book to Simon & Schuster in 1980 and it was first published in 1982, you could regain the paperback publication rights in 2017 (thirty-five years from first publication) if you serve notice on the owner anytime from 2007 to 2015 (two to ten years prior to the effective termination date). Note that the right of termination does not apply to persons who create works made for hire; the employer is deemed the author of the work for purposes of copyright.

Termination of grants or transfers are effective notwithstanding any agreement to the contrary between the person transferring the copyright and the person purchasing the copyright.

Copyright ownership in a derivative work prepared prior to the effective date of the termination of transfer does not revert back to the original author. Thus, if you transfer motion picture rights to a studio, copyright ownership in the motion picture produced by the studio will remain with the studio and will not revert back to you upon termination of the transfer of rights made to the publisher. However, the studio would probably not be able to produce a remake of the motion picture based substantially upon your novel subsequent to the reversion to you or your heirs of the copyright in the novel, without your consent. The studio will attempt to avoid this problem by obtaining an assignment from you waiving your right to terminate a transfer, but the validity of such a clause is questionable and probably will not be tested until at least 2013 (thirty-five years from the effective date of the new copyright law, 1978).

What if I co-write a novel or screenplay?

If you write a work with another author, that work generally is a "joint work." Both authors co-own the entire work. Typically, the collaborators will register the copyright in the names of both, they will have equal rights in negotiating a publication contract, each will get authorship credit and as a rule they will share equally in royalties from sale of the book and other proceeds from the exploitation of the work. It is preferable to enter a formal collaborator agreement covering points such as artistic control and division of income. In the absence of a written agreement, all collaborators normally have the power to authorize non-exclusive licenses, and the income is shared among the collaborators.

The creation of a joint work should be distinguished from so-called "ghost writing." Generally, a person who ghost writes a book is an employee for hire and is not deemed an author of the work. Any royalties paid to the ghost writer are exclusively set forth in the contract by which the writer is employed or engaged to ghost-write the work.

What happens to my copyright when my article is published in a periodical?

If you are *employed* by a magazine, under the work-for-hire doctrine, the magazine, as your employer, is deemed the author. If, on the other hand, you freelance, then the law assumes (in the absence of an express grant to the contrary) that all rights in a contribution to a periodical are presumed to belong to you as author, other than the right to use the work in the particular periodical. It is advisable to require the periodical publisher to put the proper copyright notice on your contribution. You may register contributions to periodicals as a *group* using Copyright Office Form GR/CP. However, you must meet *all* the following conditions:

1. All of the works are by the same author, who is an individual (not an employer for hire).
2. All of the works are first published as contributions to periodicals (including newspapers) within a twelve month period.
3. Each of the contributions as first published or a separate copyright notice and the name of the owner of copyright in the work (or an abbreviation or alternative designation of the owner) was the same in each notice.
4. One copy of the entire periodical issue or newspaper section in which each contribution was first published must be deposited with the application.
5. The application must identify each contribution separately, including the periodical containing it and the date of its first publication.

Note that when you apply for a single registration to cover a group of contributions to periodicals, you must submit both the basic application (Form TX, Form PA, or Form VA), along with the adjunct application Form GR/CP. The purpose of the Form GR/CP is to provide separate identification for each of the contributions and to give information about their first publication, as required by the copyright law.

What if the publisher makes editorial corrections to my submittal?

It is very common for a publisher to have its editors make changes in your submittal. The final published form may be considered a "derivative" work and the original manuscript would be the original copyrighted work. This problem is primarily theoretical, since typically a manuscript is not registered for copyright, but rather the revised and published edition is registered and assumed to be the original copyrighted work.

What if I'm hired to write a screenplay?

Writers are frequently hired to write screenplays. In such cases, the writer is termed an "employee for hire" or "writer for hire." The significance of this is that the *employer* (the person who hired the writer) is deemed the *author* of the work and owns the work unless the employment contract states otherwise. If, however, the work is not prepared by an employee in the course of his employment, the work will only be considered a "work for hire" if there is a written agreement signed by the parties to consider it a "work made for hire." Remember, in the work for hire situation, you have no termination of transfer rights as the employer is deemed author and thus the owner of all rights in the work.

In order to protect themselves, producers typically require that the writer sign a "certificate of authorship," which states that the writer in fact created the screenplay within the scope of his or her employment. Also, the writer typically will be asked to sign an "assignment of all rights" to the screenplay. A form assignment is at the end of the article.

What rights do I have in a work I have created for hire?

Without a written agreement to the contrary between you, the writer of the screenplay, and the producer, the producer who hires you will register and own the copyright in the screenplay. Thus, the producer is free to prepare derivative works from the screenplay (especially television and motion pictures) and to otherwise exploit your work in any manner desired. Note that if you are a member of the Writers Guild of America (WGA) and the producer is signatory to the WGA Minimum Basic Agreement, you will have increased rights in your creation. See the discussion on "Separation of Rights" in the chapter on the WGA Minimum Basic Agreement.

The agreement with the producer, if it is not an employment agreement, may state the screenplay is a "specially commissioned or ordered work as part of a motion picture." The result is the same as in an employment agreement—the screenplay will be considered a work made for hire for the producer.

Can I use a work made for hire as a writing sample?

Even though the producer "owns" the screenplay, the writer can use the screenplay as a writing sample, so long as the submittal of the work as a writing sample is not a *publication* as defined by the copyright law. As discussed, a publication is the distribution of copies of a work to the public by sale, rental, lease or lending. However, the limited distribution of a work for a limited purpose (e.g., to get a job) would likely not be a publication. It's a good idea to include a proper copyright notice on the screenplay, and to make clear to the person to whom you submit the screenplay that your submittal is for evaluation purposes only.

Who owns a "work for hire," if the producer fails to pay the writer the full amount agreed upon?

Unfortunately, this is an open question. The producer could argue that the writer's only remedy against the producer is to sue for the money owed under the contract, but that the copyright nevertheless remains with the producer-employer, since the copyright was vested in him by reason of his status as an "author" under copyright law.

However, the writer could argue that under principles of contract law, the writer has the right to *rescind* (nullify) the employment agreement for non-payment. Thus, the writer may claim that the contract under which he had agreed to create the work for hire is null and void, and that the copyright in the work he created is therefore his sole property. Until their dispute is resolved, both the writer and the producer may find it difficult to exploit the property. Often the producer will try to insert a provision in the writer's agreement in which the writer waives his right to rescind the agreement.

What effect does the registration of the work by an improper party have on your right to the copyright in the work?

As discussed previously, copyright registration does not in and of itself *create* a copyright, but rather is a public record of the claim to copyright in a work. The Copyright Office does not adjudicate conflicting claims to ownership in a copyright. If, however, there are conflicting claims concerning the ownership of a copyright, then in the absence of a settlement between the parties the matter must be litigated. Generally the first person to record the copyright registration or the transfer of the copyright in the Copyright Office will prevail. It is within the power of a court to order a copyright holder to execute an assignment of the copyright to the

proper author. However, courts try to avoid substantial forfeiture of property rights and may, instead, merely order that the true author receive money damages.

What is infringement?

Persons who *infringe* copyright are subject to both civil and criminal penalties. A work is *infringed* when any of the exclusive rights in a copyright are violated. Of course the copyright owner must show ownership in the copyright. Then, the copyright owner must prove the two elements which comprise infringement. The first is *access* (i.e., the plaintiff must show that the infringer had *access* to the copyrighted work). The second element is a *substantial taking* (i.e., the plaintiff must show that the infringer took or used material from the plaintiff's work). Here are some examples:

1. You write a book and enter a publication deal with Simon & Schuster. Subsequently, without permission, Copy Cat Press reproduces your book, but with cosmetic changes. Assuming that there is proof that the second publisher had access to your book (which may be presumed where the copying is so extensive as to preclude the possibility of independent origin) Copy Cat would be in violation of your and Simon & Schuster's exclusive right to reproduce copies of your work. (Even though you have transferred your publication rights, you can still sue for infringement, since you remain the beneficial owner of the copyright.)

2. You prepare an original screenplay, and submit this screenplay to an unscrupulous producer who thereafter without your consent creates a motion picture based on your screenplay. The unauthorized use of your screenplay would be an infringement of your exclusive right to prepare derivative works from your work.

When should I sue for copyright infringement?

The copyright law, like most other laws, has a "statute of limitations." In cases of infringement you have *three* years from the infringement date to bring suit. However, it is likely that if you bring suit, you will also have claims other than copyright infringement (e.g. unfair competition)—and these other claims may have *shorter* statutes of limitations. Any delay, however, can harm you. As soon as you learn of an unauthorized use of your work, see a lawyer *immediately*.

How do publishers and producers protect themselves from infringement claims?

As discussed earlier, a copyright title search is usually done before a purchaser of a literary property enters an agreement with a writer.

Additionally, a purchaser of a literary property typically will require that the writer make written warranties, including (1) that the property is original to the author; and (2) that the property does not violate the copyright of any third person. The purchaser will also require that the writer indemnify (pay back) the purchaser if claims are brought which are inconsistent with the warranties. Thus, if you take a substantial portion of the preexisting work and incorporate it in your property, you run the risk that both you and the purchaser will be sued for copyright infringement, and you will likely foot the bill.

What can I win (or lose) in an infringement suit?

The remedies provided by law in an infringement suit include both injunctions, money damages and even impounding and destruction of the infringing articles. If you can prove infringement at a preliminary stage of the suit the court may order the infringer to cease engaging in further activities which infringe on your book (i.e., cease publication and sale of your book or discontinue the exhibition of an unauthorized motion picture based on your work). This is a form of injunction. The court can also order the impounding of the allegedly infringing copies as well as the articles used to produce them. Since proving money damages is difficult, the law sets out what are termed "statutory damages," which generally run from $250 to $10,000 for a single act of infringement. In certain instances the court will also award court costs and attorneys' fees. As discussed earlier, you are entitled to statutory damages and attorneys fees only if you register your claim to copyright.

What's "fair use"?

As discussed earlier, the copyright owner has certain exclusive privileges in the copyright. Thus, a person who wishes to use the copyrighted material typically must seek permission of the copyright holder. However, the law recognizes certain limited uses of copyrighted material as long as such use is a "fair use."

In broad terms, the doctrine of "fair use" means that in some circumstances, where the use is reasonable and not harmful to the copyright owner's rights, copyrighted material may be used to a limited extent, without obtaining permission. For example, under this doctrine critics have been held to be free to publish short extracts or quotations for purposes of illustration or comment. The copyright law recognizes fair use by stating that copying for purposes such as criticism, comment, news reporting, teaching, scholarship or research, is not an infringement of copyright. Whether a use is a fair use depends on four factors: (1) the purpose and character of the use, including whether such use is of a commercial nature or is for nonprofit educational purposes; (2) the nature of the copyrighted work; (3) the amount and substantiality of the portion used; and (4) the effect of the use upon the potential market value of the copyrighted work.

The line between fair use and infringement is unclear and not easily defined. There is no specific number of words that can be safely taken without permission. Acknowledging the source of the copyrighted material does not avoid infringement unless previous permission is obtained.

The safest course is to get permission before using copyrighted material. When it is difficult to obtain permission, use of copyright material should be avoided unless it seems clear that the doctrine of fair use would apply to the situation. If there is any doubt or question, it is advisable to consult an attorney.

How much of a work can I take?

We all know that new works frequently incorporate parts of copyrighted preexisting works. The test is whether the amount of the copyrighted preexisting work that was taken was *substantial*. This rather loose standard is applied by a judge or jury when reviewing your work in comparison with the preexisting work. Again, there is no standard measure of how much of the preexisting work can be incorporated into a new work without infringing the preexisting work.

CONCLUSION

As a writer you should, at the very least, have a basic understanding of copyright law. When you write a novel or screenplay, you have certain valuable rights in that work that you can exploit. Conversely, other authors have rights in their works that you should not infringe. By knowing your rights you can protect them and avoid infringing on the rights of others.

Although hard and fast rules are often overstatements, the following should guide you as a writer:

1. *Be original.* Although you may consult previous works, and borrow ideas and facts (and perhaps limited parts verbatim under the fair use doctrine), your work should be the result of your creativity.

2. *Put copyright notices on copies.* Although technically the law requires notice only on published copies, it is prudent to put your copyright notice on *all* copies, no matter how you use them. If you are concerned about "dating" your material you may want to use Roman numerals rather than arabic. Also, if your work is published in a periodical or collection, insist on a copyright notice in your name.

3. *Put your ideas on paper.* Unless you "fix" the expression of your ideas in tangible form, they are generally not protected by copyright law.

4. *Watch out for work-for-hire agreements.* If a written agreement contains words, such as "writer for hire" or "work for hire," the employer or purchaser will be deemed the author of your work. This language should be deleted if possible.

5. *Register your works.* Whether you register with the Copyright Office or the Writers Guild, registration will provide proof that you created the work. If you enter a deal with a publisher or producer, make sure they are obligated to register your work with the Copyright Office, and also to affix proper copyright notices to copies and derivative works.

6. *Consult an attorney before making a deal.* Consult an attorney before transferring rights to your literary properties so you understand the deal, and have the opportunity to strike better terms with the publisher or producer.

Following are some of the forms discussed in this chapter.

LITERARY MATERIAL— ASSIGNMENT OF ALL RIGHTS

1. I, _____ Rona Riter _____ in consideration of.

. ___ One _____ Dollars ($ 1.00 _____) and other good and valuable consideration,

paid to me by _____ Hollywood Pictures, Inc. _____ the "purchaser"'

receipt of which is hereby acknowledged, do hereby grant, sell, assign and transfer, forever and exclusively, to the "purchaser"

that certain _____ literary work _____

entitled _____ "Star Doors" _____

(hereinafter referred to as the "work"), the copyright (common law and statutory), title and theme thereof and all now or here-after existing rights of every kind in, to and pertaining to said work, whether or not such rights are now known, recognized, contemplated, invented or discovered, and the complete, unconditional and unencumbered title in and to said work throughout the world, for all uses and purposes whatsoever.

2. I agree that in exercising said rights or any of them, the purchaser shall have the perpetual right to make and use and cause to be made and used literary, dramatic, speaking stage, motion picture, television, radio and all other adaptations of every kind of said work and of any part thereof, and to adapt, arrange, change, novelize, dramatize, make musical versions of, inter-polate, interpolate in, transpose, add to and subtract from said work and the title thereof to such extent as the purchaser in its sole discretion may desire, and may translate said work, title and adaptations into all or any languages. The purchaser is hereby granted the perpetual right, but shall not be obligated, to use my name and likeness, in advertising or otherwise, as the author of said work. The purchaser is also hereby granted the perpetual and exclusive right to use the title of said work in connection with or as the title of said work and of any literary, dramatic, speaking stage, motion picture, television, radio or other adaptations of said work or any part thereof; but the purchaser shall not be obligated to do so and may use any other title or titles which it may select as the title of said work and of said adaptations or any of them. The purchaser is also hereby granted the perpetual and exclusive right to use the title of said work in connection with or as the title of any literary, dramatic, speaking stage, motion picture, television, radio or other work not based on or adapted from said work. The purchaser shall have the exclusive right to obtain copyright and renewals and extensions of copyright in all countries upon said work and upon any literary, dramatic, speak-ing stage, motion picture, television, radio or other adaptations based in whole or in part on said work or any part thereof.

3. I hereby represent and warrant that I am the sole author and owner of said work and the title thereof; that I am the sole owner of all rights of every kind in and to said work throughout the world; that there has been no publication or any other use of said work, or any part thereof, with my knowledge or consent, anywhere in the world; that I have the sole and exclusive right to dispose of each and every right herein granted or purported to be granted; that neither said work nor any part thereof is in the public domain; that no motion pictures or any other works have been produced which have been based in whole or in part on said work or any part thereof; that I have in no way conveyed, granted, transferred or hypothecated any rights of any kind in, to or pertaining to said work or any part thereof, or any license, power, privilege or authority with respect thereto, to any person whomsoever, other than the purchaser, nor is said work subject to any involuntary liens, charges or encumbrances; that I have not done or caused or permitted to be done any act or thing by which any of the rights herein granted or purported to be granted to the purchaser have been impaired in any way; and that I will not at any time execute any other instrument or make or enter into any agreement in conflict herewith, nor will I in any way attempt to encumber the rights herein granted, nor will I do or cause or permit to be done any act or thing by which the rights herein granted or purported to be granted to the purchaser may be impaired in any way. I also represent and warrant that said work is original with me in all respects; that no incident therein contained and no part thereof is taken from or based upon any other literary, dramatic or other work or any motion picture, or in any way infringes the copyright, or any other right of any person whomsoever, and that the reproduction, exhibition or any other use by the purchaser of said work or any part thereof or any adaptation thereof or of any part thereof in any form whatsoever will not in any way, directly or indirectly, infringe or violate any rights of any person whomsoever. The foregoing warranties do not apply to any changes in said work which may be made by the purchaser.

4. I hereby appoint the purchaser my attorney-in-fact, irrevocably, and for the sole benefit of the purchaser, to institute and prosecute such proceedings as the purchaser may deem expedient to protect the rights herein granted or purported to be granted and to effect the recovery by the purchaser of damages, profits, penalties and costs for the infringement of said rights, and to secure to the purchaser the full benefit of all of the rights herein granted or purported to be granted. The purchaser may sue in its own name and may use my name, and at its option may join me as party plaintiff or defendant in any suit or proceeding brought for such purpose or purposes. All actions and causes of action for all past and future infringements of any of the rights herein granted or purported to be granted to the purchaser, and all judgments, damages, profits, penalties and costs recovered for such infringements or any of them, are hereby assigned to the purchaser.

5. I hereby agree to indemnify the purchaser against all judgments, liability, damages, penalties, loss or expense (including reasonable attorneys' fees) which may be suffered, incurred or assumed by or obtained against the purchaser by reason of any infringement or violation of any copyright or any other right of any person, resulting from any use which may be made of said

work by the purchaser, or by reason of any breach or failure of any warranty or agreement herein made by me. The foregoing agreement shall not apply to any changes in said work which may be made by the purchaser.

6. I hereby agree duly to execute, acknowledge and deliver and to procure the due execution, acknowledgment and delivery to the purchaser of any and all additional assignments and other instruments which in the sole judgment of the purchaser may be deemed necessary or expedient to effectuate the purpose or intent of this instrument.

7. All or any part of the purchaser's rights hereunder may be licensed, transferred or assigned by the purchaser. The term "purchaser" as used herein shall include the purchaser herein named and its respective successors, assigns, licensees and sublicensees. All rights, licenses, powers, privileges and authority of the purchaser hereunder may be exercised by the purchaser and/or by any person authorized or licensed by the purchaser to do so, directly or indirectly. The term "person" as used herein includes any natural person, corporation, partnership, association, company and organization. If this instrument is executed by two or more persons, this instrument shall be deemed to have been executed by them, and shall be binding upon them, jointly and severally, and each and all of the agreements, representations and warranties hereinabove set forth shall be deemed to be the joint and several agreements, representations and warranties of said persons and each of them, and all references to said persons in the singular shall be deemed to be in the plural. The purchaser shall enjoy its rights hereunder in perpetuity, or as long as any rights in said work are recognized at law or in equity, including but not limited to the full period of all copyrights and renewals and extensions of copyrights of said work.

IN WITNESS WHEREOF I have executed this instrument this_____day of_____, 19____

_____

Rona Riter

_____

STATE OF_____ } ss.

County of_____ }

On this_____day of_____, 19____, before me, _____,

a notary public in and for said county and state, residing therein, duly commissioned and sworn, personally appeared_____

_____, known to me to be the person(s) whose names(s) is/are

subscribed to the within instrument, and acknowledged to me that __he__ executed the same.

IN WITNESS WHEREOF I have hereunto set my hand and affixed my official seal the day and year in this certificate first above written.

_____
Notary Public in and for said County and State.

APPLICATION FOR COPYRIGHT REGISTRATION
for a
Nondramatic Literary Work

HOW TO APPLY FOR COPYRIGHT REGISTRATION:

- **First:** Read the information on this page to make sure Form TX is the correct application for your work.

- **Second:** Open out the form by lifting on the left. Read through the detailed instructions before starting to complete the form.

- **Third:** Complete spaces 1-4 of the application, then turn the entire form over and, after reading the instructions for spaces 5-11, complete the rest of your application. Use typewriter or print in dark ink. Be sure to sign the form at space 10.

- **Fourth:** Detach your completed application from these instructions and send it with the necessary deposit of the work (see below) to: Register of Copyrights, Library of Congress, Washington, D.C. 20559. Unless you have a Deposit Account in the Copyright Office, your application and deposit must be accompanied by a check or money order for $10, payable to: *Register of Copyrights.*

WHEN TO USE FORM TX: Form TX is the appropriate application to use for copyright registration covering nondramatic literary works, whether published or unpublished.

WHAT IS A "NONDRAMATIC LITERARY WORK"? The category of "nondramatic literary works" (Class TX) is very broad. Except for dramatic works and certain kinds of audiovisual works, Class TX includes all types of works written in words (or other verbal or numerical symbols). A few of the many examples of "nondramatic literary works" include fiction, nonfiction, poetry, periodicals, textbooks, reference works, directories, catalogs, advertising copy, and compilations of information.

DEPOSIT TO ACCOMPANY APPLICATION: An application for copyright registration must be accompanied by a deposit representing the entire work for which registration is to be made. The following are the general deposit requirements as set forth in the statute:

Unpublished work: Deposit one complete copy (or phonorecord).

Published work: Deposit two complete copies (or phonorecords) of the best edition.

Work first published outside the United States: Deposit one complete copy (or phonorecord) of the first foreign edition.

Contribution to a collective work: Deposit one complete copy (or phonorecord) of the best edition of the collective work.

These general deposit requirements may vary in particular situations. For further information about copyright deposit, write for Circular R7.

THE COPYRIGHT NOTICE: For published works, the law provides that a copyright notice in a specified form "shall be placed on all publicly distributed copies from which the work can be visually perceived."Use of the copyright notice is the responsibility of the copyright owner and does not require advance permission from the Copyright Office. The required form of the notice for copies generally consists of three elements: (1) the symbol "©", or the word "Copyright", or the abbreviation "Copr."; (2) the year of first publication; and (3) the name of the owner of copyright. For example: "© 1978 Constance Porter". The notice is to be affixed to the copies "in such manner and location as to give reasonable notice of the claim of copyright." Unlike the law in effect before 1978, the new copyright statute provides procedures for correcting errors in the copyright notice, and even for curing the omission of the notice. However, a failure to comply with the notice requirements may still result in the loss of some copyright protection and, unless corrected within five years, in the complete loss of copyright. For further information about the copyright notice and the procedures for correcting errors or omissions, write for Circular R3.

DURATION OF COPYRIGHT: For works that were created after the effective date of the new statute (January 1, 1978), the basic copyright term will be the life of the author and fifty years after the author's death. For works made for hire, and for certain anonymous and pseudonymous works, the duration of copyright will be 75 years from publication or 100 years from creation, whichever is shorter. These same terms of copyright will generally apply to works that had been created before 1978 but had not been published or copyrighted before that date. For further information about the duration of copyright, including the terms of copyrights already in existence before 1978, write for Circular R15a.

HOW TO FILL OUT FORM TX

Specific Instructions for Spaces 1-4

- The line-by-line instructions on this page are keyed to the spaces on the first page of Form TX, printed opposite.
- Please read through these instructions before you start filling out your application, and refer to the specific instructions for each space as you go along.

SPACE 1: TITLE

- **Title of this Work:** Every work submitted for copyright registration must be given a title that is capable of identifying that particular work. If the copies or phonorecords of the work bear a title (or an identifying phrase that could serve as a title), transcribe its wording completely and exactly on the application. Remember that indexing of the registration and future identification of the work will depend on the information you give here.

- **Periodical or Serial Issue:** Periodicals and other serials are publications issued at intervals under a general title, such as newspapers, magazines, journals, newsletters, and annuals. If the work being registered is an entire issue of a periodical or serial, give the over-all title of the periodical or serial in the space headed "Title of this Work," and add the specific information about the issue in the spaces provided. If the work being registered is a contribution to a periodical or serial issue. follow the instructions for "Publication as a Contribution."

- **Previous or Alternative Titles:** Complete this space if there are any additional titles for the work under which someone searching for the registration might be likely to look, or under which a document pertaining to the work might be recorded.

- **Publication as a Contribution:** If the work being registered has been published as a contribution to a periodical, serial, or collection, give the title of the contribution in the space headed "Title of this Work." Then, in the line headed "Publication as a Contribution," give information about the larger work in which the contribution appeared.

SPACE 2: AUTHORS

- **General Instructions:** First decide, after reading these instructions, who are the "authors" of this work for copyright purposes. Then, unless the work is a "collective work" (see below), give the requested information about every "author" who contributed any appreciable amount of copyrightable matter to this version of the work. If you need further space, use the attached Continuation Sheet and, if necessary, request additional Continuation Sheets (Form TX/Con).

- **Who is the "Author"?** Unless the work was "made for hire," the individual who actually created the work is its "author." In the case of a work made for hire, the statute provides that "the employer or other person for whom the work was prepared is considered the author."

- **What is a "Work Made for Hire"?** A "work made for hire" is defined as: (1) "a work prepared by an employee within the scope of his or her employment"; or (2) "a work specially ordered or commissioned" for certain uses specified in the statute, but only if there is a written agreement to consider it a "work made for hire."

- **Collective Work:** In the case of a collective work, such as a periodical issue, anthology, collection of essays, or encyclopedia, it is sufficient to give information about the author of the collective work as a whole.

- **Author's Identity Not Revealed:** If an author's contribution is "anonymous" or "pseudonymous," it is not necessary to give the name and dates for that author. However, the citizenship and domicile of the author **must** be given in all cases, and information about the nature of that author's contribution to the work should be included if possible.

- **Name of Author:** The fullest form of the author's name should be given. If you have checked "Yes" to indicate that the work was "made for hire," give the full legal name of the employer (or other person for whom the work was prepared). You may also include the name of the employee (for example, "Elster Publishing Co., employer for hire of John Ferguson"). If the work is "anonymous" you may: (1) leave the line blank, or (2) state "Anonymous" in the line, or (3) reveal the author's identity. If the work is "pseudonymous" you may (1) leave the line blank, or (2) give the pseudonym and identify it as such (for example: "Huntley Haverstock, pseudonym"), or (3) reveal the author's name, making clear which is the real name and which is the pseudonym (for example, "Judith Barton, whose pseudonym is Madeleine Elster").

- **Dates of Birth and Death:** If the author is dead, the statute requires that the year of death be included in the application unless the work is anonymous or pseudonymous. The author's birth date is optional, but is useful as a form of identification. Leave this space blank if the author's contribution was a "work made for hire."

- **"Anonymous" or "Pseudonymous" Work:** An author's contribution to a work is "anonymous" if that author is not identified on the copies or phonorecords of the work. An author's contribution to a work is "pseudonymous" if that author is identified on the copies or phonorecords under a fictitious name.

- **Author's Nationality or Domicile:** Give the country of which the author is a citizen, or the country in which the author is domiciled. The statute requires that either nationality or domicile be given in all cases.

- **Nature of Authorship:** After the words "Author of" give a brief general statement of the nature of this particular author's contribution to the work. Examples: "Entire text"; "Co-author of entire text"; "Chapters 11-14"; "Editorial revisions"; "Compilation and English translation"; "Illustrations."

SPACE 3: CREATION AND PUBLICATION

- **General Instructions:** Do not confuse "creation" with "publication." Every application for copyright registration must state "the year in which creation of the work was completed." Give the date and nation of first publication only if the work has been published.

- **Creation:** Under the statute, a work is "created" when it is fixed in a copy or phonorecord for the first time. Where a work has been prepared over a period of time, the part of the work existing in fixed form on a particular date constitutes the created work on that date. The date you give here should be the year in which the author completed the particular version for which registration is now being sought, even if other versions exist or if further changes or additions are planned.

- **Publication:** The statute defines "publication" as "the distribution of copies or phonorecords of a work to the public by sale or other transfer of ownership, or by rental, lease, or lending"; a work is also "published" if there has been an "offering to distribute copies or phonorecords to a group of persons for purposes of further distribution, public performance, or public display." Give the full date (month, day, year) when, and the country where, publication first occurred. If first publication took place simultaneously in the United States and other countries, it is sufficient to state "U.S.A."

SPACE 4: CLAIMANT(S)

- **Name(s) and Address(es) of Copyright Claimant(s):** Give the name(s) address(es) of the copyright claimant(s) in this work. The statute provides that copyright in a work belongs initially to the author of the work (including, in the case of a work made for hire, the employer or other person for whom the work was prepared). The copyright claimant is either the author of the work or a person or organization that has obtained ownership of the copyright initially belonging to the author.

- **Transfer:** The statute provides that, if the copyright claimant is not the author, the application for registration must contain "a brief statement of how the claimant obtained ownership of the copyright." If any copyright claimant named in space 4 is not an author named in space 2, give a brief, general statement summarizing the means by which that claimant obtained ownership of the copyright.

INSTRUCTIONS FOR FILLING OUT SPACES 5-11 OF FORM TX

SPACE 5: PREVIOUS REGISTRATION

• *General Instructions:* The questions in space 5 are intended to find out whether an earlier registration has been made for this work and, if so, whether there is any basis for a new registration. As a general rule, only one basic copyright registration can be made for the same version of a particular work.

• *Same Version:* If this version is substantially the same as the work covered by a previous registration, a second registration is not generally possible unless: (1) the work has been registered in unpublished form and a second registration is now being sought to cover the first published edition, or (2) someone other than the author is identified as copyright claimant in the earlier registration, and the author is now seeking registration in his or her own name. If either of these two exceptions apply, check the appropriate box and give the earlier registration number and date. Otherwise, do not submit Form TX; instead, write the Copyright Office for information about supplementary registration or recordation of transfers of copyright ownership.

• *Changed Version:* If the work has been changed, and you are now seeking registration to cover the additions or revisions, check the third box in space 5, give the earlier registration number and date, and complete both parts of space 6.

• *Previous Registration Number and Date:* If more than one previous registration has been made for the work, give the number and date of the latest registration.

SPACE 6: COMPILATION OR DERIVATIVE WORK

• *General Instructions:* Complete both parts of space 6 if this work is a "compilation," or "derivative work," or both, and if it incorporates one or more earlier works that have already been published or registered for copyright, or that have fallen into the public domain. A "compilation" is defined as "a work formed by the collection and assembling of preexisting materials or of data that are selected, coordinated, or arranged in such a way that the resulting work as a whole constitutes an original work of authorship." A "derivative work" is "a work based on one or more preexisting works." Examples of derivative works include translations, fictionalizations, arrangements, abridgments, condensations, or "any other form in which a work may be recast, transformed, or adapted." Derivative works also include works "consisting of editorial revisions, annotations, elaborations, or other modifications" if these changes, as a whole, represent an original work of authorship.

• *Preexisting Material:* If the work is a compilation, give a brief, general statement describing the nature of the material that has been compiled. Example: "Compilation of all published 1917 speeches of Woodrow Wilson." In the case of a derivative work, identify the preexisting work that has been recast, transformed, or adapted. Example: "Russian version of Goncharov's 'Oblomov'."

• *Material Added to this Work:* The statute requires a "brief, general statement of the additional material covered by the copyright claim being registered." This statement should describe all of the material in this particular version of the work that: (1) represents an original work of authorship; and (2) has not fallen into the public domain; and (3) has not been previously published; and (4) has not been previously registered for copyright in unpublished form. Examples: "Foreword, selection, arrangement, editing, critical annotations"; "Revisions throughout; chapters 11-17 entirely new".

SPACE 7: MANUFACTURING PROVISIONS

• *General Instructions:* The copyright statute currently provides, as a general rule, and with a number of exceptions, that the copies of a published work "consisting preponderantly of nondramatic literary material that is in the English language" be manufactured in the United States or Canada in order to be lawfully imported and publicly distributed in the United States. At the present time, applications for copyright registration covering published works that consist mainly of nondramatic text matter in English *must*, in most cases, identify those who performed certain processes in manufacturing the copies, together with the places where those processes were performed. *Please note:* The information must be given even if the copies were manufactured outside the United States or Canada; registration will be made regardless of the places of manufacture identified in space 7. In general, the processes covered by this provision are: (1) typesetting and plate-making (where a typographic process preceded the actual printing); (2) the making of plates by a lithographic or photoengraving process (where this was a final or intermediate step before printing); and (3) the final printing and binding processes (in all cases). Leave space 7 blank if your work is unpublished or is not in English.

• *Import Statement:* As an exception to the manufacturing provisions, the statute prescribes that, where manufacture has taken place outside the United States or Canada, a maximum of 2000 copies of the foreign edition can be imported into the United States without affecting the copyright owner's rights. For this purpose, the Copyright Office will issue an import statement upon request and payment of a fee of $3 at the time of registration or at any later time. For further information about import statements, ask for circular R62.

SPACE 8: REPRODUCTION FOR USE OF BLIND OR PHYSICALLY-HANDICAPPED PERSONS

• *General Instructions:* One of the major programs of the Library of Congress is to provide Braille editions and special recordings of works for the exclusive use of the blind and physically handicapped. In an effort to simplify and speed up the copyright licensing procedures that are a necessary part of this program, section 710 of the copyright statute provides for the establishment of a voluntary licensing system to be tied in with copyright registration. Under this system, the owner of copyright in a nondramatic literary work has the option, at the time of registration on Form TX, to grant to the Library of Congress a license to reproduce and distribute Braille editions and "talking books" or "talking magazines" of the work being registered. The Copyright Office regulations provide that, under the license, the reproduction and distribution must be solely for the use of persons who are certified by competent authority as unable to read normal printed material as a result of physical limitations. The license is nonexclusive, and may be terminated upon 90 days notice. For further information, write for Circular R63.

• *How to Grant the License:* The license is entirely voluntary. If you wish to grant it, check one of the three boxes in space 8. Your check in one of these boxes, together with your signature in space 10, will mean that the Library of Congress can proceed to reproduce and distribute under the license without further paperwork.

SPACES 9, 10, 11: FEE, CORRESPONDENCE, CERTIFICATION, RETURN ADDRESS

• *Deposit Account and Mailing Instructions (Space 9):* If you maintain a Deposit Account in the Copyright Office, identify it in space 9. Otherwise you will need to send the registration fee of $10 with your application. The space headed "Correspondence" should contain the name and address of the person to be consulted if correspondence about this application becomes necessary.

• *Certification (Space 10):* The application is not acceptable unless it bears the handwritten signature of the author or other copyright claimant, or of the owner of exclusive right(s), or of the duly authorized agent of such author, claimant, or owner.

• *Address for Return of Certificate (Space 11):* The address box must be completed legibly, since the certificate will be returned in a window envelope.

FORM TX

UNITED STATES COPYRIGHT OFFICE

REGISTRATION NUMBER
TX   TXU

EFFECTIVE DATE OF REGISTRATION
. . . .
Month   Day   Year

DO NOT WRITE ABOVE THIS LINE. IF YOU NEED MORE SPACE, USE CONTINUATION SHEET

---

(1) Title

TITLE OF THIS WORK:

If a periodical or serial give: Vol. . . . . . . No. . . . . . . Issue Date . . . .

PREVIOUS OR ALTERNATIVE TITLES:

PUBLICATION AS A CONTRIBUTION: (If this work was published as a contribution to a periodical, serial, or collection, give information about the collective work in which the contribution appeared.)

Title of Collective Work: . . . . Vol. . . . . . . No. . . . . . Date . . . . Pages. . . . .

---

(2) Author(s)

IMPORTANT: Under the law, the "author" of a "work made for hire" is generally the employer, not the employee (see instructions). If any part of this work was "made for hire" check "Yes" in the space provided, give the employer (or other person for whom the work was prepared) as "Author" of that part, and leave the space for dates blank.

1

NAME OF AUTHOR:

Was this author's contribution to the work a "work made for hire"?   Yes. . . . . .   No. . . . . .

DATES OF BIRTH AND DEATH:
Born . . . . Died . . . .
(Year)   (Year)

AUTHOR'S NATIONALITY OR DOMICILE:

Citizen of . . . . } or { Domiciled in . . . .
(Name of Country)   (Name of Country)

AUTHOR OF: (Briefly describe nature of this author's contribution)

WAS THIS AUTHOR'S CONTRIBUTION TO THE WORK:
Anonymous?   Yes. . . . . .   No. . . . . .
Pseudonymous? Yes. . . . . .   No. . . . . .
If the answer to either of these questions is "Yes," see detailed instructions attached.

2

NAME OF AUTHOR:

Was this author's contribution to the work a "work made for hire"?   Yes. . . . . .   No. . . . . .

DATES OF BIRTH AND DEATH:
Born . . . . Died . . . .
(Year)   (Year)

AUTHOR'S NATIONALITY OR DOMICILE:

Citizen of . . . . } or { Domiciled in . . . .
(Name of Country)   (Name of Country)

AUTHOR OF: (Briefly describe nature of this author's contribution)

WAS THIS AUTHOR'S CONTRIBUTION TO THE WORK:
Anonymous?   Yes. . . . . .   No. . . . . .
Pseudonymous? Yes. . . . . .   No. . . . . .
If the answer to either of these questions is "Yes," see detailed instructions attached.

3

NAME OF AUTHOR:

Was this author's contribution to the work a "work made for hire"?   Yes. . . . . .   No. . . . . .

DATES OF BIRTH AND DEATH:
Born . . . . Died . . . .
(Year)   (Year)

AUTHOR'S NATIONALITY OR DOMICILE:

Citizen of . . . . } or { Domiciled in . . . .
(Name of Country)   (Name of Country)

AUTHOR OF: (Briefly describe nature of this author's contribution)

WAS THIS AUTHOR'S CONTRIBUTION TO THE WORK:
Anonymous?   Yes. . . . . .   No. . . . . .
Pseudonymous? Yes. . . . . .   No. . . . . .
If the answer to either of these questions is "Yes," see detailed instructions attached.

---

(3) Creation and Publication

YEAR IN WHICH CREATION OF THIS WORK WAS COMPLETED:

Year. . . . .

(This information must be given in all cases.)

DATE AND NATION OF FIRST PUBLICATION:

Date. . . . .
(Month)   (Day)   (Year)

Nation . . . .
(Name of Country)

(Complete this block ONLY if this work has been published.)

---

(4) Claimant(s)

NAME(S) AND ADDRESS(ES) OF COPYRIGHT CLAIMANT(S):

TRANSFER: (If the copyright claimant(s) named here in space 4 are different from the author(s) named in space 2, give a brief statement of how the claimant(s) obtained ownership of the copyright.)

• *Complete all applicable spaces (numbers 5-11) on the reverse side of this page*
• *Follow detailed instructions attached*
• *Sign the form at line 10*

DO NOT WRITE HERE

Page 1 of . . . . pages

			FOR COPYRIGHT OFFICE USE ONLY
	EXAMINED BY:	APPLICATION RECEIVED:	
	CHECKED BY:		
	CORRESPONDENCE: ☐ Yes	DEPOSIT RECEIVED:	
	DEPOSIT ACCOUNT FUNDS USED: ☐	REMITTANCE NUMBER AND DATE	

DO NOT WRITE ABOVE THIS LINE. IF YOU NEED ADDITIONAL SPACE, USE CONTINUATION SHEET (FORM TX/CON)

PREVIOUS REGISTRATION:

- Has registration for this work, or for an earlier version of this work, already been made in the Copyright Office?   Yes . . . . No . . . .
- If your answer is "Yes," why is another registration being sought? (Check appropriate box)
  - ☐ This is the first published edition of a work previously registered in unpublished form.
  - ☐ This is the first application submitted by this author as copyright claimant.
  - ☐ This is a changed version of the work, as shown by line 6 of this application.
- If your answer is "Yes," give: Previous Registration Number . . . . Year of Registration . . . .

(5) Previous Registration

COMPILATION OR DERIVATIVE WORK: (See instructions)

PREEXISTING MATERIAL: (Identify any preexisting work or works that this work is based on or incorporates.)

{ . . . .

MATERIAL ADDED TO THIS WORK: (Give a brief, general statement of the material that has been added to this work and in which copyright is claimed.)

{ . . . .

(6) Compilation or Derivative Work

MANUFACTURERS AND LOCATIONS: (If this is a published work consisting preponderantly of nondramatic literary material in English, the law may require that the copies be manufactured in the United States or Canada for full protection. If so, the names of the manufacturers who performed certain processes, and the places where these processes were performed *must* be given. See instructions for details.)

NAMES OF MANUFACTURERS	PLACES OF MANUFACTURE
. . . .	. . . .
. . . .	. . . .
. . . .	. . . .

(7) Manufacturing

REPRODUCTION FOR USE OF BLIND OR PHYSICALLY-HANDICAPPED PERSONS: (See instructions)

- Signature of this form at space 10, and a check in one of the boxes here in space 8, constitutes a non-exclusive grant of permission to the Library of Congress to reproduce and distribute solely for the blind and physically handicapped and under the conditions and limitations prescribed by the regulations of the Copyright Office: (1) copies of the work identified in space 1 of this application in Braille (or similar tactile symbols); or (2) phonorecords embodying a fixation of a reading of that work; or (3) both.

     a ☐ Copies and phonorecords   b ☐ Copies Only   c ☐ Phonorecords Only

(8) License For Handicapped

DEPOSIT ACCOUNT: (If the registration fee is to be charged to a Deposit Account established in the Copyright Office, give name and number of Account.)

Name: . . . .

Account Number: . . . .

CORRESPONDENCE: (Give name and address to which correspondence about this application should be sent.)

Name: . . . .

Address: . . . . (Apt.)

. . . .
     (City)   (State)   (ZIP)

(9) Fee and Correspondence

CERTIFICATION: ✱ I, the undersigned, hereby certify that I am the: (Check one)

☐ author ☐ other copyright claimant ☐ owner of exclusive right(s) ☐ authorized agent of: . . . .
                                                      (Name of author or other copyright claimant, or owner of exclusive right(s))

of the work identified in this application and that the statements made by me in this application are correct to the best of my knowledge.

Handwritten signature: (X) . . . .

Typed or printed name: . . . . Date . . . .

(10) Certification (Application must be signed)

MAIL CERTIFICATE TO

. . . .
                        (Name)

. . . .
            (Number, Street and Apartment Number)

. . . .
       (City)   (State)   (ZIP code)

(Certificate will be mailed in window envelope)

(11) Address For Return of Certificate

✱ 17 U.S.C. § 506(e): Any person who knowingly makes a false representation of a material fact in the application for copyright registration provided for by section 409, or in any written statement filed in connection with the application, shall be fined not more than $2,500.

☆ U. S. GOVERNMENT PRINTING OFFICE : 1977 O - 248-641

CONTINUATION SHEET FOR FORM TX

FORM TX/CON
UNITED STATES COPYRIGHT OFFICE

- If at all possible, try to fit the information called for into the spaces provided on Form TX.
- If you do not have space enough for all of the information you need to give on Form TX, use this continuation sheet and submit it with Form TX.
- If you submit this continuation sheet, leave it attached to Form TX. Or, if it becomes detached, clip (do not tape or staple) and fold the two together before submitting them.
- **PART A** of this sheet is intended to identify the basic application. **PART B** is a continuation of Space 2. **PART C** is for the continuation of Spaces 1, 4, 6, or 7. The other spaces on Form TX call for specific items of information, and should not need continuation.

REGISTRATION NUMBER

TX   TXU

EFFECTIVE DATE OF REGISTRATION

. . . .
(Month)   (Day)   (Year)

CONTINUATION SHEET RECEIVED

Page _____ of _____ pages

DO NOT WRITE ABOVE THIS LINE: FOR COPYRIGHT OFFICE USE ONLY

(A)

Identification of Application

IDENTIFICATION OF CONTINUATION SHEET: This sheet is a continuation of the application for copyright registration on Form TX, submitted for the following work:
- TITLE (Give the title as given under the heading "Title of this Work" in Space 1 of Form TX)

. . . .

- NAME(S) AND ADDRESS(ES) OF COPYRIGHT CLAIMANT(S): Give the name and address of at least one copyright claimant as given in Space 4 of Form TX.)

. . . .

(B)

Continuation of Space 2

NAME OF AUTHOR:

Was this author's contribution to the work a "work made for hire"?   Yes...... No......

DATES OF BIRTH AND DEATH:
Born . . . . Died . . . .
(Year)   (Year)

AUTHOR'S NATIONALITY OR DOMICILE:
Citizen of . . . . } or { Domiciled in . . . .
(Name of Country)   (Name of Country)

WAS THIS AUTHOR'S CONTRIBUTION TO THE WORK:
Anonymous?   Yes....... No......
Pseudonymous? Yes....... No......

AUTHOR OF: (Briefly describe nature of this author's contribution)

If the answer to either of these questions is "Yes," see detailed instructions attached.

NAME OF AUTHOR:

Was this author's contribution to the work a "work made for hire"?   Yes...... No......

DATES OF BIRTH AND DEATH:
Born . . . . Died . . . .
(Year)   (Year)

AUTHOR'S NATIONALITY OR DOMICILE:
Citizen of . . . . } or { Domiciled in . . . .
(Name of Country)   (Name of Country)

WAS THIS AUTHOR'S CONTRIBUTION TO THE WORK:
Anonymous?   Yes....... No......
Pseudonymous? Yes....... No......

AUTHOR OF: (Briefly describe nature of this author's contribution)

If the answer to either of these questions is "Yes," see detailed instructions attached.

NAME OF AUTHOR:

Was this author's contribution to the work a "work made for hire"?   Yes...... No......

DATES OF BIRTH AND DEATH:
Born . . . . Died . . . .
(Year)   (Year)

AUTHOR'S NATIONALITY OR DOMICILE:
Citizen of . . . . } or { Domiciled in . . . .
(Name of Country)   (Name of Country)

WAS THIS AUTHOR'S CONTRIBUTION TO THE WORK:
Anonymous?   Yes....... No......
Pseudonymous? Yes....... No......

AUTHOR OF: (Briefly describe nature of this author's contribution)

If the answer to either of these questions is "Yes," see detailed instructions attached.

(C)

Continuation of other Spaces

CONTINUATION OF (Check which):   □ Space 1   □ Space 4   □ Space 6   □ Space 7

APPLICATION FOR COPYRIGHT REGISTRATION
for a
Work of the Performing Arts

FORM PA

UNITED STATES COPYRIGHT OFFICE
LIBRARY OF CONGRESS
WASHINGTON, D.C. 20559

HOW TO APPLY FOR COPYRIGHT REGISTRATION:

- **First:** Read the information on this page to make sure Form PA is the correct application for your work.

- **Second:** Open out the form by pulling this page to the left. Read through the detailed instructions before starting to complete the form.

- **Third:** Complete spaces 1-4 of the application, then turn the entire form over and, after reading the instructions for spaces 5-9, complete the rest of your application. Use typewriter or print in dark ink. Be sure to sign the form at space 8.

- **Fourth:** Detach your completed application from these instructions and send it with the necessary deposit of the work (see below) to: Register of Copyrights, Library of Congress, Washington, D.C. 20559. Unless you have a Deposit Account in the Copyright Office, your application and deposit must be accompanied by a check or money order for $10, payable to: *Register of Copyrights.*

WHEN TO USE FORM PA: Form PA is the appropriate application to use for copyright registration covering works of the performing arts. Both published and unpublished works can be registered on Form PA.

WHAT IS A "WORK OF THE PERFORMING ARTS"? This category includes works prepared for the purpose of being "performed" directly before an audience or indirectly "by means of any device or process." Examples of works of the performing arts are: (1) musical works, including any accompanying words; (2) dramatic works, including any accompanying music; (3) pantomimes and choreographic works; and (4) motion pictures and other audiovisual works. **Note:** This category does not include sound recordings, which should be registered on Form SR. For more information about copyright in sound recordings, see the reverse side of this sheet.

DEPOSIT TO ACCOMPANY APPLICATION: An application for copyright registration must be accompanied by a deposit representing the entire work for which registration is to be made. The following are the general deposit requirements as set forth in the statute:

    Unpublished work: Deposit one complete copy or phonorecord.

    Published work: Deposit two complete copies or phonorecords of the best edition.

    Work first published outside the United States: Deposit one complete copy or phonorecord of the first foreign edition.

    Contribution to a collective work: Deposit one complete copy or phonorecord of the best edition of the collective work.

These general deposit requirements may vary in particular situations. For further information about the specific deposit requirements for particular types of works of the performing arts, see the reverse side of this sheet. For general information about copyright deposit, write to the Copyright Office.

THE COPYRIGHT NOTICE: For published works, the law provides that a copyright notice in a specified form "shall be placed on all publicly distributed copies from which the work can be visually perceived." Use of the copyright notice is the responsibility of the copyright owner and does not require advance permission from the Copyright Office. The required form of the notice for copies generally consists of three elements: (1) the symbol "©", or the word "Copyright", or the abbreviation "Copr."; (2) the year of first publication; and (3) the name of the owner of copyright. For example: "© 1978 Alexander Hollenius". The notice is to be affixed to the copies "in such manner and location as to give reasonable notice of the claim of copyright." Unlike the law in effect before 1978, the new copyright statute provides procedures for correcting errors in the copyright notice, and even for curing the omission of the notice. However, a failure to comply with the notice requirements may still result in the loss of some copyright protection and, unless corrected within five years, in the complete loss of copyright. For further information about the copyright notice, see the reverse side of this sheet. For additional information concerning the copyright notice and the procedures for correcting errors or omissions, write to the Copyright Office.

DURATION OF COPYRIGHT: For works that were created after the effective date of the new statute (January 1, 1978), the basic copyright term will be the life of the author and fifty years after the author's death. For works made for hire, and for certain anonymous and pseudonymous works, the duration of copyright will be 75 years from publication or 100 years from creation, whichever is shorter: These same terms of copyright will generally apply to works that had been created before 1978 but had not been published or copyrighted before that date. For further information about the duration of copyright, including the terms of copyrights already in existence before 1978, write for Circular R15a.

HOW TO FILL OUT FORM PA
Specific Instructions for Spaces 1-4

- The line-by-line instructions on this page are keyed to the spaces on the first page of Form PA, printed opposite.
- Please read through these instructions before you start filling out your application, and refer to the specific instructions for each space as you go along.

SPACE 1: TITLE

- **Title of this Work:** Every work submitted for copyright registration must be given a title that is capable of identifying that particular work. If the copies or phonorecords of the work bear a title (or an identifying phrase that could serve as a title), transcribe its wording completely and exactly on the application. Remember that indexing of the registration and future identification of the work will depend on the information you give here.

  If the work you are registering is an entire "collective work" (such as a collection of plays or songs), give the over-all title of the collection. If you are registering one or more individual contributions to a collective work, give the title of

each contribution, followed by the title of the collection. Example: " 'A Song for Elinda' in *Old and New Ballads for Old and New People.*"
- **Nature of this Work:** Briefly describe the general nature or character of the work being registered for copyright. Examples: "Music"; "Song Lyrics"; "Words and Music"; "Drama"; "Musical Play"; "Choreography"; "Pantomime"; "Motion Picture"; "Audiovisual Work".
- **Previous or Alternative Titles:** Complete this space if there are any additional titles for the work under which someone searching for the registration might be likely to look, or under which a document pertaining to the work might be recorded.

SPACE 2: AUTHORS

- **General Instructions:** First decide, after reading these instructions, who are the "authors" of this work for copyright purposes. Then, unless the work is a "collective work" (see below), give the requested information about every "author" who contributed any appreciable amount of copyrightable matter to this version of the work. If you need further space, use the attached Continuation Sheet and, if necessary, request additional Continuation Sheets (Form PA/CON).
- **Who is the "Author"?** Unless the work was "made for hire," the individual who actually created the work is its "author." In the case of a work made for hire, the statute provides that "the employer or other person for whom the work was prepared is considered the author."
- **What is a "Work Made for Hire"?** A "work made for hire" is defined as: (1) "a work prepared by an employee within the scope of his or her employment"; or (2) "a work specially ordered or commissioned" for certain uses specified in the statute, but only if there is a written agreement to consider it a "work made for hire."
- **Collective Work:** In the case of a collective work, such as a song book or a collection of plays, it is sufficient to give information about the author of the collective work as a whole.
- **Author's Identity Not Revealed:** If an author's contribution is "anonymous" or "pseudonymous," it is not necessary to give the name and dates for that author. However, the citizenship or domicile of the author **must** be given in all cases, and information about the nature of that author's contribution to the work should be included.
- **Name of Author:** The fullest form of the author's name should be given. If you have checked "Yes" to indicate that the work was "made for hire," give the

full legal name of the employer (or other person for whom the work was prepared). You may also include the name of the employee (for example: "Music Makers Publishing Co., employer for hire of Lila Crane"). If the work is "anonymous" you may: (1) leave the line blank, or (2) state "Anonymous" in the line, or (3) reveal the author's identity. If the work is "pseudonymous" you may (1) leave the line blank, or (2) give the pseudonym and identify it as such (for example: "Huntley Haverstock, pseudonym"), or (3) reveal the author's name, making clear which is the real name and which is the pseudonym (for example, "Judith Barton, whose pseudonym is Madeleine Elster").
- **Dates of Birth and Death:** If the author is dead, the statute requires that the year of death be included in the application unless the work is anonymous or pseudonymous. The author's birth date is optional, but is useful as a form of identification. Leave this space blank if the author's contribution was a "work made for hire."
- **"Anonymous" or "Pseudonymous" Work:** An author's contribution to a work is "anonymous" if that author is not identified on the copies or phonorecords of the work. An author's contribution to a work is "pseudonymous" if that author is identified on the copies or phonorecords under a fictitious name.
- **Author's Nationality or Domicile:** Give the country of which the author is a citizen, or the country in which the author is domiciled. The statute requires that either nationality or domicile be given in all cases.
- **Nature of Authorship:** After the words "Author of" give a brief general statement of the nature of this particular author's contribution to the work. Examples: "Words"; "Co-Author of Music"; "Words and Music"; "Arrangement"; "Co-Author of Book and Lyrics"; "Dramatization"; "Entire Work"; "Compilation and English Translation"; "Editorial Revisions".

SPACE 3: CREATION AND PUBLICATION

- **General Instructions:** Do not confuse "creation" with "publication." Every application for copyright registration must state "the year in which creation of the work was completed." Give the date and nation of first publication only if the work has been published.
- **Creation:** Under the statute, a work is "created" when it is fixed in a copy or phonorecord for the first time. Where a work has been prepared over a period of time, the part of the work existing in fixed form on a particular date constitutes the created work on that date. The date you give here should be the year in which the author completed the particular version for which registration

is now being sought, even if other versions exist or if further changes or additions are planned.
- **Publication:** The statute defines "publication" as "the distribution of copies or phonorecords of a work to the public by sale or other transfer of ownership, or by rental, lease, or lending"; a work is also "published" if there has been an "offering to distribute copies or phonorecords to a group of persons for purposes of further distribution, public performance, or public display." Give the full date (month, day, year) when, and the country where, publication first occurred. If first publication took place simultaneously in the United States and other countries, it is sufficient to state "U.S.A."

SPACE 4: CLAIMANT(S)

- **Name(s) and Address(es) of Copyright Claimant(s):** Give the name(s) and address(es) of the copyright claimant(s) in this work. The statute provides that copyright in a work belongs initially to the author of the work (including, in the case of a work made for hire, the employer or other person for whom the work was prepared). The copyright claimant is either the author of the work or a person or organization that has obtained ownership of the copyright initially belonging to the author.
- **Transfer:** The statute provides that, if the copyright claimant is not the author, the application for registration must contain "a brief statement of how the claimant obtained ownership of the copyright." If any copyright claimant named in space 4 is not an author named in space 2, give a brief, general statement summarizing the means by which that claimant obtained ownership of the copyright.

INSTRUCTIONS FOR SPACES 5-9

SPACE 5: PREVIOUS REGISTRATION

• *General Instructions:* The questions in space 5 are intended to find out whether an earlier registration has been made for this work and, if so, whether there is any basis for a new registration. As a general rule, only one basic copyright registration can be made for the same version of a particular work.

• *Same Version:* If this version is substantially the same as the work covered by a previous registration, a second registration is not generally possible unless: (1) the work has been registered in unpublished form and a second registration is now being sought to cover the first published edition, or (2) someone other than the author is identified as copyright claimant in the earlier registration, and the author is now seeking registration in his or her own name. If either of these two exceptions apply, check the appropriate box and give the earlier registration number and date. Otherwise, do not submit Form PA; instead, write the Copyright Office for information about supplementary registration or recordation of transfers of copyright ownership.

• *Changed Version:* If the work has been changed, and you are now seeking registration to cover the additions or revisions, check the third box in space 5, give the earlier registration number and date, and complete both parts of space 6.

• *Previous Registration Number and Date:* If more than one previous registration has been made for the work, give the number and date of the latest registration.

SPACE 6: COMPILATION OR DERIVATIVE WORK

• *General Instructions:* Complete both parts of space 6 if this work is a "compilation," or "derivative work," or both, and if it incorporates one or more earlier works that have already been published or registered for copyright, or that have fallen into the public domain. A "compilation" is defined as "a work formed by the collection and assembling of preexisting materials or of data that are selected, coordinated, or arranged in such a way that the resulting work as a whole constitutes an original work of authorship." A "derivative work" is "a work based on one or more preexisting works." Examples of derivative works include musical arrangements, dramatizations, translations, abridgments, condensations, motion picture versions, or "any other form in which a work may be recast, transformed, or adapted." Derivative works also include works "consisting of editorial revisions, annotations, elaborations, or other modifications" if these changes, as a whole, represent an original work of authorship.

• *Preexisting Material:* If the work is a compilation, give a brief, general statement describing the nature of the material that has been compiled. Example: "Compilation of 19th Century military songs." In the case of a derivative work, identify the preexisting work that has been recast, transformed, or adapted. Example: "French version of Hugo's 'Le Roi s'amuse'."

• *Material Added to this Work:* The statute requires a "brief, general statement of the additional material covered by the copyright claim being registered." This statement should describe all of the material in this particular version of the work that: (1) represents an original work of authorship; and (2) has not fallen into the public domain; and (3) has not been previously published; and (4) has not been previously registered for copyright in unpublished form. Examples: "Arrangement for piano and orchestra"; "Dramatization for television"; "New film version"; "Revisions throughout; Act III completely new".

SPACES 7, 8, 9: FEE, CORRESPONDENCE, CERTIFICATION, RETURN ADDRESS

• *Deposit Account and Mailing Instructions (Space 7):* If you maintain a Deposit Account in the Copyright Office, identify it in space 7. Otherwise you will need to send the registration fee of $10 with your application. The space headed "Correspondence" should contain the name and address of the person to be consulted if correspondence about this application becomes necessary.

• *Certification (Space 8):* The application is not acceptable unless it bears the handwritten signature of the author or other copyright claimant, or of the owner of exclusive right(s), or of the duly authorized agent of such author, claimant, or owner.

• *Address for Return of Certificate (Space 9):* The address box must be completed legibly, since the certificate will be returned in a window envelope.

MORE INFORMATION

A NOTE ON TERMINOLOGY: The following are the meanings given to some of the terms used in the copyright statute:

• *"Works":* "Works" are the basic subject matter of copyright; they are what authors create and copyright protects. The statute draws a sharp distinction between the "work" and "any material object in which the work is embodied."

• *"Copies" and "Phonorecords":* These are the two types of material objects in which "works" are embodied. In general, **"copies"** are objects from which a work can be read or visually perceived, directly or with the aid of a machine or device, such as manuscripts, books, sheet music, film, and videotape. **"Phonorecords"** are objects embodying fixations of sounds, such as audio tapes and phonograph disks. For example, a song (the "work") can be reproduced in sheet music ("copies") or phonograph disks ("phonorecords"), or both.

• *"Sound Recordings":* These are "works," not "copies" or "phonorecords." With one exception, "sound recordings" are "works that result from the fixation of a series of musical, spoken, or other sounds." (The exception is for the audio portions of audiovisual works, including motion picture soundtracks; these are considered an integral part of the audiovisual work as a whole.) "Sound recordings" are registered on Form SR.

Example: When a record company issues a new release, the release will typically involve two distinct "works": the "musical work" that has been recorded, and the "sound recording" as a separate work in itself. The material objects that the record company sends out are "phonorecords": physical reproductions of both the "musical work" and the "sound recording."

FOR A MUSICAL OR DRAMATIC WORK, SHOULD YOU DEPOSIT COPIES OR PHONORECORDS WITH YOUR FORM PA?

• *For registration in unpublished form:*
   (1) If the work exists only in one form or the other (copies or phonorecords, but not both), deposit the work in its existing form;
   (2) If the work exists in both copies and phonorecords, deposit the form that best represents the musical or dramatic work in which copyright is being claimed.

• *For registration in published form:*
   (1) If the work has been published in the form of copies but not phonorecords, deposit two copies of the best edition. If the work has been published in the form of phonorecords only, deposit two phonorecords of the best edition.
   (2) If the work has been published in both forms, deposit two copies (**not phonorecords**) of the best edition.
   (3) If the work has been first published outside the United States, deposit one copy or phonorecord as first published.

SHOULD YOU FILE FORM PA OR FORM SR?
If the musical or dramatic work has been recorded, and both that "work," and the sound recording as a separate "work," are eligible for registration, the application form you should file depends on the following:

• *File only Form PA if:* You are seeking to register only the musical or dramatic work, not the sound recording.

• *File only Form SR if:* The copyright claimant for both the musical or dramatic work and the sound recording is the same, and you are seeking a single registration to cover both of these "works."

• *Separate applications on Forms PA and SR should be filed if:*
   (1) The copyright claimant for the musical or dramatic work is different from the copyright claimant for the sound recording; or
   (2) You prefer to have separate registrations for the musical or dramatic work **and** the sound recording.

FORM OF COPYRIGHT NOTICE ON PHONORECORDS:

For musical or dramatic works: The copyright notice for musical and dramatic works (for example: "© 1978 George Harvey Bone") is required to appear on "all publicly distributed copies from which the work can be visually perceived." There is no requirement that the notice for musical or dramatic works be placed on phonorecords reproducing them.

For sound recordings: The copyright statute provides that; whenever a sound recording is published, a special notice of copyright (for example: "℗1978 Miriam Haines") "shall be placed on all publicly distributed phonorecords of the sound recording." For further information about the requirements for copyright in sound recordings, write for Form SR.

FORM PA

UNITED STATES COPYRIGHT OFFICE

REGISTRATION NUMBER

PA   PAU

EFFECTIVE DATE OF REGISTRATION

....
(Month)   (Day)   (Year)

DO NOT WRITE ABOVE THIS LINE. IF YOU NEED MORE SPACE, USE CONTINUATION SHEET (FORM PA/CON)

(1) Title

TITLE OF THIS WORK:

NATURE OF THIS WORK: (See instructions)

PREVIOUS OR ALTERNATIVE TITLES:

(2) Author(s)

IMPORTANT: Under the law, the "author" of a "work made for hire" is generally the employer, not the employee (see instructions). If any part of this work was "made for hire" check "Yes" in the space provided, give the employer (or other person for whom the work was prepared) as "Author" of that part, and leave the space for dates blank.

1

NAME OF AUTHOR:

Was this author's contribution to the work a "work made for hire"? Yes...... No......

DATES OF BIRTH AND DEATH:
Born .... Died ....
(Year)   (Year)

AUTHOR'S NATIONALITY OR DOMICILE:
Citizen of .... } or { Domiciled in ....
(Name of Country)   (Name of Country)

WAS THIS AUTHOR'S CONTRIBUTION TO THE WORK:
Anonymous? Yes...... No......
Pseudonymous? Yes...... No......

AUTHOR OF: (Briefly describe nature of this author's contribution)

If the answer to either of these questions is "Yes," see detailed instructions attached.

2

NAME OF AUTHOR:

Was this author's contribution to the work a "work made for hire"? Yes...... No......

DATES OF BIRTH AND DEATH:
Born .... Died ....
(Year)   (Year)

AUTHOR'S NATIONALITY OR DOMICILE:
Citizen of .... } or { Domiciled in ....
(Name of Country)   (Name of Country)

WAS THIS AUTHOR'S CONTRIBUTION TO THE WORK:
Anonymous? Yes...... No......
Pseudonymous? Yes...... No......

AUTHOR OF: (Briefly describe nature of this author's contribution)

If the answer to either of these questions is "Yes," see detailed instructions attached.

3

NAME OF AUTHOR:

Was this author's contribution to the work a "work made for hire"? Yes...... No......

DATES OF BIRTH AND DEATH:
Born .... Died ....
(Year)   (Year)

AUTHOR'S NATIONALITY OR DOMICILE:
Citizen of .... } or { Domiciled in ....
(Name of Country)   (Name of Country)

WAS THIS AUTHOR'S CONTRIBUTION TO THE WORK:
Anonymous? Yes...... No......
Pseudonymous? Yes...... No......

AUTHOR OF: (Briefly describe nature of this author's contribution)

If the answer to either of these questions is "Yes," see detailed instructions attached.

(3) Creation and Publication

YEAR IN WHICH CREATION OF THIS WORK WAS COMPLETED:

Year..........
(This information must be given in all cases.)

DATE AND NATION OF FIRST PUBLICATION:

Date.....................
(Month)   (Day)   (Year)

Nation.....................
(Name of Country)
(Complete this block ONLY if this work has been published.)

(4) Claimant(s)

NAME(S) AND ADDRESS(ES) OF COPYRIGHT CLAIMANT(S):

TRANSFER: (If the copyright claimant(s) named here in space 4 are different from the author(s) named in space 2, give a brief statement of how the claimant(s) obtained ownership of the copyright.)

- Complete all applicable spaces (numbers 5-9) on the reverse side of this page
- Follow detailed instructions attached   • Sign the form at line 8

DO NOT WRITE HERE
Page 1 of .... pages

EXAMINED BY:	APPLICATION RECEIVED:	
CHECKED BY:		FOR COPYRIGHT OFFICE USE ONLY
CORRESPONDENCE: ☐ Yes	DEPOSIT RECEIVED:	
DEPOSIT ACCOUNT FUNDS USED: ☐	REMITTANCE NUMBER AND DATE:	

DO NOT WRITE ABOVE THIS LINE. IF YOU NEED ADDITIONAL SPACE, USE CONTINUATION SHEET (FORM PA/CON)

PREVIOUS REGISTRATION:

⑤ Previous Registration

- Has registration for this work, or for an earlier version of this work, already been made in the Copyright Office? Yes .... No ....

- If your answer is "Yes," why is another registration being sought? (Check appropriate box)

  ☐ This is the first published edition of a work previously registered in unpublished form.
  ☐ This is the first application submitted by this author as copyright claimant.
  ☐ This is a changed version of the work, as shown by line 6 of the application.

- If your answer is "Yes," give: Previous Registration Number .... Year of Registration ....

COMPILATION OR DERIVATIVE WORK: (See instructions)

⑥ Compilation or Derivative Work

PREEXISTING MATERIAL: (Identify any preexisting work or works that the work is based on or incorporates.)
....
....
....

MATERIAL ADDED TO THIS WORK: (Give a brief, general statement of the material that has been added to this work and in which copyright is claimed.)
....
....
....

DEPOSIT ACCOUNT: (If the registration fee is to be charged to a Deposit Account established in the Copyright Office, give name and number of Account.)

Name: ....

Account Number: ....

CORRESPONDENCE: (Give name and address to which correspondence about this application should be sent.)

Name: ....
Address: .... (Apt.)
.... (City) (State) (ZIP)

⑦ Fee and Correspondence

CERTIFICATION: ✱ I, the undersigned, hereby certify that I am the: (Check one)

☐ author ☐ other copyright claimant ☐ owner of exclusive right(s) ☐ authorized agent of: .... (Name of author or other copyright claimant, or owner of exclusive right(s))

of the work identified in this application and that the statements made by me in this application are correct to the best of my knowledge.

Handwritten signature: (X) ....

Typed or printed name. .... Date ....

⑧ Certification (Application must be signed)

MAIL CERTIFICATE TO

.... (Name)
.... (Number, Street and Apartment Number)
.... (City) (State) (ZIP code)

(Certificate will be mailed in window envelope)

⑨ Address For Return of Certificate

✱ 17 U.S.C. §506(e) FALSE REPRESENTATION—Any person who knowingly makes a false representation of a material fact in the application for copyright registration provided for by section 409, or in any written statement filed in connection with the application, shall be fined not more than $2,500.

U.S. GOVERNMENT PRINTING OFFICE:1979—281-421/10

July 1979—125,000

CONTINUATION SHEET FOR FORM PA

FORM PA/CON
UNITED STATES COPYRIGHT OFFICE

- If at all possible, try to fit the information called for into the spaces provided on Form PA.
- If you do not have space enough for all of the information you need to give on Form PA, use this continuation sheet and submit it with Form PA.
- If you submit this continuation sheet, leave it attached to Form PA. Or, if it becomes detached, clip (do not tape or staple) and fold the two together before submitting them.
- **PART A** of this sheet is intended to identify the basic application. **PART B** is a continuation of Space 2. **PART C** is for the continuation of Spaces 1, 4, or 6. The other spaces on Form PA call for specific items of information, and should not need continuation.

REGISTRATION NUMBER
PA   PAU
EFFECTIVE DATE OF REGISTRATION
. . . .
(Month)   (Day)   (Year)
CONTINUATION SHEET RECEIVED
Page _____ of _____ pages

DO NOT WRITE ABOVE THIS LINE. FOR COPYRIGHT OFFICE USE ONLY

(A)
Identification of Application

IDENTIFICATION OF CONTINUATION SHEET: This sheet is a continuation of the application for copyright registration on Form PA, submitted for the following work:
- TITLE: (Give the title as given under the heading "Title of this Work" in Space 1 of Form PA.)

. . . .

- NAME(S) AND ADDRESS(ES) OF COPYRIGHT CLAIMANT(S): (Give the name and address of at least one copyright claimant as given in Space 4 of Form PA.)

. . . .

(B)
Continuation of Space 2

☐ **NAME OF AUTHOR:**

Was this author's contribution to the work a "work made for hire"?   Yes. . . . . .   No. . . . . .

DATES OF BIRTH AND DEATH:
Born . . . . Died . . . .
(Year)   (Year)

AUTHOR'S NATIONALITY OR DOMICILE:
Citizen of . . . . } or { Domiciled in . . . .
(Name of Country)   (Name of Country)

WAS THIS AUTHOR'S CONTRIBUTION TO THE WORK:
Anonymous?   Yes. . . . . .   No. . . . . .
Pseudonymous?   Yes. . . . . .   No. . . . . .
If the answer to either of these questions is "Yes," see detailed instructions attached.

AUTHOR OF: (Briefly describe nature of this author's contribution)

☐ **NAME OF AUTHOR:**

Was this author's contribution to the work a "work made for hire"?   Yes. . . . . .   No. . . . . .

DATES OF BIRTH AND DEATH:
Born . . . . Died . . . .
(Year)   (Year)

AUTHOR'S NATIONALITY OR DOMICILE:
Citizen of . . . . } or { Domiciled in . . . .
(Name of Country)   (Name of Country)

WAS THIS AUTHOR'S CONTRIBUTION TO THE WORK:
Anonymous?   Yes. . . . . .   No. . . . . .
Pseudonymous?   Yes. . . . . .   No. . . . . .
If the answer to either of these questions is "Yes," see detailed instructions attached.

AUTHOR OF: (Briefly describe nature of this author's contribution)

☐ **NAME OF AUTHOR:**

Was this author's contribution to the work a "work made for hire"?   Yes. . . . . .   No. . . . . .

DATES OF BIRTH AND DEATH:
Born . . . . Died . . . .
(Year)   (Year)

AUTHOR'S NATIONALITY OR DOMICILE:
Citizen of . . . . } or { Domiciled in . . . .
(Name of Country)   (Name of Country)

WAS THIS AUTHOR'S CONTRIBUTION TO THE WORK:
Anonymous?   Yes. . . . . .   No. . . . . .
Pseudonymous?   Yes. . . . . .   No. . . . . .
If the answer to either of these questions is "Yes," see detailed instructions attached.

AUTHOR OF: (Briefly describe nature of this author's contribution)

(C)
Continuation of Other Spaces

CONTINUATION OF (Check which):   ☐ Space 1   ☐ Space 4   ☐ Space 6

WRITERS GUILD   WRITERS GUILD OF AMERICA, WEST, INC.
REGISTRATION   8955 BEVERLY BOULEVARD
SERVICE   LOS ANGELES, CA   90048
                                        (213) 655-2095

PURPOSE   The Guild's Registration Service has been set up to assist members
            and non-members in establishing the completion date and the identity
            of their literary property written for the fields of theatrical
            motion pictures, television and radio.

VALUE   Registration does not confer any statutory protection. It merely
            provides evidence of the writer's claim to authorship of the
            literary material involved and of the date of its completion. A
            writer has certain rights under the law the moment the work is
            completed. It is therefore important that the date of completion
            be legally established. The Registration Office does not make
            comparisons of registration deposits to determine similarity
            between works, nor does it give legal opinions or advice.

COVERAGE   Since the value of registration is merely to supply evidence, it
            cannot protect what the law does not protect. Registration with
            the Guild does not protect titles (neither does registration with
            the United States Copyright Office).

PROCEDURE FOR DEPOSIT   One (1) 8½ x 11 unbound copy is required for deposit
                          in the Guild files. When it is received, the property
            is sealed, dated, given a registration number and put on file. A
            receipt is returned. Notice of registration shall consist of the
            wording REGISTERED WGAw NO._____and be applied upon the title
            page or the page immediately following. Formats, outlines, synopses,
            treatments or scripts specifically intended for theatrical motion
            pictures, television and radio are registrable. The Guild does not
            accept book manuscripts, plays, music, lyrics, illustrations or
            articles of public record for registration. Each property must be
            registered separately. (Exception: three episodes of an existing
            series may be deposited as a single registration.) Be sure that
            the name under which you register is your full legal name. The
            use of pseudonyms, pen names, initials or familiar forms of a proper
            name may require proof of identity if you want to recover the
            material left on deposit.

DURATION   You hereby authorize the Guild to destroy the manuscript without
            notice to you on the expiration of ten (10) years from the date
            of deposit. You may, however, renew the registration for an
            additional ten (10) years if before the expiration of the first
            ten (10) year period you pay the then applicable renewal fee and
            get a written receipt therefor. The fee should accompany the
            request for renewal.

LOCATION OF REGISTRATION OFFICE: 310 No. San Vicente Blvd. (Suite 320)
                                 Los Angeles, CA 90048
                                 (corner of Beverly Blvd., one block
                                 west of La Cienega Blvd.)

                                 ALL MAIL MUST BE SENT TO THE BEVERLY
                                 BOULEVARD ADDRESS

HOURS: 10 A.M. - 12 NOON
             2 P.M. - 5 P.M.   MONDAY THRU FRIDAY

PROCEDURE FOR WITHDRAWAL   The registered copy left on deposit cannot be returned to the writer without defeating the purpose of registration, the point being that evidence should be available, if necessary, that the material has been in the Guild's charge since the date of deposit.

However, if the writer finds it necessary to have the copy returned, at least forty-eight (48) hours notice of intended withdrawal must be given to the Guild. If the copy is on micro-film, a per page charge at then current rates will be made at time of withdrawal. A manuscript will be given up only on the signature(s) of the writer(s). If the registration is in the names of more than one person, the written consent of all is required to authorize withdrawal. In case a registrant is deceased, proof of death and the consent of his representative or heirs must be presented. In no event, except under these provisions, shall any of the material be allowed to be taken from the Guild office unless a court order has been acquired.

If any person other than the writer named in the registration shall request confirmation of registration, the registration number and/or date of deposit, to see either the material deposited, the registration receipt, the registration envelope or any other material, such request shall be denied unless a court order is presented in connection therewith.

FEES $5.00 for members of WGA
         $10.00 for non-members
         $5.00 for members when registration is renewed
         $10.00 for non-members when registration is renewed

FEE MUST ACCOMPANY REQUEST FOR REGISTRATION

BLANCHE W. BAKER
REGISTRATION ADMINISTRATOR

Interpreting the Law:
Gibson v. CBS, Inc.

While it is an easy matter to state the rule of law that copyright protection is available only for the *expression* of an idea and not for the idea itself, it is quite another matter to interpret this rule and apply it to any given set of facts. The following is a summary of a case, as reported in a newsletter widely read by entertainment lawyers, which shows how one court distinguished between an idea and its expression.

ENTERTAINMENT

LAW REPORTER

Motion Pictures Television Radio Music Theater Publishing Sports

September 15, 1980   **Volume 2, Number 8**

Copyright infringement suit against CBS, on account of its broadcast of a "Tony Orlando and Dawn Show" comedy skit, is dismissed for lack of substantial similarity

The distinction between an idea and its expression was the issue in a recent copyright infringement action filed against CBS on account of its broadcast of a comedy skit on the "Tony Orlando and Dawn Show." The skit was entitled "SFX: Egg Cracking," and featured Tony Orlando as an egg white and Anne Meara as an egg yolk. In the skit, the yolk and white confront anticipated separation at the hands of an unseen cook, and they speculate about what might have been. The white had "political ambitions," and dreamed of rolling on the White House lawn on Easter Sunday. The yolk dreamed of being an egg nog at a Howard Cosell party, or even a chicken "if only we'd have stayed under mom just a few more days." The skit concludes with the yolk observing that the "most important thing" is not what happens to them, so long as they "can face it together."

Russel Gibson alleged that the "Egg Cracking" skit infringed the copyright to his lecture entitled "I am And [sic] Egg." The lecture was one-half a typewritten page in length, and was written to be delivered by a single person. It describes the plight of an egg, from the comfort of lying under a chicken, to being picked up by a "no good farmer" with a cold hand, to being put in a "little grey box with eleven strange eggs" on a freezing shelf. The egg remembers his mother's advice to be sure his sunny side is up, but he learns that it is more fun to be scrambled and "swoshed around together" with a female egg, and thus he concludes, that "Mother was wrong."

The court noted that copyright protection is available only for the expression of an idea, and not for the idea itself. In this case, the court found that the only similarities between Gibson's lecture and the CBS skit were attributing to an egg the powers of speech and feelings, the egg's experiences of lying under a chicken, in a box with other eggs and in a refrigerator, and the egg's reacting to the possibility of being cooked.

The court held that the attribution to an egg of qualities normally possessed by human beings "is of course an 'idea' and no more. The idea alone is not subject to copyright protection." The court also held that the other similarities, such as the experiences and reactions of the eggs, were "scenes a faire," that is, "sequences of events which necessarily follow from a common theme." Similarity of expression which necessarily results from the fact that a common idea is only capable of expression in stereotyped form is not copyright infringement, the court ruled.

Moreover, said the court, even if there were similarities of expression between Gibson's lecture and the CBS skit, they would be insufficiently substantial to be an infringement, in light of the substantial differences between the two. The CBS skit treated more events than the Gibson lecture. And the theme of separation which was the subject of the CBS skit did not appear in the Gibson lecture at all.

"In sum," said the court, "the only similarities between the ... material are the idea of a personified egg and of certain situations that necessarily follow from that idea. There is no substantial similarity between the expressions of the idea in the two works."

The court therefore dismissed Gibson's complaint.

Gibson v. CBS, Inc., CCH Copyright Law Reports, **Para. 25,164 (S.D.N.Y. 1980)**

Lionel S. Sobel Editor
Eileen L. Selsky Associate Editor

Copyright © 1980 by the Entertainment Law Reporter Publishing Company, 9440 Santa Monica Blvd., Suite 600, Beverly Hills, CA 90210

Reprinted with permission.

The Law: *Faris v. Enberg*

As discussed in the preceding chapter, mere ideas are not protected under the copyright laws. However, they may (or may not) be protected, depending on the factual circumstances, by other legal principles. The following is a recent, leading California case in this area which sets forth legal principles for the protection of ideas and applies these principles to the particular facts of the case.

Portions of the judge's opinion, dealing with procedural aspects of the various stages of the trial and appeal, have been deleted and the rest of the opinion has been slightly condensed.

FARIS V. ENBERG
97 Cal. App.3d 309

[Civ. No. 54583. Second Dist., Div. One. Sept. 27, 1979]
Opinion
ROTHMAN, J.

Facts

The following are the facts set forth in plaintiff's declaration. Faris conceived a sports quiz show idea in 1964, and prepared and registered a format of the idea. A few days before June 4, 1970, Faris called KTLA studios and told a secretary that he had created a sports television show that would interest Mr. Enberg. He left his name and number. The next day Enberg telephoned Faris, who told Enberg that he ". . . had a sports oriented TV show that I intended to produce and that *I desired to talk to him about participating in the show as the master of ceremonies.*" (Emphasis added.) Enberg was interested and asked when they could meet, and the

next day was agreed upon. They met at KTLA studios. Enberg was late and apologized. Faris told Enberg the format of the show and gave Enberg a copy, which Enberg read through at the meeting, and again expressed interest. Enberg asked for a copy, and Faris said it was his "creation" and "literary property." "I discussed with Mr. Enberg his prospects as to both being an MC for the show or, if he desired, actually participating with me in the production of the show and could participate then as a part owner thereof. At all times I discussed my show and Mr. Enberg's participation as a business proposal or offer to Mr. Enberg and I mentioned to him that, if he came with me, we would both make money on the show." Enberg told Faris he was going to talk the next week with some KTLA producers about a sports show. He asked Faris to leave a copy of the format for further review. Enberg took the format home to read. He kept it three to four days and talked to his wife and Gross, a producer, about the contact with Faris. Faris stated that he did not authorize Enberg to discuss the format with anyone or to give it to anyone else; that had Enberg told Faris he planned to show the format to anyone else or discuss the format with anyone else, Faris would not have left a copy with Enberg, and that had Enberg told Faris of his commitment with another sports quiz show, Faris would not have discussed the show with him or let Enberg read or have the format, and would not have "proposed a contractual relationship with him involving either his participation as an owner or acting as MC for my 'Sports Panel Quiz'. . . ."

Enberg testified that he may have revealed to the people who ultimately produced the *Sports Challenge* quiz show, that he had been contacted by someone about a sports quiz show.

Faris testified to the following: In December of 1969 Faris saw Enberg on television. Faris was thinking about his quiz show idea and thought: "It was just a question of getting the right person to do the show. Enberg impressed me. He was articulate, he was very, I thought, fine announcer, and this brought to mind—I said, that man, in my mind, suited the role of the MC for this show. . . [¶] [S]o my idea was to go to Mr. Enberg with this format in an attempt to go with me on it." He had considered many other sports personalities for master of ceremonies, and decided on Enberg. He told Enberg at the meeting that "if you will come with me and do the show, you can have a piece of the show. You can own it. You won't have to work for a salary for somebody else."

At some time following this meeting, the *Sports Challenge* show appeared on television with Enberg as master of ceremonies, and produced by Gross. There were certain differences and similarities between the show and plaintiff's idea.

Discussion

I. Plaintiff claims plagiarism, breach of implied-in-fact contract and breach of confidence. Plaintiff's idea concerning a sports quiz show was not novel and concrete and thus not subject to copyright protection. Accordingly, the claim of plagiarism is dismissed. However, the existence and the terms of an implied-in-fact contract are manifest by conduct, and there need be no showing of copyrightability. Thus, no matter how slight or commonplace is the material or idea which is revealed, the courts will not question its adequacy as a valuable exchange pursuant to a contract.

Turning, then, to consideration of the question of whether there was an implied-in-fact contract, two notable Supreme Court cases have thoroughly dealt with the subject in the area of literary works or ideas. In *Weitzenkorn v. Lesser*, plaintiff wrote a story about Tarzan and the fountain of youth, and submitted it to producer Sol Lesser. The plaintiff sued on a theory of express contract. The Supreme Court held that regardless of a work's lack of originality, it could be valuable and the subject of contract: "While the idea disclosed may be common or even open to public knowledge, yet such disclosure if protected by contract, is sufficient consideration for the promise to pay." Even if the plaintiff's story and the movie Sol Lesser produced were grossly

dissimilar, the court found that plaintiff was entitled to try to prove that defendant agreed to pay for the use of this commonplace idea. (40 Cal.2d at p. 792.)

In *Desny v. Wilder*, plaintiff submitted to Billy Wilder's secretary a story based on the life of cave explorer Floyd Collins. The Supreme Court carefully explained the subject of implied-in-fact contracts. Plaintiff called Billy Wilder on the telephone, and was told by a secretary that, because Wilder was so busy, plaintiff would have to present a synopsis for Wilder to read. Plaintiff told the secretary that he would have to be paid if they used it. His purpose was to sell the story. Plaintiff prepared the synopsis, read it to the secretary over the phone, and later Wilder produced a film which appeared to be similar to plaintiff's work. The work was not protected on any theory other than a contract express or implied from the facts. Quoting from *Stanley v. Columbia Broadcasting System*, the court ruled that "The policy that precludes protection of an abstract idea by copyright does not prevent its protection by contract. Even though an idea is not property subject to exclusive ownership, its disclosure may be of substantial benefit to the person to whom it is disclosed. That disclosure may therefore be consideration for a promise to pay. . . . [¶] Even though the idea disclosed may be 'widely known and generally understood' it may be protected by an express contract providing that it will be paid for regardless of its lack of novelty." The court limited its holding with this language:

"The idea man who blurts out his idea without having first made his bargain has no one but himself to blame for the loss of his bargaining power. The law will not in any event, from demands stated subsequent to the unconditional disclosure of an abstract idea, imply a promise to pay for the idea, for its use, or for its previous disclosure. The law will not imply a promise to pay for an idea from the mere facts that the idea has been conveyed, is valuable, and has been used for profit; this is true even though the conveyance has been made with the hope or expectation that some obligation will ensue. So, if the plaintiff here is claiming only for the conveyance of the idea of making a dramatic production out of the life of Floyd Collins he must fail unless in conformity with the above stated rules he can establish a contract to pay."

Accordingly, for an implied-in-fact contract one must show: that he or she prepared the work; that he or she disclosed the work to the offeree for sale;

under all circumstances attending disclosure it can be concluded that the offeree voluntarily accepted the disclosure knowing the conditions on which it was tendered (i.e., the offeree must have the opportunity to reject the attempted disclosure if the conditions were unacceptable) and the reasonable value of the work.

Applying these elements to the instant case, we find there is no evidence to support an implied-in-fact contract for the services of revealing plaintiff's format to him. All the evidence is to the contrary. Both participants to the conversation agreed that the format was submitted to Enberg in connection with an inquiry as to whether Enberg would act as master of ceremonies for plaintiff's television show. . . . There is absolutely no evidence that plaintiff expected, or indicated his expectation of receiving compensation for the service of revealing the format to Enberg. To the contrary, the sole evidence is that plaintiff voluntarily submitted it to Enberg for the sole purpose of enabling Enberg to make a determination of his willingness to enter into a future business relationship with plaintiff.

So far as the record before us reveals, plaintiff never thought of selling his sports quiz show idea to anyone—including Enberg. He appears at all times to have intended to produce it himself, and sought out Enberg as a master of ceremonies. He obviously hoped to make his idea more marketable by hiring a gifted sports announcer as his master of ceremonies. Not only did Faris seek to induce Enberg to join him by showing him the product, but also sought to entice him by promises of a "piece" of the enterprise for his involvement. Plaintiff never intended to submit the property for sale and did not tell Enberg that he was submitting it for sale. There is no reason to think that Enberg, or anyone else with whom Enberg spoke, would have believed that Faris' submission was an offer to sell something, which if used would oblige the user to pay.

Based on the clear holding of *Desny* an obligation to pay could not be inferred from the mere fact of submission on a theory that everyone knows that the idea man expects to be paid. Nor could it be inferred from the comment by Faris that the format was his "creation" and "literary property." In *Desny* the court held that the mere submission of an idea by a writer could not create the obligation. So, necessarily, the converse must also be the case: that knowledge on the part of the recipient that the submitter is a writer possessing his or her unprotected literary creation could not create an obligation to

pay. Plaintiff's statements that he would not have revealed the format or idea to Enberg had he known that Enberg was going to show it to anyone else were not germane since he never told this to Enberg.

Plaintiff attempted to impose a contract on the facts of this case by asserting that Enberg solicited the submission, returned plaintiff's phone call and asked to keep a copy of the format. We do not agree. Faris solicited Enberg's involvement. It would be entirely inconsistent with *Desny* to hold that an implied-in-fact contract could be created because a telephone call was returned or because a request was made for an opportunity to read the work that was unconditionally submitted.

Plaintiff argues that he is supported by the holding in *Thompson v. California Brewing Co.*, to the effect that when the recipient permits the submission of an idea with an awareness that the submitter does so in the expectation of payment if the idea is used, such is conduct from which a promise to pay may be inferred. The weakness in this argument, as already noted, is that there was no evidence that plaintiff expected Enberg to pay, and thus, Enberg could not be charged with such an awareness that plaintiff himself did not have.

In *Donahue v. Ziv Television Programs Inc.*, for example, the court found an implied-in-fact contract where the submitter of the format that eventually became the *Sea Hunt* television series had numerous conversations with the producers where compensation to the submitter was discussed. The court said that "Although the purveyor of the idea conditions his offer to disclose on an obligation to pay for it, he to whom it is disclosed must have an opportunity to reject disclosure on the terms offered." There was, the court said, strong evidence that the recipient of the disclosure "realized all along that plaintiffs expected to be paid for their idea."

II. Plaintiff has also alleged a breach of fiduciary obligation: that he "submitted in confidence to the defendants, both orally and in writing" the sports quiz show idea; that "Defendants accepted the submission of such idea in confidence, and on the understanding that they would not use the idea without the consent of the plaintiff"; and that defendants did use the idea without plaintiff's consent.

It is defendants' major contention that a literary work has to be protectable under copyright law in order to be the basis of a breach of confidence action.

We conclude that copyright protectability of a literary work is not a necessary element of proof in a cause of action for breach of confidence. An actionable breach of confidence will arise when an idea, whether or not protectable, is offered to another in confidence, and is voluntarily received by the offeree in confidence with the understanding that it is not to be disclosed to others, and is not to be used by the offeree for purposes beyond the limits of the confidence without the offeror's permission. In order to prevent the unwarranted creation or extension of a monopoly and restraint on progress in art, a confidential relationship will not be created from the mere submission of an idea to another. There must exist evidence of the communication of the confidentiality of the submission or evidence from which a confidential relationship can be inferred. Among the factors from which such an inference can be drawn are: proof of the existence of an implied-in-fact contract; proof that the material submitted was protected by reason of sufficient novelty and elaboration; or proof of a particular relationship such as partners, joint adventurers, principal and agent or buyer and seller under certain circumstances.

With these rules as a base, we consider plaintiff's contention of breach of confidence.

Among the facts mentioned and not mentioned in plaintiff's declaration were these: he told defendant that the sports quiz show format was his "creation" and "literary property"; he told Enberg that he wished to hire Enberg to be the master of ceremonies for the show; he said that he would never have told Enberg about the idea if he knew Enberg would disclose it to others, although he apparently never advised Enberg of this thought; and he did not, so far as we can tell from his declaration, tell Enberg that the material was given in confidence. We do not believe that the unsolicited submission of an idea to a potential employee or potential business partner, even if that person then passes the disclosed information to a competitor, presents an issue of confidentiality. Here, no rational receiver of the communications from Faris could be bound to an understanding that a secret was being imparted. One could not infer from anything Enberg did or said that he was given the chance to reject disclosure in advance or that he voluntarily received the disclosure with an understanding that it was not to be given to others. To allow the disclosure which took place in this case to result in a confidential relationship, without something more, would greatly expand the creation of monopolies and bear the concomitant danger to the free communication of ideas. Our conclusion that evidence of knowledge of confidence or from which a confidential relationship can be implied is a minimum prerequisite to the protection of freedom in the arts. In the instant case, there was no direct evidence that either party believed that the disclosure was being made in confidence. Only in plaintiff's own thoughts one might infer that he felt there was a confidence. But he never, so far as we can tell, communicated these thoughts to Enberg, and nothing of an understanding of confidence can be inferred from Enberg's conduct. No other special facts exist from which the relationship can be inferred: there was no implied-in-fact contract; the material was not protectable; and they were not yet partners or joint adventurers, and there was no buyer/seller or principal/agent relationship. Plaintiff might argue that he and Enberg were joint adventurers, but such was only Faris' unfulfilled hope. There was no evidence of more than a conversation which might have developed into a relationship later on. The sparcity of Faris' case is apparent. In *Blaustein* plaintiff and defendants used the same attorneys, plaintiff had been invited constantly by the defendants (Richard Burton and Elizabeth Taylor) to disclose his idea that they make a movie of *The Taming of the Shrew.* He also rendered services at their request on the project. Plaintiff's submission to Enberg was so tenuous and careless, that, as a matter of law, we find that there were insufficient facts to warrant a trial. [Case dismissed, Faris loses]

Protecting Your Ideas:
What to Do

Gilbert P. Lasky, Esq.

Suppose the following situation: An agent sets up a meeting with a producer who has agreed to hear your idea for a TV series. You give the producer an idea for an episode involving the central problem for the hero, an opposing character and maybe a major reversal or complication and resolution. The producer does not commit to any of the ideas or hire you. But four months later you see the producer's show and see a story using the same elements as you pitched. How could you have fashioned this situation so as to protect your ideas?

Writers in the media of film and television often expose themselves to the risk of having their ideas for stories, titles or characters used by others without payment. As discussed in preceding sections, ideas cannot be copyrighted, but they can be legally protected by contracts and confidential relationships. However, it is essential that you carefully follow the legally prescribed procedures for protecting your ideas.

Before disclosing the story idea orally, you should tell the producer that if what you are about to present is used by the producer, you expect to get paid. The legitimate producer should not argue with that, but you must wait for the producer's assent to the bargain. Then, after the producer has

agreed to pay you if your story is used, you should hand the idea in writing to the producer and only then make the oral presentation. The idea should be written out in as much detail as possible.

After the meeting, you should send a letter to the producer confirming the meeting and reiterating the ideas presented as well as the producer's agreement (if only a nod of the head) to pay you if the idea is used. A contract has then been formed between you and the producer, and if you discover that the producer has used the idea disclosed, you have a cause of action for a lawsuit and may be awarded damages for breach of contract. It must be emphasized that this would not be an action founded on copyright law but on contract law, and mutual agreement is essential.

Ideas can also be stolen from works which themselves are in sufficiently tangible and concrete form as to be copyrighted. A writer, for example, makes an unsolicited submission of a copyrighted screenplay to a producer, and the material is rejected. A year later, he sees a *different* story on the screen made by the same producer but which incorporates his unique title, a character or his concept. Assuming the use of these elements was not substantial enough to be the basis of an action for copyright infringement, how could the writer have fashioned the situation so as to protect his ideas?

Titles, characters and concepts in original, unpublished and unproduced dramatic works are virtually impossible to protect from unauthorized use because they are not deemed to be property to which the law affords protection. Perhaps the best protection for a unique idea, title or character is judicious disclosure through well-known and knowledgeable representatives to well-regarded,

Gil Lasky is a graduate of the UCLA Film School and has been a member of the Writers Guild of America since 1966. He is the author and/or producer of six feature films as well as writer of numerous television episodes. A member of the American Bar Association Entertainment and Sports Forum and the Academy of Television Arts and Sciences, Mr. Lasky is a partner in the law firm of Lebe, Lasky & Finer in Los Angeles and emphasizes entertainment and business matters.

honorable producers. In this respect, if the disclosed title or character is misappropriated there could be an action predicated on breach of a confidential relationship—if the representative is knowledgeable and careful to create this kind of relationship between the parties. The elements of such a confidential relationship are delineated by the court in the *Faris* case previously discussed. The remedies under such an action could be an injunction against use of the title or character, an accounting of the profits from the unauthorized use and even exemplary damages if the violation is flagrant.

Many lawsuits are instigated by irate creators who sincerely believe their ideas have been stolen by "Hollywood." Others, less scrupulous, file a legal action for its nuisance value in hopes of gaining a quick buck settlement with a studio. These litigants are frequently unsuccessful because they lack the knowledge to protect their ideas legally or else they waive their rights by way of release to a studio or network. The best protection for an author's ideas is to make the potential thief realize that the author has the legal knowledge to enforce his rights and the determination to do so.

Several other means of idea protection should be discussed briefly:

1. Keep your embryonic ideas to yourself. Other writers have been known to inadvertently use an idea previously disclosed by a friendly fellow writer.

2. Try to retain an experienced, respected representative to present you and your ideas to the potential buyer. A conscious thief will think twice before alienating a knowledgeable, powerful writer's representative, be it agent or lawyer.

3. Deal only with producers or other buyers who have good reputations. The idea thief becomes quickly known to the creative community. Avoid disclosure of ideas when in doubt.

4. If you are uncertain about what to do—ask. Before you disclose the idea or seek to enforce your rights in case of alleged theft, ask. Ask your agent, attorney or the WGA. Your ideas are precious to you. They might also be to others.

ABC Submission Form

In order to avoid lawsuits based on the claim that an idea was presented pursuant to an "implied" contract, many publishers, networks, producers and studios require those who submit ideas to sign a form stating that the recipient of the idea is under no obligation. The following is an example of such a form.

As broadcasters we wish to remain free to present to the public programs containing any and all ideas. We receive literally thousands of ideas, and we are unwilling to, and do not, assume any obligation to those who submit them whether they are used by us or not. For us to do otherwise would be progressively to curtail our ability to serve the public. We have had in the past, experiences with individuals who have claimed a right to prevent or charge for our use of submitted ideas, and because of our desire to avoid misunderstandings in this area at the outset, we ask that you read this statement of our policy and sign your name below to indicate your recognition of this policy and that any idea you submit to us is submitted pursuant to your and our express understanding and agreement that we shall have no obligation to you whether the idea is used by us or not.

For our records, would you please indicate in the space provided below (and, if necessary, continue on the reverse side) a complete description of the idea which you wish to submit to us in accordance with the foregoing policy.

American Broadcasting Companies, Inc.

Signature _____ _____

Date _____

Material:

Defamation

Tad Crawford

The First Amendment of the United States Constitution provides that "Congress shall make no law... abridging the freedom of speech, or of the press ..." This guarantee is not unlimited, however, and the writer must be aware that the content of a written work can sometimes give rise to civil or criminal liability. For example, copyright, the doctrine of unfair competition, the rights to privacy and publicity, and protection from defamation safeguard not only the writer but the writer's competitors as well. Significantly, other private citizens also have rights protecting them from invasion of privacy or defamation, which the writer will have to consider when creating work. In addition, the public at large through governmental agencies may seek to suppress works that are considered obscene or that might deny a fair trial to a criminal defendant because of excessive publicity. And school boards will sometimes act as censors of textbooks or library books thought undesirable for a student readership.

Defamation is an attack upon a person's reputation by print, writing, pictures, signs or spoken words. Whether the defamation is a libel or a slander depends on the medium in which the defamation occurs. Printed materials and films give rise to actions for libel, while spoken words give rise to actions for slander. Whether television and radio broadcasts give rise to libel or slander is gradually being resolved by statutes enacted in the various states, the importance of the issue being that a libel suit is often easier for the plaintiff than one based on slander (in which damages to reputation sometimes have to be proven, instead of simply assumed from the nature of the defamatory statement). Generally, everyone who participates in publishing defamatory material will be liable to the defamed person. While the truth of an alleged defamation is generally a defense to such an action, the burden of proving truthfulness is on the person who asserts truth as a defense.

Injury to reputation is the essence of defamation. One decision states: "Reputation is said in a general way to be injured by words which tend to expose one to public hatred, shame, obloquy, contumely, odium, contempt, ridicule, aversion, ostracism, degradation or disgrace, or to induce an evil opinion of one in the minds of right-thinking persons, and to deprive one of their confidence and friendly intercourse in society." Statements found defamatory upon their face include allegations that a person "has attempted suicide, that he refused to pay his just debts, that he is immoral or unchaste, or 'queer,' or has made improper advances to women, or is having 'wife trouble,' and is about to be divorced; that he is a coward, a drunkard, a hypocrite, a liar, a scoundrel, a crook, a scandal-monger, an anarchist, a skunk, a bastard, a eunuch, or a 'rotten egg'; that he is 'unfair' to labor, or that he has done a thing which is oppressive or dishonorable, or heartless, because all of these things obviously tend to affect the esteem in which he is held by his neighbors." The injury to reputation need only occur in the eyes of any substantial and respectable group in society, rather than society-at-large. And a statement which is defamatory at one time and place might not be defamatory in a different context.

The words used must be interpreted as they were reasonably understood in view of all the circumstances, including the entire statement which was made. The court decides whether the words could reasonably be understood as defamatory, after which the jury decides whether the words in fact were understood in that sense. Humor, ridicule, sarcasm, questions and insinuations can all be defamatory if they are reasonably understood to disgrace someone. A distinction is made between statements of fact and those of opinion. Opinion, such as abusive name-calling done in anger, may very well be considered not to contain any specific charge which could be considered defamatory. But just because a statement is made in the form of an opinion will not give protection against defamatory assertions of fact necessarily included in the opinion. A person who repeats a defamatory statement is liable for defamation, even if the person gives the original source, indicates that he or she does not believe the statement to be true, uses the customary newspaper phrase "it is alleged," or states the story is based on rumors.

A defamatory statement need not refer to a person by name in order to be actionable. The problems this can cause with fictional works based on real events or the writer's own experiences are substantial. For example, MGM made a film depicting Rasputin as the cause of the destruction of imperial Russia. In the course of the film, a character named Princess Natasha is either seduced or raped by Rasputin. Many other facts included in the film indicated that Princess Natasha in real life was Princess Irina Alexandrova. The court sustained as reasonable the jury's finding in favor of the Princess and awarding her £25,000. One justice, weighing the defendant's arguments, rejected "the contention that to say of a woman that she had been ravished by a man of very bad character, when as a matter of fact she never saw the man at all and was never near him, is not defamatory of the woman. I really have no language to express my opinion of that argument." Thomas Wolfe, whose fiction was highly autobiographical, had publication of one book held up because of the threat of a libel suit by a former mistress and, in another case, was actually sued by a former landlady and had to settle out of court despite his desire to fight the suit.

Fictional works will often use a disclaimer, such as, "All circumstances in this novel are imaginary, and none of the characters exist in real life." The problem is that such a disclaimer means little if, in fact, the characters are drawn from real life. An authoritative source states: "The fact that the author or producer states that his work is exclusively one of fiction and in no sense applicable to living persons is immaterial except as to punitive damages, if readers actually and reasonably understand otherwise. Such a statement, however, is a factor to be considered by the jury in determining whether readers did so understand it, or, if so, whether the understanding was reasonable." Punitive damages are extra damages beyond what is necessary to compensate a plaintiff for injuries suffered. They are awarded because of the acts complained of by the plaintiff are reckless or malicious. A carefully drafted disclaimer, relevant to the particular content of the book, can thus have value.

A different approach to the problem of libel in fiction is to alter the fictional characters that may be the basis for libel suits. This can work very well, since changing a work's locale, plot, and all facts of characters' lives—including appearance and mannerisms—can insure that no real persons will suffer a libel. The problem, of course, is whether the fictional work retains its integrity after the alterations. Some writers will be able to work out a compromise between what they want to say and what they dare to say, and others won't.

A lawyer's advice is a necessity if a piece is to be reworked due to fear of a libel suit. Similarly, a lawyer should be consulted if a release is to be sought from the person who might otherwise bring the libel suit. A release form would indicate that the person knows he or she will be the model for a character which may have additional fictional characteristics or experiences. The person—in return for a consideration such as a payment of money—agrees not to make a claim or sue for libel, invasion of privacy, or any other reason based on the content of the work or the advertising and promotion for the work. A problem, however, arises if the person is approached but refuses to sign the release. If the publisher or producer proceeds, the person defamed can argue for punitive damages on the basis that prior knowledge of the defamatory content is shown by the request for the release.

A different problem with fiction can arise when characters and names are completely imaginary, but happen to correspond closely with a real person. An English newspaper published a fictional article of humor about the double life of a Mr.

Artemus Jones, a blameless churchwarden who lived at Peckham with his wife except when he was secretly across the Channel at Dieppe "betraying a most unholy delight in the society of female butterflies." A real Mr. Artemus Jones sued for libel. This Mr. Jones was an unmarried lawyer who lived in North Wales. He complained only of the use of his name. The jury gave Mr. Jones a substantial award for damages. The defendant's appeals were to no avail, and the headnote to the final decision states, "In an action for libel, if the language used is, in the opinion of the jury, defamatory and people reading it may reasonably think that it refers to the plaintiff, damages are recoverable, even though the writer or publisher may not have intended to refer to any particular individual."

The requirement of reasonableness, however, saves fiction writers from facing an impossible task in the choice of names. James T. Farrell wrote a novel titled *Bernard Clare* after the name of the main character. The novel, while clearly fictional, draws in part on Farrell's own experiences as a young man journeying from Chicago to New York in order to become a writer. The character's name derived from County Clare in Ireland and was intended to connote an Irish background. A newspaperman named Bernard Clare claimed that he had been libeled by the novel. This real Bernard Clare had worked in Minnesota, Michigan and Wisconsin, and had nothing in common with Farrell's fictional character except sharing the same name. The court granted Farrell's motion for summary judgment, stating, "It would be an astonishing doctrine if every writer of fiction were required to make a search among all the records available in this Nation which might tabulate the names and activities of millions of people in order to determine whether perchance one of the characters in the contemplated book designated as a novel may have the same name and occupation as a real person. . . . It is inconceivable that any sensible person could assume or believe from reading this book of fiction that it purported to refer to the life or career of the Bernard Clare who was a newspaper writer in Minneapolis."

Defamatory statements directed at a large group will not be considered to defame an individual member of the group. To avoid unchecked group defamation in attacks on various minority groups, some states have enacted criminal statutes to punish such defamation. An individual can sue for defamation when the group defamed is small. "All of A's sons are murderers" is a defamation for which each son can sue individually. But the statement that "Some of A's sons are murderers" would be a much more difficult statement upon which to bring suit because not all of the sons are defamed and the ones defamed are not identified.

The First Amendment provides important limitations on the extent to which actions for defamation can successfully be pursued. The right of a public figure, in particular, to sue for libel is limited to false statements made with actual malice or reckless disregard of the truth. The term "public figure" is itself subject to definition. For example, a woman successfully sued a magazine for unfavorably misreporting the grounds of her divorce decree. Although the woman was often mentioned in society columns and actually gave news conferences because of the widespread reporting of her divorce proceedings, the Supreme Court reasoned she was not a public figure because she had no major role in society's affairs and had not voluntarily joined in a public controversy with an intention to influence the outcome. Similarly, when a magazine accused a prominent lawyer of having framed a policeman as part of a Communist conspiracy to discredit the police, the attorney was determined not to be a public figure. The Supreme Court stated, "The communications media are entitled to act on the assumption that public officials and public figures have voluntarily exposed themselves to increased risk of injury from defamatory falsehoods concerning them. No such assumption is justified with respect to a private individual."

The Supreme Court determined that the states should have discretion to determine the standard of liability for defamation where a private individual is involved in a matter of public interest, so long as the states require some negligence or fault on the part of the person accused of the defamation. Thus, where a matter of public interest is involved, a public figure will have to show actual malice or reckless disregard for the truth to recover for defamation while a private individual will only have to show negligence (assuming negligence has been selected as the relevant state standard). Where a private person is defamed on a matter not of public interest, there is no requirement even to show an intent to defame. Recovery in such a case is allowed on the basis of the defamation alone and malice or reckless disregard for the truth is only relevant in fixing punitive damages.

Damages for defamation can be lessened by a retraction of the defamatory statement. The retraction must be a complete and unequivocal attempt to repair the injury to reputation which has taken place. The retraction should be given the same prominence and publicity as the defamation, and come as soon after the defamation as possible. Such a retraction can be used to show that the plaintiff's reputation was not so badly damaged or that there was an absence of the malice necessary for punitive damages. In many states statutes limit the amount of damages which can be recovered if a retraction is made or if no retraction is requested by the injured person.

Only the living person who has been defamed may bring the suit for defamation, not assignees or heirs. Statutes in a number of states do make defamation of the dead into a crime, but these statutes have been held not to give surviving relatives a right to sue.

Invasion of Privacy
(and Other Theories of
Liability Facing Writers)

Stephen F. Rohde, Esq.

INTRODUCTION

In recent years screenwriters and authors have increasingly turned to the daily headlines for inspiration and story ideas. Major motion picture and television productions and best-selling books have reenacted, in dramatic and documentary formats, the lives of the famous and notorious—Lee Harvey Oswald, Caryl Chessman, Senator Joseph McCarthy, Francis Gary Powers, Dr. Martin Luther King, Jr., Karen Ann Quinlan, Gary Thomas Rowe, Jr., John Dean, Richard Nixon, Karen Silkwood and Gary Gilmore. The coverage of the news events that have surrounded these individuals and that will surround others will no longer be confined to the daily newspaper or the nightly news program. Screenwriters and authors are vigorously attempting to engage the attention of their audiences with factual reenactments of historical and current events, and the label "docudrama" is well fixed in the artistic lexicon.

At the same time, the law has proved quite flexible in offering a wide variety of legal theories for those who believe they have been damaged by their portrayal. Despite the First Amendment guarantees of freedom of speech and press, the courts have recognized the right of certain persons to be let alone and to exact money damages for the breach of that right.

Aside from the well-recognized actions for defamation (see the preceding chapter), the law has created separate causes of action based on invasion of privacy, the right of publicity, and most recently and distressingly, the tort of imitation. This chapter seeks to describe the basic elements of these theories of liability facing writers and to suggest some potential defenses. Space does not permit a comprehensive analysis and, indeed, it will be immediately apparent that each case turns on its own peculiar facts with the law often furnishing suitable arguments to sustain a predetermined result based on fundamental concepts of fair play.

INVASION OF PRIVACY

Lawyers are taught that as far as the common law goes, invasion of privacy is of relatively recent vintage, by which the scholars mean December 15, 1890, when the *Harvard Law Review* published an article by a future member of the United States Supreme Court, Louis D. Brandeis, and his law partner, which argued that a right of privacy existed, the violation of which was actionable in court. (This was the age of "yellow journalism" and apparently Brandeis' partner was upset with the Boston newspapers' coverage of his private social affairs.)

In one fashion or another, more than forty states have now accepted a right of privacy, and in California and New York it is established by statute.

Stephen F. Rohde, Esq., has his own law practice in Beverly Hills, where he specializes in entertainment and constitutional law, including First Amendment cases and civil litigation in the areas of copyright, defamation, invasion of privacy, unfair competition and contractual disputes. He is a graduate of Northwestern University and Columbia Law School and a frequent lecturer and writer of law-related articles.

The everpresent urge of lawyers and judges to compartmentalize has resulted in a generally accepted breakdown of the right of privacy into four categories:

1. Unreasonable intrusion upon another's seclusion.
2. Unreasonable publicity given to another's private life.
3. Misappropriation of another's name or likeness.
4. Publicity which unreasonably places another in a false light before the public.

There is a certain overlap in these categories, and any particular publication or broadcast may give rise to an alleged violation of the right of privacy under more than one heading. The common thread is the protection of the legitimate right to be let alone. The key word is "legitimate," and it is the clash between the bold assertions of the writer insisting upon his right to portray the newsworthy and the outrage of the private citizen exposed to public view which ignites litigation.

Unreasonable Intrusion Upon Another's Seclusion

This tort consists of violating one's private space at home, in the office, or elsewhere, by direct surveillance or electronic eavesdropping. In some cases, the tort is combined with an action for physical trespass, and recently newsmen and journalists have been charged with trespass for refusing to leave the scene of an accident or crime.

Actions against writers for invasion of privacy by intrusion are rare but not unheard of. At least two prominent examples are in the law books and are instructive, particularly for the writer who is intent upon competing with Woodward and Bernstein.

In 1963, two employees, one male and one female, of *Life* magazine obtained entry into the home of A. A. Dietemann (a disabled veteran with little education who was engaged in the practice of healing with clay, minerals and herbs) through the misrepresentation that the female employee wanted Dietemann to examine a lump in her breast. While so distracted, Dietemann was secretly photographed by *Life's* male employee who used a hidden camera. The conversation was transmitted by radio transmitter hidden in the female employee's purse to a tape recorder in a parked au-

tomobile occupied by another *Life* employee and officials from the district attorney's office and the State Department of Public Health. After Dietemann pled *nolo contendere* to misdemeanor charges, *Life* published an article titled "Crackdown on Quackery," including two of the surreptitious photographs.

Dietemann sued Time, Inc., the publisher of *Life* magazine, and recovered $1,000 in general damages, which was affirmed on appeal. Basing its decision on both invasion of privacy and intentional infliction of emotional distress, the appellate court found that under California law the surreptitious electronic recording of one's conversation causing him emotional distress and the unreasonable penetration of one's mental tranquility are actionable. The Court rejected Time, Inc.'s claim that the First Amendment immunized it from liability because the Constitution "has never been construed to accord newsmen immunity from torts or crimes committed during the course of news gathering." (*Dietemann v. Time, Inc.*, 449 F.2d 245 [9th Cir. 1971].)

An earlier case demonstrates that liability depends upon whether the journalist is directly involved in the intrusion and not on whether he or she publishes the fruits of the intrusion. In a long-forgotten precursor of Watergate, columnists Drew Pearson and Jack Anderson were accused of receiving copies of numerous documents purloined from the files of Senator Thomas Dodd of Connecticut by Dodd's own staff members; that Anderson was aware of the manner in which the copies had been obtained and that Pearson and Anderson thereafter published six newspaper columns containing information gleaned from these documents.

The trial court found that the contents of the columns bore on Dodd's qualifications as a United States senator and his relationship with certain lobbyists for foreign interests and, as such, did not constitute an invasion of privacy under the rubric of unreasonable publicity given to another's private life, discussed on pages 95 and 96.

As to invasion of privacy by intrusion, the court recognized the existence of such a tort and while assuming, without deciding, that Dodd's employees committed an improper intrusion when they removed confidential files with the intent to show them to unauthorized outsiders, the court found Pearson and Anderson free from liability for invasion of privacy for knowingly receiving and publishing the stolen documents. Of particular importance to writers, the court held that since the columnists' role in obtaining the documents did not make them liable to Dodd for intrusion, the subsequent publication, itself no invasion of privacy, cannot reach back to render that role wrongful. (*Pearson v. Dodd*, 410 F.2d 701 [D.C. Cir. 1969].)

Unreasonable Publicity Given to Another's Private Life

This branch of invasion of privacy is probably what most people think of when they complain that a publication has violated their right of privacy. Thus, the revelation that Betty Sue is pregnant with her Uncle Jack's child in the local society column is plainly an invasion of privacy. But, then again, this absolute statement might be affected if Betty Sue and Jack were famous rock stars who proudly proclaimed the inalienable right to communal life shorn of all official regulations. Then, the first line of defense to an action for public disclosure of private facts comes into play—the truthful publication of matters of *public interest*.

It should be noted that in this aspect of the right of privacy a plaintiff need not prove that a false statement was published, as is a requirement in a defamation action. Indeed, it has been said that it is the very truth of the private matter which makes the public revelation all the more painful, presumably because the harm has been done and cannot be erased by a denial or retraction. Frankly, even the decision to bring suit in such circumstances is a calculated risk since it may give wider currency to the embarrassing disclosure.

One legal treatise summarizes the elements of this tort as follows:

> One who gives publicity to a matter concerning the private life of another is subject to liability to the other for unreasonable invasion of his privacy, if the matter publicized is of a kind which
>
> (a) would be highly offensive to a reasonable person, and
> (b) is not of legitimate concern to the public.

A writer faced with a problem in this context should have little difficulty with the concept of "publicity," which includes oral and written communications to the public at large, or to a substantial number of persons, or with the concept of "private life" which is meant to exclude information which is already public or which a plaintiff leaves open to the public eye. Serious problems arise, however, when a writer attempts to decide what is "highly offensive to a reasonable person" and what is "not of legitimate concern to the public." Take for example, Mike Virgil, a body surfer from Newport Beach, California.

In the summer of 1969, staff writer Thomas Curry Kirkpatrick was dispatched by *Sports Illustrated* to do a story about the sport of body surfing as practiced at the Wedge, a public beach near Newport Beach, California, reputed to be the world's most dangerous site for this adventure. Kirkpatrick heard about Mike Virgil and his daredevil attitude. The following summer Kirkpatrick interviewed Virgil several times and arranged for photographs to be taken of him with other body surfers. Before publication, a *Sports Illustrated* staff member contacted Virgil to check and verify the article. While not disputing the truth of the article or the accuracy of the statements about him and while admitting that he had known that his picture was being taken, Virgil indicated that he thought the article was going to be limited to his prominence as a surfer at the Wedge and that he did not know that it would contain references to some rather bizarre incidents in his life that were not directly related to surfing. In spite of Virgil's objections, the article was published in 1971. Virgil's name and photographs were published, as well as a wide variety of his exploits, including putting out cigarettes in his mouth and diving off stairs to impress women, hurting himself in order to collect unemployment so that he would have time for body surfing at the Wedge, fighting in gang fights as a youngster and eating insects.

Virgil sued Time, Inc., the publisher of *Sports Illustrated*, for invasion of privacy based on the public disclosures of embarrassing private facts. After complicated legal proceedings reaching all the way to the United States Supreme Court and back to the trial court, Virgil's case was thrown out, but not before several judges offered a variety of opinions which created more questions than answers.

Thus, the court noted that talking freely to a writer, knowing the listener to be a member of the press, can be construed as a consent to the publication of what is said, unless such implied consent is withdrawn prior to the act of publication. This, of course, creates all manner of problems, not only for the writer working under a deadline, but for one whose galleys or script has already been printed or filmed, but not yet released.

The court valiantly attempted to define what is "newsworthy" and of "legitimate concern to the public." The privilege extends to both voluntary public figures and to those involuntary public figures who have not sought publicity or consented to it, but who "through their own conduct or otherwise have become 'news.' " The privilege also extends to all matters of a kind "customarily regarded as news" and also to giving information to the public for purposes of "education, amusement or enlightenment, where the public may reasonably be expected to have a legitimate interest in what is published." Of course, these sorts of legalisms communicate very little meaning to the lay writer and boil down to defining "newsworthy" as that which is "customarily regarded as news."

Ultimately, in Virgil's case, the court ruled that whether something is a matter of legitimate public interest depends upon the customs and conventions of the community, and the line is to be drawn when the publicity ceases to be the giving of information to which the public is entitled and becomes "a morbid and sensational prying into private lives for its own sake, with which a reasonable member of the public, with decent standards, would say that he had no concern." Applying these standards to the revelations about Virgil's exploits, the court found that they were not sufficiently offensive to reach the very high level of offensiveness necessary to lose the newsworthy privilege and that while the facts were generally unflattering and perhaps embarrassing, they were simply not offensive to the degree of morbidity or sensationalism. Accordingly, the court dismissed Virgil's suit without allowing it to be submitted to the jury. One wonders whether the jury would have found the article to be an invasion of privacy, and one wonders still more how attorneys can properly counsel writers given the subjective issues at stake. (*Virgil v. Time, Inc.*, 527 F.2d 1122 (1975), *cert. denied*, 425 U.S. 988, 96 S.Ct. 2215 (1976), on remand, 424 F. Supp. 1286 [S.D.Cal. 1976].)

Misappropriation of Another's Name or Likeness

This branch of the right of privacy protects against the unauthorized use of one's name, photograph or likeness for advertising or commercial purposes. Certain applications of this theory of liability would not affect writers, such as an action against an advertising agency, newspaper or magazine for using the name and photograph of a famous athlete or movie star to advertise a product or service without having first obtained permission.

In some states statutes have been enacted to deal specifically with this problem. For example, in California any person who knowingly uses another's name, photograph or likeness, in any manner, for purposes of advertising products, merchandise, goods or services, or for purposes of solicitation of purchases of products, merchandise, goods or services, without such person's prior consent, or the consent of the parent or legal guardian of a minor, shall be liable for any damages sustained by the person or persons injured plus a statutory penalty of $300. Under the law, one must be "readily identifiable" with the naked eye, and the statute does not prohibit photographs of sporting events, crowds, audiences at the theater, glee clubs, baseball teams and the like. There are other limitations in the statute, including one of particular importance to writers, which provides that the use of name, photograph or likeness in connection with "any news, public affairs, or sports broadcast or account, or any political campaign, shall not constitute a use for purposes of advertising or solicitation." Once again, however, writers and their attorneys are left to speculate as to the meaning of "news" or "public affairs." (California Civil Code §3344.)

But a recent United States Supreme Court decision should give pause to writers and, particularly, journalists—"The Human Cannonball case." It seems that Hugo Zacchini was appearing at the Geauga County Fair in Burton, Ohio, in the summer of 1972, where he was regularly shot from a cannon into a net some 200 feet away. Members of the public attending the fair were not charged a separate admission fee to observe his act. A freelance reporter for Scripps-Howard Broadcasting Co., the operator of a local television station, videotaped Zacchini's fifteen-second act, which was broadcast on the eleven o'clock news that night, together with favorable commentary.

Zacchini sued for unlawful appropriation of his professional property, and the United States Supreme Court upheld his complaint and ordered the matter to trial. The Supreme Court rested its decision heavily on the fact that Zacchini's "entire act" had been broadcast, thereby violating Zacchini's right of personal and exclusive control over the commercial display and exploitation of his personality and the exercise of his talents. While acknowledging that entertainment as well as news enjoys First Amendment protection, the Supreme Court cast aside the constitutional defense with the suggestion that all that was at stake was the requirement to pay Zacchini for the commercial use of his "entire act." It appears to have escaped the Supreme Court's attention that if taken to its logical conclusion, every public figure who purposefully exposes his enterprises to public view could exact from newspapers, journalists, television stations and writers in general, a tax in the form of money damages for satisfying the legitimate public interest in such matters. Ironically, the Supreme Court appears to have endorsed the epithet of "checkbook journalism." (*Zacchini v. Scripps-Howard Broadcasting Co.*, 433 U.S. 562, 97 S.Ct. 2849 [1977].)

The related issues involving the so-called right of publicity are treated separately below.

Publicity Which Unreasonably Places Another in a False Light Before the Public

Closely akin to defamation, this aspect of the right of privacy imposes liability on a writer for creating a false image of an individual or placing him or her in a false light whether or not the publication rises to the level of defamation. Increasingly, actions for false light invasion of privacy are being combined with actions for defamation in an attempt to avoid the burdensome legal requirements that have limited defamation suits.

The United States Supreme Court first dealt with this area in *The Desperate Hours* case. In 1952 the Hill family was held hostage by three escaped convicts in their home for almost 20 hours. The Hills were thrust into the public eye after they were released unharmed, and Mr. Hill actively discouraged attempts to expose his family to public scrutiny. Shortly thereafter, Joseph Hayes published *The Desperate Hours*, a novel depicting the experience of a fictional family held hostage by three escaped convicts. In the fictional version, unlike the Hills' experience, the family was subjected to verbal and physical abuse. In connection with the opening of a play based upon the novel, *Life* magazine published an article in which staged photographs dramatized the fictional incidents in the very house in which the Hill family had been held captive.

The Hills filed suit against *Life* magazine, not for defamation, since no defamatory accusations had been made against them, but for placing their family in a false light in the public eye. Although a lower court rendered a judgment awarding the

Hills compensatory damages, the United States Supreme Court reversed the decision, enunciating the rule that in matters of *legitimate public interest* a publication in the news media could only result in liability for a false light invasion of privacy where its falsity was actually known to the writer prior to its publication, or the writer wrote the article with a reckless disregard for its truth. If the writer was merely negligent in verifying the truth of the article, the news publication would be protected under the First Amendment, and there would be no liability. This is the same rule that was previously established in connection with defamation in the landmark Supreme Court case of *New York Times Co. v. Sullivan*. (*Time, Inc. v. Hill*, 385 U.S. 374, 87 S.Ct. 534 [1967].)

RIGHT OF PUBLICITY

For certain analytical purposes, the right of publicity should be treated separately from the right of privacy, although the former plainly overlaps the misappropriation and certain aspects of the false light branches of the latter. The major difference between the two doctrines is that several courts have decided that the right of publicity may be assigned and passed to one's heirs or beneficiaries, whereas the right of privacy may not. What might otherwise seem to be a rather technical distinction may have a substantial impact on the ability of screenwriters and authors to portray historical figures and prominent persons now deceased.

The most recent and authoritative analysis of the right of publicity came from the California Supreme Court in cases involving Bela Lugosi and Rudolph Valentino.

In a four-to-three decision, the California Supreme Court held that the right of publicity is personal to the individual who may during his lifetime create a business, product or service with a secondary meaning associated with his name and/or likeness. If this right is exercised during one's lifetime by entering into agreements or licenses for the exploitation of such business, product or service, it may be legally protected under the laws of unfair competition against those who violate such rights without permission. If the right of publicity is not exercised during one's lifetime, it expires upon one's death and cannot be passed to one's heirs or beneficiaries. Thus, the heirs of Bela Lugosi were denied the right to recover damages from Universal

Pictures for exploiting Bela Lugosi's characterization of Count Dracula (in a mask and other forms of merchandising) beyond the terms of the original employment agreement between the parties.

The Chief Justice of the Supreme Court, Rose Bird, and two of her colleagues vigorously dissented, arguing that the right of publicity was a property right, not a personal right, since it dealt with the loss of potential financial gain from purposefully exposing one to the public rather than damages for embarrassment and mental anguish suffered by one who chose not to be exposed; that the right of privacy extended to the likeness of an individual in his portrayal of a fictional character, such as Count Dracula; and that whether or not the individual has exercised the right during his lifetime, it may be passed on to his heirs or beneficiaries with overall legal protection during the individual's lifetime and for a period of 50 years thereafter. Given these arguments, the dissenters would have sustained the judgment against Universal. (*Lugosi v. Universal Pictures*, 160 Cal. Rptr. 323 [1979].)

The case involving Rudolph Valentino is of particular importance to screenwriters and authors. In November 1975, ABC broadcast a film produced by Spelling-Goldberg Productions titled *Legend of Valentino: A Romantic Fiction*. The nephew of Valentino, Jean Guglielmi, sued for invasion of the right of publicity in Valentino's name and likeness. The California Supreme Court unanimously agreed that Valentino's nephew had no case. Chief Justice Bird and the other two dissenters in the Lugosi case joined in the decision on the grounds that the First Amendment protected the television film and its advertising from liability. The justices distinguished between books and films portraying famous people (whether they are fictional or factual) and the use of one's name or likeness in connection with the sale of commercial products such as plastic toys, pencil sharpeners, soap products, target games, candy dispensers and beverage stirring rods. Since the Valentino case involved the use of a celebrity's identity in a constitutionally protected medium of expression, irrespective of the debate over whether the right of privacy had passed to Valentino's heirs, the lawsuit was barred by the First Amendment. (*Guglielmi v. Spelling-Goldberg Productions*, 160 Cal. Rptr. 352 [1979].)

Given the sharply divided opinions of the justices in these cases and inconsistent rulings in other jurisdictions around the country, the portrayal of public figures, living or dead, is still fraught with complex legal problems.

TORT OF IMITATION

One of the most disquieting developments in this area is the recent assertion that television producers can be held liable for crimes committed by viewers who are allegedly "inspired" to imitate the fictional crimes depicted on television. This new theory of liability has already been asserted in two separate cases, and it remains to be seen whether the courts will bar such claims on First Amendment grounds.

In September 1974, NBC broadcast the television movie *Born Innocent*, in which a fifteen-year-old inmate of a state home for wayward girls was depicted as being sexually attacked in a shower by four other inmates. Three days later, at Baker's Beach in San Francisco, four children made a similar attack on a nine-year-old girl. The victim's family took no legal action against them but, instead, sued NBC for $11 million.

In 1977, a fifteen-year-old Florida youth, Ronny Zamora, defended himself against charges of murdering an eighty-three-year-old woman on the grounds that he had been driven temporarily insane by "involuntary intoxication" induced by such allegedly violent televison shows as *Kojak*. The jury rejected this defense and convicted Zamora, who was sentenced to twenty-five years in prison. Zamora's lawyer turned around and filed a $25 million lawsuit against ABC, CBS and NBC alleging that violent television programs "taught" Zamora to be a criminal and requesting the networks to pay a total of $1 million for each year that he must serve behind bars.

Both lawsuits have been dismissed. In the *Born Innocent* case an earlier appeal was reversed, with the appellate court holding that the victim was entitled to proceed to trial on the issue of whether the requisite incitement was present. But their decision was reversed in a later appeal and NBC ultimately prevailed.

The very pendency of these matters runs contrary to fundamental principles for determining civil liability for personal conduct and violates First Amendment guarantees of freedom of expression. The courts have never accepted the notion that, because some people may react violently to what they see or read, a given book or movie can be censored or its creator made to pay damages. To do otherwise would be absurd, for there is no telling who will be provoked to violence by exposure to the most unlikely of stimuli. For example, it is reported that Heinrich Pommerenke, a German rapist and mass slayer of women, carried out his ghastly deeds after seeing—of all things—Cecil B. DeMille's *The Ten Commandments*. During the scene in which Jewish women dance around the gold calf, Pommerenke's suspicions about the opposite sex were confirmed; and upon leaving the movie theater, he slew his first victim in a nearby park. More recently, a fifty-eight-year-old Frenchman confessed that he had killed his uncle by poisoning a bottle of red wine, using a recipe from an Agatha Christie murder mystery.

Can anyone seriously contend that Cecil B. DeMille or Dame Agatha Christie would be civilly liable for having "incited" these crimes? Unless our Constitution assures screenwriters and authors that the exposition of any idea—including depictions of the seamy side of human existence—will not subject them to multimillion-dollar jury verdicts, free expression will not be "chilled," it will be "frozen."

The law is plain that government cannot forbid or proscribe even advocacy of the use of force, much less the mere description of it, except where such advocacy is, in the words of the United States Supreme Court, "directed to inciting or producing imminent lawless action and is likely to incite or produce such action." Only the most irresponsible critic of television and motion pictures would contend that writers and producers have intentionally directed their programs in order to provoke criminal action or have advocated using force or violating the law. The new paternalism that would censor the content of television and motion pictures out of professed concern for our children is misguided, for it places the primary responsibility for children's upbringing with the government and the courts, rather than with parents and their children. Crime and antisocial behavior are serious matters, but solutions to difficult problems are never found in the repression of ideas.

Rights to a Life Story

Stephen Farber

When William Arnold, a young film critic for the *Seattle Post-Intelligencer*, went to see a revival of *Come and Get It* in the summer of 1973, he could not have guessed that a casual night at the movies was about to engender an obsession that would dominate his life for the next decade. But that night he came under the spell of Frances Farmer, the film's long-forgotten star, and he resolved to learn more about her. Five years later, McGraw-Hill published his book about Farmer's tragic life and death, *Shadowland*. From the time he began researching the biography, Arnold says, he imagined it as a movie; he was excited by the cinematic possibilities in this story of a beautiful and talented young actress persecuted because of her fiery temperament and her radical politics, and eventually committed to a mental institution, where she was abused and probably lobotomized. Writing the book was for him a means to an end; he hoped one day to work on the screen version of Frances Farmer's story.

Now, almost nine years after Arnold's obsession took hold, the Frances Farmer story has indeed been turned into a major motion picture, starring Jessica Lange. (Universal Pictures has released it). But Arnold, who believes that his book awakened interest in the subject, has no credit line in the movie. Mel Brooks's company, Brooksfilms, made *Frances* without buying *Shadowland*. The story of how this happened is the nightmare that every author fears, one that raises questions for all writers who deal with biographical or historical material.

Stephen Farber, former film critic for New West, *is a contributor to* Saturday Review *and* The New York Times.

As Hollywood looks to real people and real incidents for the inspiration for more and more films and television movies, debate over the legal rights of authors who provide the original research on these stories will intensify. The courts are likely to be clogged with lawsuits by biographers and historians who believe that producers have capitalized on their research without acknowledging their contributions.

This is not a new problem, but in the past it was resolved without litigation. One famous instance was that of the two *Harlows* in 1965. Joseph E. Levine paid $100,000 for Irving Shulman's biography of Jean Harlow and planned an expensive, big-screen version starring Carroll Baker. But before the Levine *Harlow* was completed, promoter Bill Sargent announced that he was making a black-and-white Electronovision movie called *Harlow*, starring Carol Lynley. Sargent's *Harlow*, covering the same basic story as Levine's, was filmed in eight days and rushed into the theaters two months before the Levine opus.

Levine fumed publicly, but there was not much he could do except take out full-page ads crying: "Let there be no confusion! The only 'Harlow' produced by Joseph E. Levine and Paramount Pictures will open August 11. It's the *only* 'Harlow' starring Carroll Baker, the *only* 'Harlow' filmed in breathtaking Technicolor, the *only* 'Harlow' produced at the world-famous studios of Paramount Pictures." But the only lawsuit filed in the case was by Sargent against Paramount and five theater chains for allegedly keeping his quickie *Harlow* out of movie theaters.

After the Andes plane crash in 1972, when the survivors resorted to cannibalism in order to stay alive, United Artists paid a hefty sum of money for the rights to *Alive*, a best-selling book on the crash by Piers Paul Read. John Schlesinger was hired to direct. At the same time, producer Allan Carr got hold of a Mexican film called *Survive*, based on another book about the plane crash. Carr re-edited and dubbed the movie, Paramount released it, and that killed the projected film of *Alive*. The people who had hoped to make *Alive* had no legal recourse.

The outcome of these disputes has not discouraged others from seeking redress. The *Shadowland* case, for example, is currently in federal district court in Los Angeles, where William Arnold and producer Noel Marshall, to whom Arnold had sold the movie rights to his book, have filed a $5 million suit against Brooksfilms and the movie's producers, Jonathan Sanger and Marie Yates, charging them with copyright infringement as well as violation of contractual relations. The judgment in the case may well affect future rulings in this thorny field of authors' rights in regard to factual material.

Arnold has read the script of *Frances*, and he thinks he has an open-and-shut case. "They actually used dialogue that I had constructed in the book," he says. "It amazes me that they were so stupid; but maybe they know something I don't. In the book I advanced several theories about Frances Farmer. I argued that her case grew directly out of the left-wing labor movement in the Pacific Northwest, that she was committed by a right-wing judge, that she was not really insane but was a victim of the psychiatric and legal establishment. They incorporated all of those ideas into the screenplay."

Arnold's lawyer, Jay Plotkin of Los Angeles, acknowledges that "as a general rule of law, you cannot protect facts, per se. Those become part of the public domain. But *Shadowland* is not purely factual. It has certain things in common with a work of fiction, which *is* protectable. There are a lot of things in the book that Bill conjured; he took the facts and imagined scenes that *might* have taken place. Our contention is that the producers lifted the whole concept of Bill's book as well as some specific details that he had invented himself."

In affidavits on file in federal court, Brooks and Sanger state that they were familiar with *Shadowland* but that they instructed screenwriters Eric Bergren and Chris DeVore to take a different approach to the Farmer case. Sanger says he told the screenwriters that he wanted to downplay the theory of a political and psychiatric conspiracy, which is at the heart of Arnold's book. To establish a fresh slant on the material, Sanger approached Lois Kibbee, a friend of Farmer's, and got a signed release from her for exclusive use of her reminiscences. The screenwriters conducted additional research in Seattle and interviewed a private detective, Stewart Jacobson, who claimed to have had a close relationship with Farmer; they created a character based on Jacobson, who had not appeared in Arnold's book.

Questioned about the case, Sanger says, "I was interested in the Frances Farmer story long before I read Arnold's book. I never considered it a particularly well written book, and there was nothing special in *Shadowland* that we wanted to use. The reports of her arrests and commitment are part of the public record. As for the book's conspiracy theory, I don't think there are easy villains or heroes in this story. Frances was as much responsible for her fate as the people around her."

The director of the film, Graeme Clifford (the film editor on *The Man Who Fell to Earth* and the recent *Postman Always Rings Twice*), says that he also has been interested in Farmer for many years. As a matter of fact, other film projects on the actress's life had been considered even before Arnold's book appeared. In 1974 a film on Farmer was announced, with Glenda Jackson starring and Ida Lupino directing, but it never materialized. Two television movies, one for CBS and one for ABC, were in the works at various times, but neither got the go-ahead. The CBS movie was to be based on Farmer's autobiography, *Will There Really Be a Morning?*, published in 1972, two years after the actress's death. In one of the amusing complications of the case, an attorney representing Sama Productions, the company that originally owned the rights to *Will There Really Be a Morning?*, threatened Arnold's partner, Noel Marshall, with a lawsuit if he made a film of *Shadowland*. Sama Productions claimed that *Shadowland* infringed the copyright of the Farmer autobiography.

All of this appears to verify the defendants' claim that Frances Farmer is not the exclusive property of William Arnold or any single writer. However, there are special circumstances in the *Shadowland* controversy that would seem to strengthen Arnold's case. As Jay Plotkin points out, "In many lawsuits regarding copyright infringement, it is difficult to establish that there was any contact between the two parties to the suit. Here there is an incredible bridge between the two camps." Plotkin intends to introduce documents to try to establish that Marie Yates, the coproducer of *Frances*, acted as Arnold's agent, helping him to get *Shadowland* published and to sell the movie rights to Noel Marshall. Yates also is said to have brought the book to the attention of Sanger and even to have set up a meeting between Arnold and Mel Brooks.

Arnold describes his own relationship with Brooks: "I first interviewed Brooks in late 1977, when *High Anxiety* was released. I was with him for ninety minutes, and it was a great interview. At the end of the interview, he actually kissed me. During the course of that interview, another reporter who was there mentioned *Shadowland*, and Brooks said he would be interested in reading it. I told Marie Yates to get him a copy of the manuscript." Some time later, Arnold met again with Brooks. That meeting did not go well, and they parted on a discordant note. "The next thing I knew," Arnold says, "Brooks and Marie Yates were working together on their own Frances Farmer movie." (Brooks has declined to discuss the case.)

In their affidavit, Brooks and Yates acknowledge their contact with Arnold, and this may help Arnold to prove his charges of contractual violations. In many cases of suspected plagiarism, the courts are inclined to dismiss the charge of copyright infringement but still award the plaintiff some damages under the separate charge of breach of contract.

But Arnold and his attorneys want to win on the copyright charge as well. They believe this case could be a landmark in the field of copyright law. "I think Mel Brooks wants to set a precedent," Arnold says. "He is trying to prove that the author of a work of nonfiction has no rights at all."

Actually, that is pretty much the conclusion that the courts have already reached. Judges have consistently held that "ideas are free as air" and that "factual information is in the public domain." Richard E. Marks, an agent and attorney with Ziegler, Diskant Inc., a major literary agency in Los Angeles, agrees that "the law is definitely in favor of the free flow of information and ideas." John Diamond, an attorney who handled copyright cases for Simon & Schuster for seven years, adds, "It is almost a truism that a book based on fact is unprotectable. Of course, you cannot lift huge portions of the text, huge portions of dialogue. But when two writers simply use common facts, the courts have found that there is no infringement."

Two recent court decisions give a strong indication of where the courts stand on the copyright of biographical or historical material. The first case revolved around the movie *The Hindenburg*. In 1962,

A. A. Hoehling published a book called *Who Destroyed the Hindenburg?* in which he hypothesized that the dirigible was sabotaged by an anti-Nazi zealot who wanted to embarrass Hitler's regime. Ten years later, Michael Macdonald Mooney published another book, *The Hindenburg*, which also advanced the theory of sabotage; Mooney acknowledged that he had read Hoehling's book before writing his own. Universal bought Mooney's book and eventually made a film about the Hindenburg directed by Robert Wise. Hoehling sued both Mooney and Universal for stealing his ideas.

In rejecting Hoehling's claim, Judge Irving R. Kaufman of the U.S. Court of Appeals in New York declared that in situations where "the idea at issue is an interpretation of an historical event, our cases hold that such interpretations are not copyrightable as a matter of law. . . . Such an historical interpretation, whether or not it originated with Mr. Hoehling, is not protected by his copyright and can be freely used by subsequent authors." Judge Kaufman concluded, "In works devoted to historical subjects, it is our view that a second author may make significant use of prior work, so long as he does not bodily appropriate the expression of another."

This principle was further clarified in a recent case. Gene Miller had written *83 Hours Till Dawn*, a true story about a woman who was kidnapped and buried alive. He put in a great deal of original research, including extensive interviews with the victim. Then Universal produced a "Movie of the Week" for ABC called *The Longest Night*. Although it was based on the same story, Universal had not purchased the book. Miller sued, and the lower court ruled in his favor. But a U.S. court of appeals reversed that ruling, declaring, "Labor of research by an author is not protected by copyright." In other words, the appeals court argued, the mere fact that Miller had done original research did not give him exclusive rights to the story.

Mel Brooks and Jonathan Sanger were involved in a related case a year before they embarked on the Frances Farmer movie. They made *The Elephant Man* while the Broadway play on the same subject was running, but they did not buy the rights to the play. Sanger insists that he had hired screenwriters to work on the story of the elephant man before the play appeared: "Our script was registered in March of 1978, and the play opened in January of 1979." Besides, John Merrick's story had already been the subject of several books, and so it belonged to the public domain. The only real controversy revolved around the title. The producers of the play sued Sanger and Brooks to prevent them from calling their movie *The Elephant Man*. "We finally reached a settlement with them," Sanger says. "They *had* made the title popular, and even though I think we probably would have won the case in the end, it might have dragged on and there was always the chance that we might lose. We wanted to use the title, so we agreed to give them a modest fee."

ABC Motion Pictures is currently preparing a theatrical movie on the life and death of Karen Silkwood, to be directed by Mike Nichols and to star Meryl Streep. Two books about Silkwood have already been published, one by Richard L. Rashke and one by Howard Kohn. Others are in the planning stages. But the producers have bypassed all of the authors. "We used primary sources," says Robert Bookman, vice-president of ABC Motion Pictures. "The film is based on research, court records, and interviews that we conducted ourselves. We did not feel that it was necessary to buy a book. Besides, most of the books take a strong point of view. We want to present all the information and let viewers draw their own conclusions." Howard Kohn, for one, says he wishes that he had been involved in the film project but recognizes that he has no exclusive rights to the subject matter.

Is there, then, any protection for an author who puts in years of labor telling a true-life story? Richard Marks of Ziegler, Diskant, which represents a number of journalists and authors who try to sell nonfiction books to the movies, says, "We advise our writers to create some unique slant on the story. And, of course, if you get an exclusive release from the subject of the story, that helps, too. Even then a producer could still sidestep the author of the book. But often it's an advantage for a company to buy the book. Usually a movie company wants to hang its hat on something concrete before embarking on a film."

In many instances, it is more convenient to buy the book. "The reason you go to an author," suggests attorney John Diamond, "is to avoid a lawsuit. Even if a studio expects to win the suit in the end, it's frequently cheaper to buy the book and avoid all the court costs."

The issues in these copyright cases are extraordinarily complex, and it is impossible to make absolute judgments about right and wrong. Attorney Kenneth Kulzick, who frequently represents the studios in such cases, makes a compelling case for the free flow of information: "Wouldn't it be terrible if we had only one history? I think any First Amendment lawyer would cringe at the prospect. That would be like Russia. I find it disturbing when a writer tries to fence off a historical figure. Who's to say that his book is definitive? I think we all benefit from having access to different viewpoints of the same material." Kulzick, who is not involved on either side of the *Shadowland* case, says, "I know a lot about Frances Farmer, and I've never read that book. Just because a writer opens up a subject doesn't mean he owns it. Someone else might come along and do it better."

As Kulzick suggests, there are strong legal and ethical arguments for allowing considerable leeway to the media to offer as many perspectives on factual events as possible. At the same time, one can sympathize with the anger of an author like William Arnold, who immersed himself in his subject for years and now feels his work has been exploited without being acknowledged. "When I read the script of *Frances*," he recalls, "I got physically ill. I felt as if I'd been raped."

In the copyright field, perhaps there's one law that everyone would agree on: Author beware.

Legal Liability: What to Do

Jeffrey L. Nagin, Esq.

1. If the work is fictional, avoid the use of real names.

A. Avoid accidental identification. Names of all characters, companies, organizations, products, etc. which are utilized should be "cleared" (checked to make sure they are not the same as or confusingly similar to the names of actual persons, companies, etc.). Names can be checked through telephone books covering the area in which the character is portrayed as living. If the character's occupation is given (i.e., army officer, dentist, attorney) a check should be made with the appropriate body (army, dental society, state bar) to insure that there is no name conflict. Where the character's name and occupation are given, a check should be made over a wide geographical area, even if the character's city of residence is identified. Similarly, addresses, telephone numbers, auto license plate numbers, social security numbers, etc. which are used should be cleared by determining through the applicable entity (telephone company, Social Security office, Department of Motor Vehicles) that no such number has been used. As an alternative, a "number" having less or more than the appropriate number of digits, such as a seven- or eleven-digit social security number may be utilized. In a pinch, producers have been known to use their own social security, army serial or telephone numbers. Please note that any Errors and Omissions insurance that you may obtain to cover problems in this area assumes and is subject to your clearing names, numbers, etc. There are firms that specialize in providing this type of clearance procedure. One of these firms recently cleared for my office such diverse items as the names of current New York City street gangs and the names of World War II-era British flying officers.

B. Avoid intentional use of real names. If the work is intended to be fictional, the use of the names of real individuals, companies, products, organizations, etc. should be avoided. Using the name of an actual company or organization may not present a problem, so long as the company or organization named is not disparaged. Thus, describing your villain as having graduated from USC Law School is probably not going to cause any difficulties; describing him as the Dean of the Law School might. As several of the cases cited above and below indicate, however, where it is clear from the nature of the material that the entire story is fictional, including the involvement of the actual individual, organization or company involved, more latitude *may* be permitted. Courts in various jurisdictions are not consistent in this area; therefore, great care should be exercised before proceeding. (See sections 2A and 2B below.) Note the distinction between the use of a real name in an otherwise fictional work and the fictionalization of the biography of an individual which is discussed below.

2. If the work is fictional, avoid identification with individuals.

A. Close similarity of name and other identifiable characteristics. Slight changes in the name of a character which clearly indicate the actual character being depicted are generally not sufficient. Thus, making the villain of your piece the president of an identified local motion picture studio and

Reprinted with permission from Contract to Courtroom: Recent Developments in Entertainment Litigation *(Syllabus from the 25th Annual Program on the Legal Aspects of the Entertainment Industry—Co-sponsored by the Beverly Hills Bar Association and the University of Southern California Law Center). Copyright © 1978 Jeffrey L. Nagin. All rights reserved.*

changing one or two letters in his name would probably not help you a great deal. In addition, if the character is described in such a fashion as to make it clear who is being depicted even though the name has been substantially altered, a court may well find that the reading or viewing public will understand that the character is none other than the plaintiff. Thus, for example, if you carefully describe the villain of a political novel and your description (age, height, weight, hair color, moustache, scars) perfectly matches that of a certain United States Senator, even though you have changed his name, the Senator would have a pretty good argument if he maintained that everyone knew that it was he who was being depicted.

B. Avoid setting and circumstances which will make for identification, even if work is denominated as fictional. Even if a character is not identified using the name of an actual individual, the story may be based upon actual events which are either so well-known or so unique as to leave little doubt as to who was being depicted. In the *Yousoupoff* case, for example, the character was sufficiently identified by the circumstances that surrounded her (her royal blood, her position in the court of the Czar, her involvement with Rasputin, etc.), that the court found that even though she was not identified by name the viewing public could well come to the conclusion that Yousoupoff was, in fact, the character being depicted. In the *Simpson* case, the plaintiff was one of two guards who accompanied a notorious gangster to prison. Years later, defendant's television program involved the "fictional" story of the same gangster's attempted "escape" with the aid of one of his guards. Obviously, one of the two actual guards could be seen as having been depicted in an unfavorable way. Note that in situations in which it may have been one of several people who were depicted, if the group is small enough, they may all be able to recover.

C. Privacy may be invaded even though neither name nor likeness is used. People may be identified by many means other than the use of their name and likeness. Thus a person's accoutrements, if sufficiently distinctive may, if depicted, identify the person. In *Motschenebacher v. R. J. Reynolds Tobacco Co.*, the distinctive look of a driver's racing car was the basis for identifying the driver.

D. Prior book may be basis for identifying. Even though the person who has been identified in a book has his name and other details about him changed in a subsequent motion picture or televi-

sion program which is based upon the book, a court may hold that the person has had his privacy invaded or has been defamed if the viewing public identifies the motion picture or television program with the prior book and the character was sufficiently identified in the book so that the people viewing the motion picture or television program would know who was being depicted, even though the person would otherwise not be identifiable solely on the basis of the motion picture or television program.

3. Fictional dialogue, if it is substantially consistent with facts, doesn't invade privacy.

In creating a book, motion picture or television program involving real characters and real situations, obviously some of the dialogue between the characters involved must be invented, either because the actual dialogue is unknown or for dramatic purposes. So long as the dialogue that is created is consistent with the actual facts, it probably would not constitute an invasion of privacy. Dialogue having nothing to do with the major plot line, but which would be normal given the relationship among the characters ("Would you care for some tea?") is acceptable. However, inventing dialogue between two characters involving intimate details of their sex life, or involving major invented events, which conversation has nothing to do with the factual story line, will cause problems (in fact it will probably cause problems even if it does have something to do with the story line).

4. Even if work is factual, avoid name confusion by appropriate qualification.

It would be advisable in factual situations to adequately identify the people being portrayed so as to minimize the possibility of there being unintentional confusion between such persons and other people with similar names. As indicated in the cases below, the use of a name may be dangerous if more than one person with that exact name (or nicknames in the case of an unusual nickname) exists. Qualifying the name may amount to adding a middle initial, or indicating the age, occupation or marital status of the person being depicted. The degree of qualification that is required may depend upon the circumstances. For example, if you are writing about a dentist named John Smith in a small city in which there are four dentists named John Smith, it would certainly be wise to clarify by the use of other identifying material which doctor Smith was being referred to.

5. Avoid disclosure of "private" facts.

A. Can invade privacy. If the person involved is not a public figure or someone who is generally considered "newsworthy" or a person in whom the public has a great deal of interest, the disclosure of "private" facts may constitute an invasion of privacy which might be actionable.

B. Incorrect statement concerning private aspects of "public figure's" life may be outside New York Times *requirement that actual malice or reckless disregard be established in order to sustain recovery for false light statements.* It is important to remember that public figures have a "public" and a "private" life. Statements which might not be actionable, in the absence of actual malice or reckless disregard, with respect to a public official's "public" life, may well be actionable if made with respect to the public figure's "private" life, if such statements turn out to be incorrect. What we see here is the public figure's "private" life having a greater degree of protection than the public figure's "public" life.

C. Courts have generally sustained, against a privacy claim, factual presentations concerning persons in whom the public has an interest. There is an ongoing conflict between an individual's right of privacy, his right to be "let alone," and the right of a free press to provide the public with information about persons who are deemed "newsworthy." Exactly when a person's private life becomes "newsworthy" is a subject of some debate, but it would appear that persons who inject themselves into the news, who seek the limelight, are entitled to less protection than those who are thrust into public view as the result of circumstances not necessarily of their own choosing.

6. Avoid disclosures of names or likenesses of non-public figures when not required.

The "non-public" figure is entitled to a greater degree of protection in the privacy area than the public figure. In this connection, although the subject matter with which the private individual is involved may be newsworthy or a matter of public interest, the individual's involvement with that subject matter may not be a matter of public concern. Thus, for example, if one were doing a series of articles on mental hospitals in southern California, the subject matter of mental hospitals might be newsworthy, but the fact that a given individual was a patient at one of the mental hospitals involved would not be deemed newsworthy unless he were, for example,

a candidate for public office. People who may have once been public figures or newsworthy may cease to be public figures after some period of time and therefore become entitled to greater protection.

7. Availability of Insurance

A. Types of risks covered. Generally, Errors and Omission insurance in the entertainment/publishing area covers the insured against costs (including judgments, settlements and attorneys' fees) arising as a result of a successful or unsuccessful claim involving invasion of privacy, libel, slander and other forms of defamation, copyright infringement (including unauthorized use of titles, formats, characters and breach of implied contract in submission cases). The insurance does not cover breach of contract action, leaving the insured responsible, for example, for claims made by a person whose name, likeness or life story was used in a manner inconsistent with the terms of a specific agreement between such person and the insured and for claims made by someone based upon the insured's alleged breach of a contract granting certain rights with respect to copyrighted material, even though the latter claim may be pursued as an infringement of copyright. The insurance companies writing this type of insurance, and there are very few of them, require the insured and/or his attorney to exercise reasonable diligence in complying with generally accepted clearance procedures (or the insurance company's own suggested procedures if the insured or his attorneys are neophytes in this area).

While it is generally the producers or publishers who obtain the policies, they typically cover employees, including writers who are rendering services pursuant to an employment relationship. Writers who furnish services or materials as independent contractors (as in the case of an author who sells a producer motion picture rights to a book) are not covered as insureds. However, in the latter case, the author could ask to be specifically named as an additional insured under the producer's or publisher's policy.

B. Insurance company requirements. The insurance company may well decline coverage of a known "risky" situation, may impose a higher premium or a higher individual deductible with respect to claims originating from certain persons or entities, or may impose a higher aggregate deductible. The companies will require a title report and confirmation that clearance procedures have been complied with. In addition, in cases involving known risks, the companies may require their own review of the material in question. To the extent that the name, likeness or biographical incidents of the life of individuals are utilized, the insurance companies require that releases be obtained which permit the uses contemplated.

Writers can also attempt to reduce their liability by including disclaimers in their work and by obtaining releases from potential claimants—see the preceding chapter on defamation; and by limiting the warranties in their contracts—see the section on Contracts, especially the portion of the chapter on the WGA Minimum Basic Agreement concerning Article 28.

Contracts

INTRODUCTION TO THE LAW OF CONTRACTS

Laurence M. Marks

1. You have a meeting with someone from the story department of a production company to discuss one of your story ideas that has not yet been put on paper. After the meeting an executive of the production company requests that you put your idea into written form and expand it to full screenplay length. Is there a contract between you and the production company? How much must the production company pay you if you comply with their request? What is the production company's recourse if you do not perform as requested?

2. Your agent has a phone conversation with the attorney for a production company in connection with the employment by the production company of your writing services. At what point in the discussions, if at all, is there a binding contract?

3. After your agent has reached an oral understanding with the production company for you to render services to said company, a 30-page written agreement arrives at your attorney's office. Your attorney sends a letter to the production company's attorney containing fifty "comments" (i.e., requested changes) necessary to be made before the agreement will be acceptable to you. These comments contain everything from modifications of the delivery dates for the revisions to changes in the definition of net profits. Is there a binding agreement if all the changes are not made? If some of the changes are made? If none of the changes are made?

4. After the execution by you of a written agreement to provide your writing services to a production company, you get an offer elsewhere at twice the price. Can you accept the other offer? What are the production company's rights if you do accept the other offer? Can the production company force you to work for them? Can they sue you for money damages? Can they prevent you from taking the better job, even though they may not be able to require you to work for them? Is the production company required to mitigate its damages?

5. What if the agreement in Paragraph 4 above was for the sale of a literary property that you had previously written? Could the production company require you to sell the property to them?

6. The literary property in Paragraph 5 above is delivered to the production company by you, but you do not receive the last payment due you pursuant to the written agreement. Can you reclaim the literary property? Can you prevent the release of the motion picture based upon the literary property?

7. A motion picture based on your screenplay does not contain the screen credit that was agreed upon in the contract executed in connection therewith. Can you require the production company to recall all the release prints presently in circulation to change the prints to conform to your agreement? Can you claim money damages for the improper screen credit?

8. Pursuant to your employment agreement, you are to receive five percent of the net profits from the first motion picture based upon your screenplay. The movie costs $5 million to make and has presently grossed $40 million, but as yet your participation statements show that the picture is not yet in a profit position. Can this be?

Laurence M. Marks is an entertainment attorney with the Century City law firm of Donnenfeld & Brent. He received his B.A., summa cum laude, and his J.D. from the University of California at Los Angeles. He is a member of Phi Beta Kappa.

What actions can you take? What are your potential remedies?

9. You have an oral agreement with your agent whereby he is to receive a ten percent commission on all monies you earn. You subsequently enter into a writing agreement that was procured strictly by your own efforts. The compensation payable to you pursuant to said agreement is $100,000. Must you pay your agent ten percent of the $100,000?

The above are just a few examples of why writers must have a basic understanding of contract law. True, you can employ attorneys, but they will not be with you in every meeting. Even with competent legal advice, it is just that, advice, and the final decision is always yours and yours alone. This chapter endeavors to give the reader a very basic understanding of contract law.

A contract may be brought into being by a written agreement, an oral agreement—or by understanding, by actions, or, in certain instances, by failure to act. Contracts stated in words, whether oral or written, are termed "express" contracts, while contracts whose existence and terms are manifested by conduct are "implied" contracts.

> For example, if you ask an attorney for legal advice, there is an implied agreement that you will pay the attorney for the advice requested.

A binding contract contains a promise (composed of an offer and an acceptance) and consideration.

An offer may be withdrawn at any time before it is accepted unless there has been consideration in exchange for the holding open of said offer for a designated period of time. If the party to whom an offer is directed communicates a rejection of said offer to the party making the offer, or proposes a counteroffer for acceptance by the party originally making the offer, which varies the terms of the original offer, the original contract is deemed rejected and can no longer be accepted.

> For example, if a producer makes you an offer to employ your writing services for $100,000 for twelve weeks of work, with the first draft to be delivered on June 1, and you agree, but add that you cannot deliver the first draft until June 3, you are deemed to have rejected the original offer and it can no longer be accepted. Your statement can be deemed a counteroffer which the producer may accept or reject. The party receiving an offer to enter into a contract must make an absolute and unqualified acceptance of the offer and communicate such acceptance to the offering party in a way that

the offering party would reasonably interpret as an acceptance of the offer.

The second major element required for a binding contract is that there be consideration that must be legally sufficient.

> For example, if a producer asks a writer to give him a free option on a literary property and the producer is not required to do anything in exchange for the option, the contract is illusory and the writer may sell the property to whomever he desires. Not much would be required on the part of the producer for there to be sufficient consideration to make this a valid and binding agreement. The producer may, for example, merely agree to use "reasonable efforts" to shop the script around to potential markets.
>
> If a would-be producer offers to shop a script around for a screenwriter in exchange for a consideration of one-half of the writer's share of any net profits from any motion picture based upon said screenplay, then whether or not the producer is the one who generates the picture deal, there is a contract between the writer and the producer whereby the writer has obligated himself to pay the producer one-half of any net profits he may receive from a motion picture based on the story idea, whether or not the motion picture is generated by the producer's efforts. Of course, it would be more likely for the writer to agree to share his revenues with the producer if, and only if, the producer is the source of the motion picture deal which generates revenue to the writer.

The actual amount or type of consideration need not be stated in the contract so long as there is a method by which it may be reasonably ascertained (i.e., custom in the industry, reasonable value of the product or services rendered, etc.).

> For example, if a contract states that the writer's credit shall be given in all paid advertising, subject to the standard industry exclusions, a court of law would look to the customary excluded advertising in the motion picture industry to determine what was intended by this phrase.

If one party to a contract reserves an absolute right to cancel or terminate the contract at any time, he has really given up nothing and the contract is illusory and therefore unenforceable.

> For example, if a writer agrees to write a script upon notice by producer but reserves the absolute right not to do so if he does not feel like it at the time, then, there is no binding contract, but merely

an agreement to agree to do something in the future or not at all.

A contract may come into existence even though certain terms are not enumerated if there is a clear standard by which a court of law could infer what the parties, in good faith, intended the non-enumerated terms to be.

Many times, in the motion picture industry, a production company will make an oral agreement between itself and a writer for the writer to provide services to the production company. It is clearly understood between the parties that the oral agreement contains merely the most basic terms and that a complete written agreement will follow containing all of the terms of the agreement. In this case the oral agreement may be a binding contract if enough of the basic terms are outlined and there is a clear standard by which a court of law could imply the missing elements. In some cases, it may be enough to have a binding contract if the money, credit and delivery dates have been agreed upon.

For example, your agent and the producer have reached agreement on the financial terms, delivery dates and credit provisions for you to provide your writing services to the producer. The written, 30-page contract arrives, and your attorney commences "discussions" with the attorney for the producer. The two attorneys cannot reach agreement on the net profits definition, the types of excluded advertising, the pay or play provisions, or the turnaround provisions. The two attorneys have not reached an agreement; nor is the contract signed as the commencement date for the writer's services quickly approaches. You, as the writer, would be very concerned as to whether or not you should commence work. The issue of whether or not there is a binding contract based on the oral discussions between the agent and the producer and the points agreed upon between the attorneys is a question subject to many interpretations. The producer could properly contend that the basic points were agreed upon and the rest is subject to good faith negotiation with an eye to the custom and usage in the industry. The writer could contend that (a) it was not intended that there be a deal until there was a signed agreement; (b) there are major points that the parties have not reached agreement upon; or (c) any other legal position that may be applicable to this situation. If the writer didn't commence his writing services and the case went to court, the jury would decide who was right. But more often, negotiations, threats and cajoling from both sides will cause an agreement to be reached in the last hours before services are to commence.

When a court of law is called upon to interpret a contract's terms, it will look to the intent of the parties at the time the contract was entered into. If the contract or any of its terms are ambiguous, such ambiguities are usually interpreted against the party whose attorney drafted the agreement. In certain conditions and circumstances (i.e., the motion picture, television or book publishing industries) custom and usage can be used to interpret contract terms that are ambiguous or missing.

For example, if a motion picture literary purchase agreement provides for reservation by writer of the customary publication rights, then the interpretation of exactly what rights have been reserved by the writer and what rights are transferred to the producer can be determined by looking at custom and usage in the industry. For example, a reservation of publication rights by a writer usually leaves the producer with the ability to take excerpts from the work not to exceed 7,500 words for use in publicizing and exploiting the motion picture based upon the screenplay.

You should be careful to inform yourself of all the provisions of any agreement that you intend to sign. If you had an opportunity to so inform yourself, you cannot later claim that you were misled, unless there was fraud or misrepresentation by the other party to your agreement. Many times you will think that you and the other party have reached complete agreement on the terms of the contract, but you must be very careful to make sure that the other party's written interpretation of your mutual oral understanding is the same as yours.

A contract that has not yet been completely performed may be altered by the parties. For example, a screenwriter executes a writing agreement with a producer that calls for him to turn in a first-draft screenplay on June 1. On May 20, both parties, realizing that the June deadline will not be met, agree to change the delivery date of August 1. This is a modification of the agreement whose performance was not yet due.

When one party waives the requirements of the other party to do or refrain from doing something, then the other party is no longer required to do or refrain from doing such thing. This is called a waiver. If a producer makes no demand for performance by a writer on the date designated for such performance, a court of law might determine that the producer had waived that condition of the contract requiring performance on said date and that the producer should accept performance within a reasonable time thereafter.

If one party has *substantially* performed his or her obligations under the terms of the contract, the lack of complete performance may be termed an "immaterial breach" and the non-breaching party to the contract may be required to perform fully and later sue the breaching party for the value of the difference between the breaching party's substantial performance and the breaching party's full performance.

> For example, if a writer delivers his final draft of a screenplay two days late and the two additional days merely cause producer to incur $5,000 in additional expenses, producer is still required to pay writer his agreed upon compensation. The producer may later sue for his $5,000 loss. (If said delay had caused the cancellation of the production and writer had been aware of such possible outcome of his delay; a mere two-day delay may be deemed a material breach thereby excusing performance by producer). If producer gives writer paid advertising credit in a single paid ad in a size that is fifty percent of the size of the title, when seventy-five percent was the agreed-upon size, producer may be sued for damages; but writer may still have to perform any services still required of him pursuant to the terms of the agreement.

A material breach of an agreement by one party may completely excuse performance by the non-breaching party. For example, if a writer does not deliver the first-draft screenplay, the producer does not have to pay the writer the agreed-upon compensation.

In addition to having his or her performance excused, the non-breaching party has a choice of potential remedies:

1. The non-breaching party may sue for damages (i.e., enough money to place the non-breaching party in the same position he would have been in had the contract been properly performed). For example, if producer tells writer, before writer commences services, that he will not pay writer the agreed upon consideration, writer may refrain from commencing his writing services and sue the producer for the agreed-upon compensation, less any monies writer was able to earn during the proposed period of his writing services. The writer is required to seek other comparable employment during this period in order to "mitigate" his damages.

2. In addition to the damages referenced in Paragraph 1 above, the breaching party may also be liable for all losses resulting from the breach, which a reasonable person with knowledge of the breaching party should have foreseen at the time of the contracting as being likely to result from the breach. For example, a writer contracts to provide a finished screenplay to the producer no later than June 1, with full knowledge that producer will be entering into a pay or play acting agreement with a major star containing a stop date for the artist's services of September 1. Writer was further aware that it would require the full period from June 1 through September 1 for required actor's services to be completed. If writer's delay causes producer to have to renegotiate and pay for the actor's additional services necessary to complete the production, writer may be liable for these increased costs in addition to all other costs or losses incurred by producer as a result of writer's delay.

(a) The losses the producer may recover are only those losses which are reasonably certain of computation. In the example above, writer would have to pay the additional salary paid to the actor and *all* the costs of the additional days of production necessitated by writer's delay. It would be unlikely, however, that producer could recover the additional net profits he claims the picture would have generated had it been released during the peak Christmas season as originally scheduled. The amount of net profits that a picture will generate is very speculative and is not capable of reasonably certain computation.

(b) The non-breaching party will not be permitted to recover damages he could have avoided by reasonable efforts on his part. For example, if a writer under contract to a production company realizes that the production company is in breach and will not be using his/her services for the twelve-week term of the agreement, the writer must exercise reasonable efforts to locate and accept a comparable position. Any reasonable expenses incurred by the writer in connection with such efforts will be compensated, in addition to writer's other losses, in the lawsuit for the breach of the original agreement.

3. If the object of the contract is of such a unique nature that money damages cannot make the non-breaching party whole, then the non-breaching party may be able to sue for specific performance under the agreement. For exam-

ple, if the non-breaching party had entered into a contract to purchase a literary property and the breaching party then refused to sell the property, the court, in a lawsuit for the breach of the agreement, may require the breaching party to transfer the property to the non-breaching party for the consideration agreed to in the contract. This decision by the court would be based upon the fact that each piece of literary property is totally unique unto itself, and no amount of money or other piece of property may place the non-breaching party in the position he would have been in had the contract been properly performed. If, on the other hand, the breaching party had entered into an agreement to provide his writing services to the non-breaching party, a court of law would not require the writer to pro-vide such services but would limit producer's remedies to a recovery of money damages. The courts of this country will not *require* an individual to provide services to another, as this would be akin to forced labor, however, the courts may issue an injunction prohibiting the writer from working for any company other than the producer, which in effect forces the writer to work for the producer or not at all.

This article should not be looked at as an all-inclusive dissertation on the law of contracts but merely as an introduction to some of the aspects of the field of contract law. The articles that follow analyze the various specific provisions of the types of contracts you may be confronted with during your literary career.

A GUIDE TO THE WGA 1981 THEATRICAL AND TELEVISION BASIC AGREEMENT

Molly Wilson

MINIMUM BASIC AGREEMENT

The Minimum Basic Agreement (MBA) is unique in many respects, and is recognized as perhaps the most complex collective bargaining agreement in the entertainment industry. While the typical labor contract addresses the traditional issues of wages, hours and working conditions, the special needs of the writer in television and motion pictures demand a contract that goes far beyond normal collective bargaining terms. The MBA therefore deals with rights in material, purchases of literary material, speculative writing and writing credits, among others.

The MBA is incorporated in its entirety in every "covered employment" as defined below. Thus, the MBA overrides terms in an individual writing contract that are in conflict with the MBA. Similarly, any covered deal automatically provides all of the benefits and protections set forth in the MBA. Of course, a writer is free to negotiate and contract for better than minimum terms (except with respect to credit provisions).

Molly (Margaret) Wilson joined the WGAw as Associate Resident Counsel in May 1979. She has also practiced labor law at the firm of Silber, Benezra & Taslitz. She is a graduate of the UCLA School of Law and received her undergraduate degree in Russian Studies and Language from the University of California at Riverside.

WHAT SITUATIONS COME WITHIN WGA JURISDICTION?

If a writer is hired to write something for a signatory company, that employment relationship is governed by the MBA, even if the writer is not a member of the WGA.

However, writers often, without any assignment or direction from a producing company, initiate the creation or development of a literary property that is subsequently offered for sale to a producer. If the writer sells the property and renders no personal services with respect to adapting or revising the material, no employment relationship has been established.

In this case, the MBA does not govern the terms of the sale of the literary material unless the writer is considered a "professional writer" and the material has not been previously exploited. The term "professional writer" is defined in the MBA in terms of an accumulation of prior professional writing credits in television, motion pictures, legitimate stage or publishing. If the material sold to the producer was not written by a professional writer, or was previously published (e.g., a movie based on a best-selling novel) or exploited in any other medium, the terms of the MBA will *not* apply.

Even if the sale is being made by a professional writer and is of unexploited material, there are a few provisions of the MBA that do not apply, such as the requirement that the producer contribute to the WGA pension and health funds.

GEOGRAPHICAL APPLICATION OF THE MBA

There are limitations on the applicability of the MBA, based on the following geographical factors: (a) whether or not the writer lives in the United States; (b) where the deal for the writer's services or the acquisition of literary material is made; and (c) where the writer's services are rendered.

The MBA applies to writers in the following situations:

1. With respect to a writer who lives in the United States, if the "deal is made" in the United States, and if at the time the deal is made the writer is present in the United States, the MBA will apply regardless of where the services are to be rendered. If the writer is a permanent resident of the United States but is temporarily abroad and if the deal is made by the writer's agent or other representative who is in the United States at the time the deal is made, the deal is within the scope and coverage of the MBA. The MBA applies even if the deal is made by the writer's representative in a communication by telephone, mail, or cable with a representative of the production company who is outside of the United States.

2. The MBA applies to a deal made with a writer who lives in the United States and is transported abroad by the production company, if the literary purchase deal or the writing employment deal is made while the writer is abroad as the result of being so transported.

3. The MBA also applies to the employment of a writer (whether or not such writer lives in the United States) where the writer's services are required by the production company to be performed, and are performed, in the United States under the supervision and direction of the production company.

A "deal is made" within the meaning of the foregoing provisions when agreement is reached between the production company and the writer as to the monetary terms of the deal. The time and place of the formal signing of the written contract or deal memorandum is not determinative with respect to whether the MBA applies to the purchase or employment deal.

MINIMUM INITIAL COMPENSATION FOR COVERED EMPLOYMENT AND LITERARY PURCHASES

Television Freelance Minimums

Basic flat deal minimums. The MBA provides minimum rates of compensation for TV freelance employment, which depend upon the literary element written, the length of the program or segment, and whether the production is classified as "low-budget" or "high-budget." The minimum initial compensation payable to the writer also varies according to the date, or the "period," in which the writing (or the purchase, in case of a literary acquisition) occurs. The minimums escalate, with the highest minimums being applicable to employments and literary acquisitions occurring during the later periods of time covered by the MBA.

The minimum rates are for one writer, except that a bona fide team of writers is considered a unit and can be paid the minimum compensation for one writer. A team is defined as two writers who offer, prior to employment, to collaborate.

The literary elements: Minimum rates of compensation are specified for the writing of a story, teleplay, story and teleplay, narrative synopsis, rewrite, polish, format, bible and other literary elements. Most of those terms are self-explanatory. "Story" is defined as:

> "story indicating the characterization of the principal characters and containing sequences and action suitable for use in or representing a substantial contribution to a final script."

"Rewrite" means the writing of significant changes in plot, story line or interrelationship of characters in a teleplay. "Polish" means the writing of changes in dialogue, narration or action, but not including a rewrite.

A "format" is defined as a written presentation that sets forth the following:

"the framework within which the central running characters will operate and which framework is intended to be repeated in each episode, the setting, theme, premise or general story line of the proposed serial or episodic series and the central running characters which are distinct and identifiable including detailed characterizations and the interplay of such characters. It may also include one or more suggested story lines for individual episodes."

A "bible" is a format for a mini-series or multi-part closed-end series, but is much more detailed than a traditional format. It must satisfy the definition of format and also meet the following criteria:

"(i) It is in much greater detail than a traditional format, and includes the context, framework, and central premises, themes and progression of the multi-part series or serial.

"(ii) It sets forth a detailed overall story development for the multi-part series or for the first broadcast season of the serial (or such lesser period as may be contracted for with the writer) and includes detailed story lines for (A) all of the projected episodes of the multi-part series or (B) most of the projected episodes for the first broadcast season of the serial (or such lesser period as may be contracted for with the writer).

"(iii) The characters must be not only distinct and identifiable, but must be set forth with detailed descriptions and characterizations."

Schedule of installment payments: With respect to so-called "flat deals" (i.e., where the writer is employed to write literary material for a particular theatrical or television production), the MBA provides a schedule of installment payments. The installments are percentages of the aggregate compensation due the writer for the literary material that is to be delivered. Upon the writer's delivery of each literary material (e.g., story, first-draft teleplay, final-draft teleplay), he must be paid not less than the applicable percentage of total compensation. The production company is thereby precluded from withholding all compensation until the writer has completed the literary material. Payment must be made to the writer promptly after the company's receipt of the literary material; the MBA prescribes a late charge of one and one-half percent per month on delayed payments.

Except in the case of the writer's default or failure to deliver the literary material, payment to the writer of at least Guild minimum compensation is guaranteed. In no event can the production company make payment of the minimum compensation contingent upon its approval of the material, or upon the securing of financing for the project, or upon a network order for a production based upon the material, or upon actual production of a film, or upon any other condition. The company can, however, make the payment of *overscale* compensation (compensation above applicable minimum) conditional upon actual production, broadcast and like contingencies.

Literary purchases. If the production company purchases literary material from a professional writer, the minimum payable for the purchase of such material is the same as the flat deal minimum for employment to write such material. Moreover, if the production company obtains an option to purchase literary material from a professional writer, the company cannot, prior to the exercise of its option, employ a second writer to render any writing services on the optioned material, unless the amount paid by the company to the professional writer for the option is at least ten percent of applicable minimum purchase price for the literary material which was optioned.

Higher minimums payable in certain circumstances. The MBA prescribes special, higher initial minimums in certain situations, due to the fact that the material is being written for a particular kind of production. The principal categories of such special, higher minimums are as follows:

Pilot script: A pilot script is a story or story and teleplay intended to be used for the production of a pilot film which is to serve as the basis of a proposed serial or episodic series. A pilot script usually sets forth the framework intended to be repeated in subsequent episodes, including the setting, theme, and premise of the proposed serial or series and its central running characters. A writer employed to write a pilot script must be paid an amount not less than one hundred fifty percent of the otherwise applicable minimum initial compensation (including going rate and bonus if applicable).

Back-up script: A writer employed to write a "back-up" script must receive initial compensation of not less than one hundred fifteen percent of the otherwise applicable minimum initial compensation (including going rate and bonus if applicable). A back-up script is a story and/or teleplay designed to serve as an episode of a proposed episodic series and written in anticipation of, but prior to the company's actual receipt of, the order for production of the series from a network.

Spin-off script: If a writer is employed to write a story or story and teleplay for an episode of an existing series which episode is intended to be used as the basis of a spin-off series the writer must be paid at least one hundred fifty percent of the otherwise applicable minimum basic compensation (including going rate and bonus if applicable).

As outlined above, the initial minimum compensation for pilot scripts, back-up scripts and spin-off scripts is higher than the standard MBA minimum compensation applicable to other types of productions. This excess compensation is *not* included, however, for the purpose of computing re-run and other residual payments which are triggered by the re-use of the program.

Additional terms of freelance television employment. *No cut off in teleplay employment:* The MBA provides that the company shall have no right to cut off the writer in teleplay employment (i.e., between first draft, final draft and revisions).

Reading time and obligations of freelance writers re revisions: Television freelance writers are typically employed to write a story and teleplay, or a story with option for teleplay (i.e., the writer can be cut off after the story is delivered if the producer doesn't like it). In these situations, the MBA prescribes the number of revisions of story and teleplay to which the company is entitled and imposes time limits within which the company can request such revisions.

Generally speaking, the payment of story minimum gives the company the right to request one revision of story. The request for revision must be made within fourteen days of first submission.

If the writer is also employed to write the teleplay, the company may request a second revision of the story, as long as such revision is incorporated into the teleplay. Otherwise, the company must pay one-half of story minimum for a second revision of the story.

A very significant time limit in story and teleplay employment is that the company has only fourteen days after submission of the story within which to instruct the writer to commence the teleplay. Similarly, the company must request a teleplay based on a format or bible within fourteen days after the format or bible is submitted.

Payment of teleplay minimum entitles the company to two sets of revisions to the teleplay. For thirty-minute programs, the first revision must be requested within fourteen days after first submission of the teleplay. If the company requests the first revision within seven days of the first submission of the teleplay, it may make a second request for revision within seven days after submission of the first revision. For programs over thirty minutes in length, the first revision must be requested within twenty-one days of submission. If the first request for revision is made within fourteen days, the company may make a second request for revision within seven days after submission of the first revision.

None of the foregoing revisions can amount to a new story or story line.

Week-to-week and Term Employments

A writer may be employed on a week-to-week or term basis to render writing services on one or more productions. Staff writers are frequently employed in this manner. The MBA provides minimum weekly compensation depending upon the number of guaranteed weeks of employment, provided that in no event may the week-to-week or term writer receive less for the material written by him/her on such week-to-week or term basis than he/she would have received had he/she written the same material on a freelance basis at minimum compensation.

Theatrical Minimums

Flat deal minimum compensation. As in television employment, the MBA also provides a schedule of initial minimum basic compensation for the writing of a treatment, story, screenplay, rewrite, polish and other literary elements of a theatrical motion picture. There are also separate minimum compensation schedules for low-budget and high-budget theatrical motion pictures. A high-budget motion picture is one the cost of which equals or exceeds $2.5 million, while a low-budget motion picture is one that costs less than $2.5 million.

As in television, payment of minimum compensation must be guaranteed, and cannot be conditioned upon acceptance or approval of the literary material, or upon any other contingency. If the writer is not paid within seven days of when it is due, interest automatically accrues.

Motion picture writers may also be employed on a week-to-week or term basis at specified weekly rates, although that form of employment is now seldom used.

Maximum period of employment. The MBA specifies the maximum period of time determined by a formula that a writer employed on a flat deal basis to write theatrical motion picture material can be required to render services. The rationale of the limitation is that a freelance writer employed on a flat deal basis must earn at least as much as he would have if employed on a weekly basis.

Termination for late delivery. If a writer is late in delivering material, and the delay was not caused by the company's instruction or directions, the company may terminate the employment *prior to the delivery* of the material. The company then can retain the ownership of any material previously delivered for which appropriate payment was made.

ARTICLE 14 (WRITERS EMPLOYED IN ADDITIONAL CAPACITIES)

A substantial number of WGA members enter into term contracts in television under which they render services as a producer, executive producer or story editor in addition to functioning as a writer. The general thrust of Article 14 is to provide a premium rate of weekly minimum compensation to be applicable to such employees. In addition, a "program fee" is payable to the "hyphenated" employee (e.g., writer-producer) for each program produced during the term of his or her employment.

RESIDUALS AND OTHER ADDITIONAL COMPENSATION FOR SPECIFIC USES

Television Payments

Reruns and foreign telecasts. With respect to the reruns of television programs, the Guild residuals are based on a declining percentage of the ap-

plicable minimum for each successive run of a program. Residuals for reruns in domestic syndication range from forty percent of the applicable minimum scaling downward to as little as five percent per run beginning with the thirteenth run of a program. For foreign telecasting, a writer will receive from fifteen percent to thirty-five percent of the applicable minimum compensation depending on the total gross revenues derived from foreign telecasting. Residuals for reruns on network prime time can be as high as one hundred percent of the applicable minimum compensation.

Use of "excerpts" or "clips." The use of an excerpt from a television program is deemed a domestic rerun or foreign telecast (depending upon the territory in which the excerpt is exhibited) of the program from which the excerpt is taken. Except in special exempted cases, such use triggers the company's obligation to pay the writer the full rerun or foreign telecast payment. In the excepted cases, either no additional payment is payable to the writer or a reduced payment is required, computed in accordance with a formula for each particular use. The principal exempted cases are:

- excerpts used for promotional, trailer, news or review purposes (provided that the running time of the excerpt does not exceed a specified length);
- excerpts used as "stock shots";
- excerpts used for purposes of recapping a story in the context of a serial, etc. (subject to certain time limitations);
- excerpts used as "flashbacks" in the context of a serial, etc. (subject to certain time limitations);
- excerpts used in so-called "compilation" television programs (for example, *25 Years of Lucy on Television*); a special payment formula is provided by the MBA for such use.

Theatrical exhibition of a television motion picture. If a television film is exhibited theatrically outside the United States, the credited writer must be paid an amount equal to one hundred percent of the minimum initial compensation applicable to the literary material written by him for the program. If a television film is exhibited theatrically in the United States, or both in the United States and in a foreign country or territory, the credited writer must be paid not less than one hundred fifty percent of the minimum initial compensation applicable to the literary material written by him.

The production company and the writer may agree in their contract that all or any portion of the compensation paid to the writer over and above twice the applicable initial minimum may be applied as a pre-payment to be credited against amounts due for theatrical exhibition.

Additional compensation for certain uses of material to which separated rights do not apply. The MBA provides that even in cases where separation of rights does not apply (discussed below), additional compensation is payable to the credited writer for certain specified uses of the story or teleplay material written for an established series or one-time television program. Additional compensation is payable to the writer of such material if the company produces or authorizes the production of a theatrical motion picture, radio program, dramatic stage production, printed publication, phonograph record or other audio recording, or merchandising item based upon such material.

The publication payment is twenty-five percent of the company's net receipts from the exercise of the publication rights. The merchandising payment is five percent of the company's net receipts. The definition of "merchandising" applicable to this area is rather restrictive, however, as it covers only "any object or thing first described in literary material written by the writer."

Character payments: Additional compensation is also due to a writer who creates and introduces into an existing serial or episodic series a new character who is fully developed and fully described in the material written by the writer. If it is a principal character who is distinct and identifiable, and the character is thereafter used in subsequent episodes of the same series, the production company must pay the writer a character payment for each subsequent episode of such series in which the character appears. (The writer of a pilot is not entitled to such character payments.)

If the production company uses such character as the central character having a continuing role in a new and different serial or episodic type television series (i.e., a "spin-off"), the company must pay the writer who created and introduced such character in the first series a per-episode royalty for each episode of such new and different series which is produced and broadcast.

Supplemental markets. Writers are entitled to additional compensation from the licensing of television and theatrical motion pictures to "supplemental markets" (including pay television, video cassette and video disc distribution). Such payments, equivalent to one and two-tenths percent of the company's gross receipts derived from the licensing, apply to all films produced since 1981.

Theatrical Residuals

Free television release. Writers of theatrical motion pictures receive one and two-tenths percent of the gross receipts derived from the licensing of such films to free television.

Merchandising payments. If the company exploits the merchandising rights in the literary material written by the writer, the writer is entitled to a merchandising payment of five percent of absolute gross. Such payments apply even if the writer is not entitled to separation of rights. The definition of "merchandising" applicable in this area also includes the sale of photo novels and comparable items.

Supplemental markets. As in the television area, the supplemental markets (pay TV, video cassette, etc.) payment is one and two-tenths percent of the company's gross.

Collection of Residuals

The Guild systematically polices payments of television and theatrical residuals, use of excerpts, supplemental markets payments and others. However, occasionally uses of literary material for which additional payment is due (such as merchandising, publication and character payments) go undetected. Thus, all writers should try to stay informed of uses of their literary material and report payments that are due and unpaid to the Guild.

SEPARATION OF RIGHTS

As an employee for hire, the writer in television and motion pictures does not own the copyright. To offset this lack of statutory protection to the writer in the area of property rights, the Guild has successfully negotiated for the inclusion of the concept of separation of rights in the MBA. The basic premise of the provisions is that, with respect to original material (i.e., material that is not based on source material such as a novel, play, etc.), certain rights, other than the primary television or screen rights for which the material is written, are reserved to the credited writer of the story of the particular television or theatrical film.

As for theatrical motion pictures, the reserved rights are limited to publication and dramatic (i.e., legitimate stage) rights. In television, all rights other than the television film rights and the television sequel (i.e., series) rights are reserved to the writer. In addition to providing for certain reserved rights, the separation of rights articles of the 1981 MBA also provide for certain monetary benefits for the writer resulting from the exploitation of various ancillary rights' on the part of the company.

These articles are perhaps the most complicated in the MBA, and the serious student of separation of rights is directed to the actual text of the MBA. Only a short summary is provided here.

Theatrical

In the theatrical area, a writer of an original story or original story and screenplay is initially entitled to separation of rights.

Publication rights. The writer acquires a royalty-free license to these rights. However, the writer may not exercise these rights until the expiration of six months from the general release of the motion picture or three years after the date of the employment or purchase agreement, whichever is earlier.

However, the producer retains a limited right to publish material for the purpose of advertising, publicity or exploitation of the picture and the right to author a paperback novelization to be published in connection with the exploitation of the motion picture. The writer must be given the first opportunity to write the novelization, and whether he writes it or not, will be entitled to an advance and royalty from the publication of the novelization.

Dramatic rights. "Dramatic rights" are the live stage production rights. Initially, the producer has the right to exploit a large stage production, but if he fails to do so within two years after general release of the motion picture, then these rights revert to the writer. In any event, the writer will be entitled to royalty payments if a stage show is produced.

Sequel payments. The writer does not actually have sequel rights, but is instead entitled to certain payments if the company produces a motion picture or television sequel.

If the sequel is a theatrical motion picture, the employed writer receives twenty-five percent of the initial fixed compensation for the writing services, and the writer who sells literary property receives fifteen percent of the initial fixed payment for the material.

If the sequel is a television series or a one-time television program, the writer receives (subject to certain offsets) the sequel payments provided in the MBA for each episode broadcast.

Television

The writer of a format, story or story and teleplay for a television program may be entitled to separation of rights. Television writers entitled to separation of rights retain all rights other than the television film and television sequel rights. Where separation of rights applies, the production company owns the exclusive film television rights in the literary material for four years from the date on which the writer delivers the material. Thereafter, the company and the writer own the film television rights in the material non-exclusively. The non-exclusive rights include the right to continue to exhibit in perpetuity the television film based on the literary material and to remake the film for television purposes.

The company also has the exclusive right, for a limited time, to commence the exploitation of the television sequel rights in the material (the right to produce an episodic series or a serial based on the material).

If the production company commences exploitation of the television sequel rights within the period allowed, the television sequel rights remain vested in the company; otherwise, they revert to the writer.

If the production company exploits the television sequel rights by producing a series based on the literary material, it must pay the writer who is entitled to separation of rights at least a minimum sequel payment for each episode produced and broadcast.

If a series episode is rerun, the writer entitled to separation of rights is paid an additional sum for each such rerun. The rerun sequel payment is computed in terms of a percentage declining in accordance with the residual formula.

Rights acquired by a production company in a format revert to the writer, unless within twenty-four months after delivery of the format the company engages the writer to write a story and teleplay based on the format.

Except for the television rights acquired by the production company as described earlier, all other rights in the literary material are reserved to the writer with separation of rights, subject to certain "hold back" periods during which the writer cannot exercise his reserved rights.

The rights reserved by the writer include legitimate stage rights, theatrical motion picture rights, publication rights, merchandising rights, radio rights and live television rights.

If at any time before the writer disposes of or exploits his reserved rights the company desires to acquire any of such rights, the company must negotiate with the Guild for such rights. If the production company refuses to accept the price quoted by the Guild, the writer may dispose of the rights elsewhere, subject to a right of first refusal by the production company.

The company has the right to negotiate directly with the writer to acquire the reserved theatrical motion picture rights, publication rights and merchandising rights, provided that the amounts to be paid to the writer for such rights cannot be less than the applicable minimum prices specified in Article 16.B(3)(e) of the MBA.

The minimum for theatrical motion picture rights is two and one-half percent of the bona fide budgeted direct cost of the motion picture or $20,000, whichever is greater. In the case of publication and merchandising rights, the minimum is six percent of the "absolute gross" (that is, the monies remitted by the manufacturer or publisher).

If the foregoing enumerated rights are acquired by the company, but the company fails to commence exploitation of the acquired rights within four years from the date of delivery of the literary material or three years from the exhibition of the first film of the series, whichever period is shorter, then the unexploited rights revert to the writer, subject to a right of first refusal on the part of the company if the writer thereafter offers such rights for sale.

Separated rights in television are subject to the "upset price" provisions of the MBA. If the initial compensation paid to the writer who is entitled to separation of rights is at least equal to the "upset price" (a sum that is substantially higher than the standard minimum), then the production company may bargain freely with such writer for the acquisi-

tion of the separated rights and may "buy out" any or all such rights, subject to the continuing obligation to pay the writer the prescribed minimum sequel payments.

The company must meet two requirements to acquire the separated rights: (1) the reserved rights acquired by the production company must be expressly specified in a separate contract, and (2) a separate purchase price must be paid to the writer as consideration for acquiring his reserved rights. The separate purchase price must be expressly set forth in the separate agreement. No minimum amount is prescribed for such separate purchase price, and it is often nominal.

The writer should be aware that he or she is not required to sell the separated rights simply because the company has paid an amount equal to or greater than the upset price. Such payment merely gives the company the right to negotiate freely for them.

SPECULATIVE WRITING

The MBA secures to the writer a guarantee that he or she will be paid at least the minimum compensation applicable for the literary material written or sold, except in instances of default or clear departure from directions given by the company. Payment of such minimum amount can not be conditioned upon the company's approval of the work submitted, or upon the company's ability to finance or decision to produce a production based on the material, or any other contingency.

The MBA specifically prohibits "speculative writing," whereby the writer writes material without any firm guarantee of payment and where payment is made contingent upon the occurrence of any other event. So long as at least MBA minimum is paid for the material, however, nothing prohibits the writer and the company from agreeing that additional sums or bonuses shall be payable upon the occurrence of specified events, such as production of a program based on the script, network order of a series, and the like.

Where the writer, without encouragement, solicitation or other instigation by the production company, writes literary material on his own initiative and thereafter voluntarily submits such material to the company for consideration, the writing will *not* be deemed prohibited speculative writing.

THE TWO-MEETING RULE

In the television area, the MBA recognizes that it is a common practice for the company and writers to discuss the writer's ideas as well as ideas and material suggested by the company. The MBA therefore contains rules to prevent the company from going beyond the bounds of permissible "pitching." They provide that certain kinds of contacts between a writer and a production company will create firm commitments on the part of the company to pay for the writing of the literary materials discussed by the writer and the company during the course of such contacts.

If no commitment is made by the production company in its initial interview with the writer, then a second interview between the writer and the production company concerning the same assignment may only be with a person who is empowered (subject to the negotiation of mutually acceptable terms) to make the final decision to engage the writer for an assignment. In no event may there be a third interview between the writer and the company with respect to an assignment unless a firm commitment has been made prior to such third interview or is made in such third interview.

If in the first interview the writer proposes, or "gives," a story, then a second meeting at the request of the company concerning that story is deemed to constitute a story commitment at minimum compensation. If at the request of the company the writer gives a story by telephone, in person, or otherwise, then a meeting on that story at the request of the company constitutes a story commitment. In any event, the writer can not be required to deliver any material written by him until all the terms and conditions relating to the employment or purchase of such material have been agreed upon.

As used in the foregoing provisions, the term "interview" does not include a telephone request by the company addressed to the agent or the writer which is solely for the purpose of obtaining general information concerning the writer's availability for employment or concerning the writer's credits, or an appointment solicited by the writer in order to convey such information to the company.

PRECAUTIONS TO TAKE IN DEALINGS WITH A COMPANY BEFORE A CONTRACT OR DEAL MEMO HAS BEEN COMPLETED

The Guild legal staff handles a great many speculative writing claims and claims based on the two-meeting rule. Many of the speculative writing claims arise when a company asks the writer to develop an idea and to come back later to discuss it. The writer, eager to obtain an assignment, complies and does extensive writing. The company then claims that the writer voluntarily prepared and submitted the material.

This unfortunate situation can be avoided if the writer refuses to do any writing until at least a deal memorandum has been prepared, as required by Article 19 of the MBA and Working Rules 3(a) and 4. Without a written contract, the writer should at a minimum keep records of the content of each conference, including telephone conversations, noting instructions and suggestions given.

The claims arising under the two-meeting rule usually hinge upon two factors: (1) whether a story was actually given at the first meeting, and (2) who requested the second meeting. If, in fact, in the first meeting the writer did present a story, even if orally, with principal characters and a developed story line, another meeting at the request of the producer, concerning that story, will constitute a story commitment under Article 20.B.2. of the MBA.

An excellent practice is to keep a working daily calendar and record all telephone conversations in substance, also noting who called whom. This may be important in that, in certain instances, a second meeting may be considered initiated by the company through a telephone call if the conversation deals with the story as pitched at the first interview. Another simple, but too often overlooked, practice in the situation described above is to retain copies of all written material, including initial notes and scribbles. It is extremely important as evidence, and oftentimes crucial at an arbitration, to have the writer's original notes as well as copies of all delivered material in case the company asserts it never received the writer's material.

One last suggestion is to record the name and have the individual at the production company sign for any material deposited with the company. This receipt could prove invaluable if the issue of delivery is raised at some later date.

GRIEVANCE AND ARBITRATION

As is typical of most collective bargaining agreements, the 1981 MBA provides for grievance and arbitration of disputes. The prescribed procedure has essentially three steps; the first is a conference between representatives of the Guild and of the company in which a good faith attempt is made to resolve the matter. Failing resolution at that step, a dispute is litigated through an adversary proceeding before a grievance committee consisting of three persons appointed by the company and three appointed by the Guild. The grievance committee is empowered to reach a decision that is binding on all parties. However, due to the make-up of the committee, the potential for deadlock is always present. In the event that the dispute is not resolved by the grievance committee, the matter is then tried before a sole neutral arbitrator selected from a specified list of arbitrators set forth in the 1981 MBA. The persons serving as arbitrators are, in general, attorneys with particular expertise in the entertainment industry. The arbitrator is empowered to grant a final and binding award.

The MBA places some limitations on the nature of disputes that can be handled through the grievance and arbitration process. With the exception of unpaid salary claims up to maximum limits specified in the MBA, individual disputes are not subject to arbitration, and the writer must pursue his legal remedies through the courts. Thus, the bulk of the grievances and arbitrations handled by the Guild involve the interpretation and application of the MBA itself.

In the cases that are covered by the arbitration provisions of the MBA, the Guild legal staff represents the Guild and the writer without charge to the writer. The other costs of arbitration, including the arbitrator's fee and the cost of a transcript, is also borne by the Guild and the company. A writer who feels he or she has an arbitrable claim should send a complete written statement to the legal department or call the Guild's legal department coordinator.

NOTICE TO OTHER WRITERS EMPLOYED ON SAME MATERIAL

If the writer so requests, the company must inform the writer of the names of all other writers then or previously employed by the company on the same material, or from whom the company purchased the material on which the writer is employed. When a new writer is assigned to any material, the company *must* notify all other writers who are then employed on such material.

It is of course in the writer's interest to inquire the names of previously assigned writers, and indeed Working Rule 12 requires the writer to do so. That working rule also requires the new writer to notify the other writers of his or her assignment.

WRITTEN CONTRACTS

Article 19 of the MBA requires the company to render a written contract to the writer within specified periods of time after employment. The time limits vary according to the type of employment and the type of contract used. The company must also file a copy of such contract with the Guild. Related working rules require the writer to file a copy of written employment contracts with the Guild and to work only pursuant to a written contract.

LOCATION EXPENSES

If a writer is required to perform services on location sufficiently far away from the studio that overnight accommodations are necessary, the company must furnish first-class transportation, board and accommodations.

In the above situations, the company must provide travel insurance.

WARRANTIES AND INDEMNIFICATION

The company may require the writer to warrant in the individual employment contract that the written material is original and does not defame, invade the privacy of or otherwise violate rights of third parties. However, the writer may not be required to warrant or indemnify with respect to any claim that the literary material defamed or invaded the privacy of any person, unless the writer knowingly used the name or personality of such person or should have reasonably known that such person would or might claim that his personality was used.

The *company* must indemnify the *writer* against claims or actions respecting material assigned to the writer by the company. Moreover, the company must cover or name the writer as an additional insured on its errors and omissions policies.

PENSION AND HEALTH

The company must contribute six percent of "gross compensation" paid to an employed writer to the pension plan, and four percent to the health fund. Such contributions are not required with respect to amounts paid a writer in a literary purchase deal.

Moreover, pension plan and health fund contributions are not payable on Article 15 and Article 51 payments (residuals, certain additional minimum compensation and supplemental markets payments). No pension and health fund contributions are required upon compensation in excess of $150,000 in connection with a single theatrical motion picture.

In the case of a writer who works through a loan-out company (see the chapter on Taxes), the loan-out company is initially responsible for the contributions, but the production company is obligated to reimburse the loan-out upon proof of payment.

CREDITS

Form

Writing credit can be given only in the technical forms authorized by Theatrical and Television Schedule A of the MBA. In the theatrical area, the standard credits are "screenplay by," "story by" and "written by" (which subsumes the screenplay and story credits).

For television programs, the standard credits are "teleplay by," "story by" and "written by." In addition, a writer entitled to separated rights with respect to a television series or serial may be given a continuing credit in the form "created by," or, in some circumstances, "developed by." Writers employed in the additional capacity of story editor for an established episodic series or serial may receive credit in the form "story editor," "story consultant" or "story supervisor."

The Guild requirements concerning form of credit apply only to unexploited literary material, not to source material.

Credits on Screen

The writing credits on the main title of a theatrical motion picture must appear on a title card immediately preceding the cards on which appear credit to the producer, if the credit to the producer immediately precedes that of the director. Otherwise, the card on which writing credits appear must immediately precede that of the director. The writing credits on the print of a television program must appear immediately prior to or following the director's credit.

In general, the writing credits on screen must be in the same size and style of type as the credits to the producer and director. The writing credit must also receive parity of time on screen.

Credits in Advertising and Publicity

Writing credit must be given in most publicity and advertising in connection with a motion picture or television program whenever the producer or director is mentioned, and generally in the same size and style of type. Where a production or presentation type of credit is given to a director or producer (such as "A Sam Jones Production" or "A Sam Jones Presentation") in advertising for a theatrical motion picture, the writing credit receives special treatment in terms of size and style of type relative to the main (artwork) title and the producer and/or director credits.

Pseudonyms

A writer for a theatrical motion picture who is guaranteed payment of less than $125,000 may elect to receive credit in a reasonable pseudonym. In television employment, the writer may use a pseudonym if he or she is paid less than three times the applicable minimum. In either case, the right to use the pseudonym must be invoked within specified time limits.

Caveat: The foregoing discussion is not a substitute for the actual text of the MBA and is intended only as a general overview. If the reader has any questions regarding interpretation of the MBA, or as to the duties or responsibilities of WGA members, he or she should consult an attorney or call the WGA Legal Department. Any interpretations herein are those of the author and do not necessarily represent the views of the Guild.

HIGHLIGHTS OF THE 1981 AMENDMENTS TO THE WGA BASIC AGREEMENT

Term: March 2, 1981–February 28, 1985

Compensation increases (Screen and Television)

Effective March 2, 1981 (retroactive)	12%
Effective July 1, 1982	12%
Effective July 1, 1983	11%
Effective July 1, 1984	9%*

*In "Long Form" Television (over 60 minutes)—an additional 4-percent premium effective July 1, 1984

"Going Rate and Bonus" concept eliminated.

Examples	*Old MBA*	*Now*	*Effective 7/1/84*
High-Budget Screenplay	$26,326	$36,656	$40,000
Network Prime Time			
30 min. Story Option Teleplay	6,739	9,384	10,229
60 min. Story Option Teleplay	9,972	13,885	15,135
90 min. Story Option Teleplay	13,477	18,765	21,204
120 min. Story Option Teleplay	17,546	24,431	27,607
One-Hour Variety	3,614	5,032	5,486
One-Hour Daytime Serial			
Weekly Package	9,139	12,725	13,870
Script Fee	905	1,261	1,374

Pension and Health

Increase in pension contribution from 5 percent to 6 percent effective March 2, 1982.

Ceiling on contributions in screen increased from $100,000 to $150,000.

Productions for Pay-TV and Video Cassettes/Video Discs

Initial compensation: 100 percent of free-TV minimums

2 percent of accountable receipts (plus pension and health) after recoupment based on $1,000,000 per hour in tape and $1,250,000 per hour in film (recoupment scaled proportionately downward for programs paying less than network prime-time minimum and proportionately upward on overscale contracts).

Recoupment figures increase 12 percent on July 1, 1982, 11 percent on July 1, 1983, and 9 percent on July 1, 1984. Grosses from video cassettes and video discs are included in accountable receipts from the first dollar.

Instructional and Informational Material
Writers of instructional and informational material for video cassette/video discs in the home market now covered.

Improved Coverage
Previously, WGA had three separate freelance agreements: the Freelance Film MBA with the Majors, an inferior Network MBA and an inferior Network Documentary MBA. These three documents have now been merged into a single document with uniform, industry-wide application. As a result, negotiations which were formerly the exclusive province of the networks (e.g., serials, variety, quiz, documentary) will henceforth be subject to industry-wide bargaining.

Non-Discrimination
A three-part program (emphasizing minority writers) consisting of:
1. A study of patterns of minority employment.
2. A script submission program.
3. A training program for neophyte writers.

Travel Insurance
Ordinary travel: increased from zero to $150,000
Air travel: increased from $50,000 to $250,000
Helicopter: increased from $50,000 to $350,000

Merchandising (Screen)
Expanded to include payment of 5 percent of gross receipts from sale of photo novels and comparable items.

Writing Teams (Screen)
Company may no longer split minimum between two writers *assigned* by company to collaborate. Each must receive full minimum.

Payment (Screen)
Automatic interest if writer not paid within seven days.

Paperback Novelization (Screen)
Company may no longer charge for use of the logo and title more than one-sixth of the gross monies payable to the writer when the writer makes the deal.

Turnaround (Screen)
Company may no longer capriciously prevent writer from re-acquiring unproduced original material. A writer's right to re-acquire original material subject to the 1981 MBA commences after five years (reduced from seven).

Rewrite of Original Screenplay (Screen)
Original writer has right to do first rewrite.

Credits (Screen)
Writer receiving less than $125,000 (formerly $75,000) has unilateral right to use pseudonym.
If a producer or director receives an oversize credit in a quotation from a review in advertising, writer is entitled to parity.

Improved arbitration procedures including Guild access to print of film. Participating writers to receive final shooting script automatically.

Allocation of Hyphenate Salary (Television)

Not less than 50 percent of the salary of a "two-hatted" hyphenate must be allocated to writing services—enhances hyphenate's pension benefits and increases income to health fund.

Right to View Cut (Screen and Long-Form Television)

All participating writers have right to view final director's cut.

Freelance Access (Television)

On episodic series, company must interview one freelance writer for each episode unassigned at time of network order.

Separation of Rights (Television)

Period of company's exclusive television rights reduced from four to three years on 30-minute, 60-minute and topical long-form original material.

Comedy-Variety (Television)

Establish limitation on duration of writer's services on a special. Increase in third run residual from 50 percent to 75 percent.

Quiz & Audience Participation

Writers of questions and answers for quiz and audience participation programs now covered on industry-wide basis.

Daytime Serials (Television)

Two weeks paid vacation per year for associate writers.

Immediate increase in minimums for long-term story projections of up to 114 percent.

Established minimum compensation for writer substituting for head writer and for breakdowns.

Improved flashback provisions.

MOTION PICTURE AGREEMENTS

Nicholas LaTerza, Esq.

LITERARY OPTION/PURCHASE AGREEMENT

An initial step in the development of a motion picture often involves the acquisition by the producer of the right to use an existing novel, screenplay, play, story, song (or some other "literary property") as the basis of the proposed film. Since at this stage of production, the producer is uncertain whether he will be able to obtain financing for the picture or whether he will be able to interest a suitable director, cast members or other "above the line" creative elements, he will want to minimize his investment. Therefore, instead of purchasing the motion picture rights to a literary property, he will merely obtain an option to purchase these rights. An option is the right given by an owner of property to a prospective purchaser to buy the property at a given price for a certain fixed period of time. The contractual provisions discussed in this article are drawn from a modern "short form" literary option/purchase agreement. ("Long form" agreements, with much more detailed provisions are not

Nicholas LaTerza, Esq., is an associate with the law firm of Manatt, Phelps, Rothenberg & Tunney, specializing in the area of theatrical motion pictures and television. Previously, he was with the law firm of Kaplan, Livingston, Goodwin, Berkowitz & Selvin, and clerked for the Honorable Jessie W. Curtis at the Federal District Court in Los Angeles. He is also currently an adjunct professor of law at Southwestern University Law School, where he teaches copyrights. He earned B.A. and M.A. degrees in English literature at Villanova University and received his J.D., cum laude, at the University of Toledo Law School.

uncommon, although their use within the industry has declined over the past few years.)

Literary Option/Purchase Agreement

As of (Date)

Dear Sirs:

This will confirm the agreement between the undersigned, _____ ("Purchaser"), and you ("Owner") with respect to the literary work entitled _____ (which, together with the title, themes, contents and characters, and all translations, sequels, adaptations and other versions thereof, whether now existing or hereafter created, is hereinafter called the "Property"), written by _____ ("Author"), published by _____ ("Publisher") on or about, in the United States and registered for copyright in the name of in the United States Copyright Office, registration number, as follows:

The foregoing introductory paragraph identifies the parties involved (indicating that throughout the text of the agreement they will be referred to as "Purchaser" or "Producer" and "Owner" or "Author," respectively) and the property to be acquired, including specific references to the publisher of the work (if previously published) and the copyright owner and identification number. Often specifically indicated is that the rights being acquired include rights in all elements of the work (i.e., the plot, title, themes, contents, characters, translations and adaptations).

1. In consideration of the sum of _____ (receipt of which you hereby acknowledge) you hereby grant to Purchaser a one year exclusive and irrevocable option to purchase all motion picture, television and allied rights (as specified in Paragraph 4 hereof) in the Property (the "Rights"). The initial option period shall commence on

_____ and may be extended to and including _____ by the payment to you of an additional _____ at any time prior to expiration of the initial option period. Purchaser may further extend the option period to and including _____ by the payment to you of an additional _____ at any time prior to _____. During the initial option period and extensions thereof, Purchaser shall have the right to engage in preproduction with respect to motion pictures and/or other productions intended to be based on the Property.

PARAGRAPH 1: This paragraph specifies the amount paid for the option and the length or term of the option period. Although deals of this type vary widely, the option payment is usually a relatively small percentage (between 5 percent and 15 percent) of the purchase price. The option term may also vary, but typical provisions include a one-year option term, with the right to extend for one or two additional one-year periods, subject to the purchaser's payment of an additional sum prior to the expiration of the prior option period. Often the extension payment is the same amount as the initial option price, although it may be less.

2. If Purchaser exercises its option, the _____ aforesaid payments with respect to the option will apply toward and be credited against the purchase price of the Rights, which shall be _____ payable upon the earlier of exercise of the option or the date of the commencement of principal photography of the "Picture" (as hereinafter defined). The option, if exercised, shall be exercised by written notice to you and payment to you of _____ less the credited option payments upon exercise of the option or commencement of principal photography of the first motion picture based upon the Property, whichever earlier occurs, at any time prior to the expiration of the option period as extended.

PARAGRAPH 2: The option payments themselves (including the initial and extension payments, if any) may or may not be applicable toward the ultimate purchase price; however, it is common for the initial option price (but not the extension payments) to be applied toward the purchase price, if the option is exercised. If the extension payment is applicable toward the purchase price (as in this agreement), the producer would always prefer to extend the option rather than exercise it, unless of course, he is ready to start production, in which case he will usually be required to exercise the option and pay the purchase price.

In the event the option is not exercised, the owner of the rights, of course, keeps the option money and all rights in the property as well. Typically, during the period in which the producer has an option to buy the property, he also has the right to engage in "pre-production" of the movie. This right is necessary in order that the producer may secure financing or the execution of agreements regarding the services of the creative elements to be utilized in the production. The purchaser may also retain the services of a writer during the option period to develop the property into a screenplay on which the picture will be based. However, once principal photography commences, most agreements, as noted above, provide that the option will be deemed exercised and that the purchase price becomes payable.

3. You shall be entitled to the following payments in addition to the purchase price subject to the occurrence of the conditions specified:

(a) If the first motion picture based on the Property (the "Picture") is a television motion picture (including a so-called "novel for television," "mini-series," "movie of the week" or other "long-form" television production, but excluding a television series or serial or an episode or aggregate of episodes thereof) the length of which exceeds two hours of broadcast time, an additional one-time payment of _____ for each full half-hour of broadcast time by which the length of such television motion picture exceeds two hours, payable within 30 days after initial broadcast if broadcast on network television, or within 120 days after initial broadcast if otherwise broadcast;

PARAGRAPH 3: In addition to the purchase price, the owner will often bargain successfully for a bonus to be paid if and when his literary property is actually exploited. The amount of the bonus will often depend upon the medium of exploitation.

PARAGRAPH 3(a): This paragraph provides for a bonus in the event a television mini-series is produced. Typically, at the present time, the bonus for a movie for television is $20,000. The time of payment of the bonus is also a consideration, and an owner would normally request the payment be made within ten days of the commencement of principal photography. Of course, the owner may have entered into this agreement on the basis that purchaser was producing a theatrical motion picture. In this case, owner would want a provision in the agreement making it clear that purchaser had no right to produce a television motion picture or mini-series.

(b) If the Picture is produced as and intended to be a television motion picture, but is placed in general theatrical release in the Domestic Territory before and/or after its initial television exhibition in the Domestic Territory, a one-time payment of _____ payable within 90 days after the first such general theatrical release. If the Picture is produced as and intended to be a television motion picture, but is placed in general theatrical release in the Foreign Territory before and/or after its initial television exhibition in the Foreign Territory, a one-time payment of _____ payable within 90 days after the first such general theatrical release. As used herein, "Domestic Territory" means the United States of America and, if Purchaser so elects in its sole discretion, Canada, and "Foreign Territory" means the world outside of the Domestic Territory. As used herein, "general theatrical release" means the exhibition of the Picture in motion picture theaters pursuant to an overall pattern of distribution of the Picture throughout the applicable territory. General theatrical release shall not include, and no payment shall be due under this subparagraph with respect to: (i) exhibition of the Picture where the audience does not pay an admission or similar charge to view same, or (ii) so-called "non-theatrical" exhibition, or (iii) isolated or limited exhibition, including, by way of illustration, exhibition at film festivals or at screenings for distributors or members of the television or motion picture industries, or limited exhibition for award consideration purposes;

(c) If the Picture is produced as and intended to be a theatrical motion picture, and in fact is placed in general theatrical release in the Domestic Territory prior to its initial exhibition on television in the Domestic Territory, an additional sum equal to the difference between _____ and the aggregate of all sums theretofore paid by Purchaser under this agreement (excluding the _____ payment, if any, for the second extension of the option period), payable within 90 days after such general theatrical release;

PARAGRAPH 3(b) and (c): The foregoing payments, similar to those set forth in subparagraph (a), are by way of bonuses in the event that the property is utilized as the basis for a motion picture, eventually exhibited theatrically, whether or not the picture, as initially produced is intended for theater exhibition.

(d) If Purchaser produces or causes to be produced a sequel motion picture based on the Property (as hereinafter defined), the following additional sums:

(i) if the sequel is produced as and intended to be a television motion picture, _____, payable upon commencement of principal photography, plus a one-time payment of _____ for each full half-hour by which the length of such sequel motion picture exceeds two hours of broadcast time, payable within 30 days after initial broadcast if broadcast on network television, or within 120 days after initial broadcast if otherwise broadcast;

(ii) If such sequel motion picture is produced as and intended to be a theatrical motion picture, and in fact is placed in general theatrical release in the Domestic Territory prior to its initial exhibition on television in the Domestic Territory, _____ (less any sum paid under subparagraph 3[d][i]), payable within 90 days after such general theatrical release;

(iii) A "sequel" means a motion picture or television production (other than the Picture, and other than a program which is an episode of a television series or television serial) which (1) includes as principal characters one or more of the characters which are principal characters in the Property and which have appeared as principal characters in a prior production produced hereunder based on the Property, and (2) which depicts such characters as participating in events which are different from those in which such characters participated in the Property or any prior production produced hereunder based on the Property, or any remake of such prior production, and (3) which contains a plot and storyline substantially different from that in the Property or any such prior production or remake thereof. A segment of any "mini-series," "novel for television," or other similar "long-form" television production, or of a regular television series, shall not be deemed a sequel hereunder;

(e) If Purchaser produces or causes to be produced a remake motion picture based on the Property (as hereinafter defined), the following additional sums:

(i) If the remake is produced as and intended to be a television motion picture, _____, payable upon commencement of principal photography, plus a one-time payment of _____ for each full half-hour by which the length of such remake motion picture exceeds two hours of broadcast time, payable within 30 days after initial broadcast if broadcast on network television, or within 120 days after initial broadcast if otherwise broadcast;

(ii) If such remake motion picture is produced as and intended to be a theatrical motion picture, and in fact is placed in general theatrical release in the Domestic Territory prior to its initial exhibition on television in the Domestic Territory, _____ (less any sum paid under subparagraph 3[e][i]), payable within 90 days after such general theatrical release;

(iii) A "remake" means a motion picture or television production (other than the Picture, and other than a program which is an episode of a television series or television serial) which includes substantially the same characters in substantially the same plot and storyline as any production based on the Property previously produced hereunder. The remake of a sequel as hereinabove defined shall be a remake hereunder;

(f) If Purchaser produces or causes to be produced a regular television series (i.e., other than a "mini-series," "novel for television" or similar multi-part production) which is based on the Property, and which features as a principal character a person who appears as a principal character in the Property, and which is broadcast on a national television network within the United States during prime-time on a one episode per week or less frequent basis, the following royalty for each new program of such series which is produced and broadcast: for a one-half-hour program, _____; for a one-hour program, _____; for a 90-minute program, _____; for a program longer than 90 minutes, _____. For each of the second through sixth runs of such program in the United States and Canada, Purchaser shall pay an additional sum equal to 20% of the applicable royalty; no further sum shall be payable with respect to the seventh or any subsequent runs of any such program. A "run" shall be defined in accordance with the definition of "run" in the 1977 Writers Guild of America/ Producers Basic Agreement. Initial run royalty payments under this subparagraph shall be made within 30 days after the initial broadcast of the program involved, or in the case of reruns, within 120 days after broadcast;

(g) If Purchaser produces or causes to be produced a "spin-off" regular television series (as hereinafter defined), Purchaser shall pay royalties in accordance with the terms and conditions of the immediately preceding subparagraph, except that the amount of such royalty payments shall be equal to 50% of the applicable amount set forth therein. A "spin-off" television series shall mean a regular television series (i.e., other than a "mini-series," "novel for television," or other multi-part television production) which features as a principal character a character who appears as a principal character in the Property and as a character in a previously produced and broadcast television series of the kind set forth in the immediately preceding subparagraph, and which series is broadcast on a national television network within the United States during prime-time on a one episode per week or less frequent basis.

PARAGRAPH 3(d), (e), (f) and (g): The seller of the rights will usually attempt to bargain for specific payments, in addition to the payments due if a theatrical motion picture is produced based on the work, in the event that the producer later produces a television movie, mini-series or other long-form TV production, or conventional series or series "spin-off" based on the property. In addition, the seller will attempt to secure a promise of a specific payment in advance, in the event any motion picture sequel or remake of the original picture based on the property is produced. The compensation for sequels and remakes is usually expressed in some percentage of the compensation which will be payable on exercise of the option and out of profits of the initial production (including fixed compensation, deferments and profit participations, if any). Although this compensation is specifically bargained for and may vary from agreement to agreement, the compensation for remakes is often between twenty-five percent and thirty-five percent of the original compensation, while for sequels it may be as high as fifty percent. The compensation for a television sequel or remake may likewise be included and is very often expressed as a fixed sum (usually no more than ten to twenty-five percent of the original purchase price) for a two-hour TV movie, with additional pro rata payments for more lengthy long-form or mini-series programs.

Finally, agreements of this type will often include a schedule for payments in the event that a television series or series "spin-off" is produced based on the work. These payments will usually be expressed in terms of the length of the series program, with a specific sum payable for each half-hour show, hour show, and each show longer than one hour. These sums are specifically bargained for, but the sum payable per show is significantly less than the sum payable for a TV movie, since the budget for an individual television series episode usually cannot accommodate a large payment for the original owner of the underlying work.

Regarding series compensation, there will usually be included provisions regarding compensation payable for reruns. Usually, the owner will receive twenty percent of the episodic royalty for each of the first five reruns and nothing thereafter.

(h) A sum equal to 5% of any "net profits" derived from the Picture and each sequel motion picture as hereinabove defined and from a regular television series (other than a "spin-off") for which royalties are payable to you hereunder; and a sum equal to 2½% of any "net profits" derived from each remake motion picture as hereinabove defined and from a "spin-off" regular television series for which royalties are payable to you hereunder. "Net profits" shall be defined, accounted for and paid according to Exhibit A if the Picture is produced as and intended to be a theatrical motion picture, or Exhibit B if the Picture is produced as and intended to be a television motion picture, or Exhibit C if the first production hereunder is a regular television series. The net profit definition applicable to any subsequent production hereunder in connection with which you are entitled to a percentage of net profits shall be Purchaser's then standard definition, as of the time of commencement of principal photography, for the type of production involved.

PARAGRAPH 3(h): Here, the seller has secured a profit participation, i.e., an actual percentage of the "net profits" from the exploitation of the picture. Net profit participations are quite common. The participation may at times be expressed as a share of the gross proceeds generated by the picture. However, the "gross" participation is somewhat rare, normally accorded only to the owners of a property thought to have extraordinary promise.

Note that net profit definitions relating to theatrical and television motion picture and series exploitation would be attached as exhibits to this agreement. The precise definition of "net profits" is rather significant. Although there are customary definitions utilized through the industry, the definition is usually a significant bargaining point which is often heavily negotiated. An extensive treatment of net profit definitions is beyond the scope of this article; however, certain general observations may be made.

Each major studio utilizes a standard, rather exhaustive, net profit definition, perhaps several pages in length and which enumerates in detail the various costs to be deducted from gross receipts before "net profits" will be deemed earned. Where the producer acquiring the property is an independent producer unaffiliated with a major studio, he will usually provide that the definition of net profits applicable to the agreement will be the same definition which he receives from his financiers and/or distributor (usually a major or mini-major). Owners will usually attempt to exclude from their net profit definitions any deductions attributable to "over-budget penalties" and "cross-collateralization," or "abandonment charges," described below.

The definition of net profits between the producer and the studio will usually provide that if the picture goes over budget an additional amount (usually equivalent to the amount that the picture went over budget) will be charged as an expense to the picture, thus reducing net profits. Since a writer has no control over production costs, it is unfair for the writer to be subject to this overbudget penalty.

Producer's agreements with major studios are often "multi-picture" deals and provide that the losses from one picture made by the producer at that studio can be charged against the profits of other pictures made by the producer under the overall agreement. More than a few writers who have had successful pictures have ended up with no profits because an earlier picture, with which they had no connection, lost money for the same studio and producer. Any reference to such a cross-collateralization provision, as it affects the producer, should be deleted from a writer's net profit definition.

Producers may have more than one project in development at a given studio. Of the many projects which get started in development, only a few make it to the screen. The others are "abandoned." Sometimes, the studio's agreement with the producer will provide that the development costs associated with abandoned projects will be charged against the profits of a completed and successful motion picture. Again, the writer's profit participation should not be diminished due to the costs of someone else's abandoned projects.

In the event there is no single financier or distributor, the independent producer/purchaser will usually provide for a definition of net profits similar to that utilized by the majors. Net profits will be expressed in terms of the total gross revenues generated from the exploitation of the picture, less all the costs incurred in producing and distributing the picture. These costs usually include all production costs, distribution costs and fees, interest and financing charges incurred in financing the film and a small percentage (between five percent and fifteen percent) of the negative cost of the picture, which is payable to the producer as an overhead charge.

Authors with profit participations will usually attempt to include in the agreement the so-called "most favored nations" clause. A provision of this type requires that the profit-participant writer receive a no less favorable net profit definition than any other profit participant in the picture. If, in an agreement with a major star, the producer-purchaser of the rights accords a definition more favorable to the star than contained in the writer's agreement, the writer will be entitled to the same definition as the star when his profits are computed, regardless of how profits are defined in (the writer's) agreement. On the other hand, the writer may, himself, secure a very favorable net profit definition. If an actor or director who is a profit participant bargains successfully for a "most favored nations" clause, he will get the benefit of the writer's definition. For this reason, producers are loath to give a writer (usually the first creative party involved in the project) a net profit definition that he or she cannot afford to give to the actors and director, who will almost always be hired later on and who, of course, will also be asking for "most favored nations" treatment.

4. Upon exercise of the option, Purchaser shall own, exclusively and forever, throughout the universe, all rights in the Property not expressly reserved to you in Paragraph 5 hereof, including without limitation the following: all motion picture rights, all television rights, (except live television rights reserved under Paragraph 5 hereof), and all allied and incidental rights, including without limitation sequel and remake rights, music publishing rights, soundtrack album rights, merchandising rights, and promotional and advertising rights (including without limitation the right to broadcast, over radio, television, and all other media, advertisements with respect to productions produced hereunder, and also including 7,500 word synopsis and excerpt publication rights). The rights herein granted include the right to distribute, transmit, exhibit, broadcast, and otherwise exploit all productions produced pursuant to this agreement by means of any and all media and devices whether now known or hereafter devised, and in any and all markets whatsoever. Purchaser may in its discretion make any and all changes in, additions to, and deletions from the Property. Purchaser may use Author's name, likeness, and biographical material in and in connection with the exploitation of the rights granted under this agreement. Nothing contained in this agreement shall be construed as requiring Purchaser to exercise or exploit any of the rights granted to or acquired by Purchaser under this agreement.

PARAGRAPH 4: In some instances, the purchaser may, upon exercise of the option, acquire all rights in the property. More usually, the purchaser will acquire the right to produce and exploit theatrical and television motion pictures based on the property. In addition, the purchaser will also acquire certain so-called "allied and incidental rights" which are needed to exploit the picture itself and all "subsidiary rights" in the film (which include primarily novelizations, soundtrack albums and merchandising). Novelization rights will generally not be granted if the work itself is an existing novel. The purchaser will obtain the right to advertise and promote the motion picture in all media and to publish synopses of the work, usually within a 7,500-word limitation, which are intended to promote the picture. The prior publisher of the work (if any) will usually execute a release permitting the producer to exercise these limited publication rights. However, major publishers have recently added to such "releases" a provision expressly forbidding the exercise of such publication rights that would compete with their commercial exploitation of the work as a publication.

Agreements of this type usually also include a provision that relieves the producer from having any actual obligation to produce or distribute any work based on the property, even if the rights are acquired upon exercise of the option. Finally, the purchaser will obtain the right to revise or rewrite the property as he sees fit, without the owner/author's permission. The producer is generally the person with the final say over the creative aspects of the production, and it is rare indeed for the owner/author of a property to bargain successfully for creative control in the picture to be produced based on the property.

5. You reserve the following rights in the Property, subject however to the terms and conditions set forth below, and it being understood and agreed that the rights reserved by you shall not relate to or include any adaptation, version, revision of, or change in, the Property made by or with the authorization of Purchaser:

(a) All publication rights in the Property (except the limited publication rights granted to Purchaser for advertising, promotion, and exploitation purposes as set forth in Paragraph 4 above); and

PARAGRAPH 5(a):Where the property is an existing book, the owner must of course retain the right to publish this book. The purchaser will be granted no interest in that publication. If the property is an original screenplay, it is customary for the writer to have the right to publish the screenplay (for whatever that's worth). However, the producer will want the right to publish a novelization based on the final screenplay. Assuming this deal is covered under the WGA, the provisions concerning novelization in the MBA will apply. These provisions are discussed in the chapter on the WGA Minimum Basic Agreement.

(b) Live television rights, legitimate stage rights, and radio rights (except the limited radio rights granted to Purchaser for advertising, promotion, and exploitation purposes as set forth in Paragraph 4 above). You agree not to exercise, or to authorize or permit the exercise of, or to sell, license, or otherwise dispose of any of the reserved live television rights, legitimate stage rights, or radio rights referred to in this subparagraph until after the expiration of the "holdback period" as hereinafter defined. If the first production produced by Purchaser under this agreement is a theatrical motion picture, then the holdback period shall mean the period commencing on the date of this agreement and expiring five (5) years after the first general theatrical release of said motion picture in the United States, or seven (7) years after the date of this agreement, whichever first occurs. If the first production produced by Purchaser under this agreement is a television motion picture or other television production other than a television series or a television serial, then the holdback period shall mean the period commencing on the date of this agreement and expiring five (5) years after the first national television broadcast of said television production in the United States, or seven (7) years after the date of this agreement, whichever first occurs. If the first production produced by Purchaser under this agreement is a television series or a television serial, then the holdback period shall mean the period commencing on the date of this agreement and expiring two (2) years after the date on which the last episode or program of said television series or television serial is initially telecast (i.e., telecast on a "first-run" basis), provided however that in no event shall said holdback period expire earlier than seven (7) years following the date of this agreement. At any time that you are entitled to exercise or dispose of any rights reserved under this subparagraph, Purchaser shall have the right to acquire such rights upon such bona fide terms and conditions as you are offered by and are prepared to accept from a third party at any time within 30 days after you notify Purchaser in writing (which you shall be obligated to do) of such terms and conditions. In that regard the "first-refusal" procedures set forth in Paragraph 9 hereof with regard to disposal of "recaptured rights" shall be applicable with respect to your disposal of reserved rights under this subparagraph.

PARAGRAPH 5(b): The right to exploit the property on live television or on radio (these rights are generally not worth very much) or on the legitimate stage (this right can be worth something) are typically reserved to the owner. In addition, the author will reserve the right to produce author-written sequel books based on the work and the right to exploit the sequel book by basing a motion picture, television program, etc., on it. The purchaser will usually require the seller to agree to a "holdback period" regarding the seller's rights (other than publication). The holdback period for all reserved rights is typically five years after the initial release of the picture, or seven years after the date on which the buyer exercises its option, whichever first occurs. In some instances, the holdback period may be shorter (such as three and five years, respectively).

Aside from rights in the work itself, the owner/author may reserve certain prerogatives affecting their exploitation. For example, an author may obtain a right of first negotiation and first refusal regarding his services as to sequels or remakes of any picture based on the property. Therefore, if the motion picture is successful enough to warrant a remake or sequel, the producers involved will have to deal with the original writer, at least in terms of an initial negotiation, in order to produce the later picture.

The purchaser may bargain for a right of "first negotiation and first refusal" regarding the standard reserved rights (i.e., live TV, radio and legitimate stage). This provision, if successfully bargained for, will give the purchaser the right to buy these reserved rights at terms no more favorable to the owner than terms which the owner is willing to accept from a third party. The owner retaining the rights will have the obligation to first present an offer to the purchaser and thereafter to inform the purchaser of any offer which he is willing to accept from a third party in order that the owner may exercise his first refusal rights.

6. You hereby represent and warrant that: (a) the Property was written solely by and is original with Author; (b) neither the Property nor any element thereof infringes upon any other literary property; (c) the production or exploitation of any motion picture or other production based on the Property will not violate the rights to privacy of any person or constitute a defamation against any person, nor will production or exploitation of any motion picture or other production based thereon in any other way violate the rights of any person whomsoever; (d) you own all rights in the Property as specified in Paragraph 4 hereof free and clear of any liens, encumbrances, claims or litigation, whether pending or threatened; (e) you have full right and power to make and perform this agreement; and (f) the Property has not previously been exploited as a motion picture, television production, play or otherwise than in book form, and no rights have been granted to any third party to do so. You shall indemnify Purchaser against any loss or damage (including reasonable attorneys' fees) incurred by reason of any breach or claim of breach of the foregoing representations and warranties. The term "person" as used herein shall mean any person, firm, corporation or other entity.

PARAGRAPH 6: The owner of the work is almost without exception required to give to the purchaser certain warranties, representations and indemnities regarding the work. The term "warranty," as customarily understood regarding consumer items, is similarly applicable in agreements of this type. Just as the maker of an appliance will give a warranty to a buyer to the effect that the appliance will be usable for the purpose for which it was intended, the seller of a literary work usually must make analogous promises to his buyer.

In the case of literary properties, the owner gives a warranty to the buyer to the effect that the work will be usable for the purposes for which the buyer intends it, i.e., to make movies based on the property without interference from either the seller or third parties. The customary warranties include promises that the property is original with the owner; it does not itself infringe any other works; and that a motion picture based on the property will not infringe the rights of any other person, including copyrights, and rights of privacy; and, that the work contains no libelous statements. The owner will also be required to warrant that he has the right to convey to the purchaser the rights being granted in the property and that the rights are not subject to any other claims, encumbrances or threatened litigation.

The owner will also almost always be required to indemnify the purchaser against any loss or damage which might occur as a result of a breach or failure of these warranties. An indemnity is an obligation on the part of the owner to pay over to the purchaser an amount equal to any loss or damage (usually including reasonable attorneys' fees) that the purchaser sustains in the event that the warranty is breached. For example, if after the movie is released, a third party sues the purchaser on the basis that the movie infringes the copyright in the third party's book, the owner granting the indemnity will be required to pay the cost of defending this action and any damages that the third party may be awarded in court or which the producer of the movie (purchaser) may have to pay to settle the claim short of litigation.

With respect to such indemnities, owners of literary properties will usually try to limit their liability to the sum they are paid for the work. Purchasers will usually resist the inclusion of a limiting provision of this sort in the agreement, since the potential liability of the producer will in all likelihood far exceed the purchase price for the rights. (It should be noted, however, that "errors and omissions" insurance in connection with the movie is almost always secured to the producer from claims of this type, other than those arising from willful misconduct. The owner should ask to be named as an additional insured under this policy.) The purchaser of the rights will usually similarly agree to indemnify the seller from any loss sustained as a result of infringing material appearing in the movie which is added to the property by the producer/purchaser.

7. Subject to applicable WGA requirements, Purchaser agrees to accord Author credit on the positive prints of the Picture, and of any other productions based on the Property, and in all paid advertising issued by Purchaser with respect thereto in which the screenwriter receives credit, substantially as follows:

(a) If the production has the same title as the title of the Property, such credit shall read: "Based on the book by _____."

(b) If the production does not have the same title as the Property, such credit shall read: "Based on the book '_____' by _____."

Author's screen credit shall appear on a separate card, and any credit accorded by Purchaser to Author shall appear in the same size of type in which the screenwriter's credit appears. Subject to the foregoing, all matters regarding such credits shall be determined by Purchaser in its sole discretion. Any casual or inadvertent failure by Purchaser, or any failure by any third party, to comply with the provisions of this paragraph shall not be deemed to be a breach of this agreement by Purchaser. In the event of a breach of Purchaser's obligations under this paragraph, it is expressly agreed that your sole remedy shall be to seek damages in a court of competent jurisdiction, and that in no event shall you be entitled to obtain any injunctive or other equitable relief or undertake any legal efforts to restrict Purchaser's right to exploit the Property.

PARAGRAPH 7: Generally, the Writers Guild controls all matters dealing with credit, and so the size, form and placement of credit are not subject to contractual agreement between the producer and the writer. However, where a producer acquires material for use as a basis for a motion picture (this is called "source material"), the producer may contractually agree to give the author credit, but only pursuant to certain prescribed forms. "Based on the book by _____" is such an approved form.

Note that purchaser has limited his liability only to money damages if the proper credits are not accorded to the owner/author. This limitation is essential since, if credits are improperly displayed or omitted entirely, the party to be credited could theoretically have a court enjoin the distribution and exploitation of the film entirely.

The provisions set forth above contain the primary "deal points" in agreements of this type. In addition, these contracts usually include certain "boilerplate" provisions as follows:

8. At Purchaser's request, you will execute or cause the execution of any and all additional documents and instruments reasonably necessary or desirable to effectuate the purposes of this agreement (including, without limitation, a short-form assignment covering Purchaser's acquisition of the rights in the Property, which assignment shall be in form satisfactory to Purchaser's counsel and suitable for recordation in the United States Copyright Office). You agree to secure, and maintain in force for the full term legally allowed, copyright protection throughout the world in and to the Property, and to prevent the Property from being injected into the public domain; you agree to renew and extend (or cause the renewal and extension of) the aforesaid copyrights in and to the Property, and you grant to Purchaser for the duration of said renewal period or period of extension the same rights as are granted to Purchaser hereunder during the original term of copyright with respect to the Property. If you shall fail to cause said renewal and/or extension to the fullest extent permitted by all applicable copyright laws, or shall otherwise fail to execute any reasonably necessary additional documents or instruments (as provided in the first sentence of this Paragraph 8), then in such event you irrevocably appoint Purchaser as your attorney-in-fact with the right and authority (but not the obligation) to execute and file all such additional documents and instruments in the name of and as agent for you, including without limitation any additional document or instrument which may be necessary to secure, protect, renew, or extend the aforesaid copyrights and/or any additional document or instrument which may be necessary to vest in Purchaser the aforesaid rights in the Property for the full term legally allowed by copyright.

PARAGRAPH 8: The seller/owner of the rights will usually agree to cause the execution of additional documents (e.g., short-form assignment agreements to be recorded in the Copyright Office) in order to facilitate protection of the rights granted to purchaser. The author also usually agrees to maintain the copyright in the published work in order not to jeopardize the rights which he has granted to the buyer. In this connection, the purchaser will usually obtain from the seller a "power of attorney," which will enable the purchaser himself to execute the necessary documents on behalf of the seller in order to protect the copyright in the event that the seller fails to do so.

9. All rights granted and agreed to be granted to Purchaser under this agreement shall be irrevocably vested in Purchaser and shall not be subject to rescission by you or any other party for any cause, nor shall said rights be subject to termination or reversion by operation of law or otherwise, except to the extent, if any, that the provisions of any copyright law or similar law relating to the right to terminate grants of, and/or recapture rights in, literary property may apply. If, pursuant to any such copyright law or similar law, you or any successor or any other legally designated party (all herein referred to as "the terminating party") becomes entitled to exercise any right of reversion, recapture, or termination (the "termination right") with respect to all or any part of the rights granted or to be granted under this agreement, and if the terminating party exercises said termination right with respect to all or part of said rights (the "recaptured rights"), then from and after the date on which the terminating party has the right to transfer to a third party all or part of the recaptured rights Purchaser shall have the first right to purchase and acquire the recaptured rights

from the terminating party. If the terminating party is prepared to accept a bona fide offer from a third party with respect to all or part of the recaptured rights, then in each such instance the terminating party shall make a written offer to Purchaser, specifying in such offer all of the terms and conditions which the terminating party is prepared to accept and the name of the third party who made the offer to the terminating party, and the terminating party shall offer Purchaser the right to enter into an agreement with the terminating party with respect to the recaptured rights on the aforesaid terms and conditions. Purchaser shall have thirty (30) days from the date of its receipt of such written offer within which to notify the terminating party of its acceptance of such offer (provided however that Purchaser shall not be required to meet any terms or conditions which cannot be as easily met by one person as another, including without limitation the employment of specified persons, etc.). If Purchaser shall acquire from the terminating party all or part of the recaptured rights, then the terminating party agrees to enter into appropriate written agreements with Purchaser covering said acquisition. If Purchaser shall elect not to purchase the recaptured rights from the terminating party, then the terminating party may dispose of said recaptured rights, but only to the aforesaid third party and only upon the terms and conditions specified in the aforesaid written notice given by the terminating party to Purchaser, it being understood and agreed that the terminating party may not dispose of said recaptured rights either to (1) any other proposed transferee or (2) upon terms and conditions which are more favorable to any transferee than the terms and conditions previously offered to Purchaser hereunder, without again offering to enter into an agreement with Purchaser (1) on the terms offered to such other transferee and/or (2) on such more favorable terms and conditions offered to said proposed transferee, whichever of (1) and/or (2) shall apply. Any such required offer made to Purchaser by the terminating party shall be governed by the procedure set forth in the preceding four sentences of this Paragraph 9. The unenforceability of any portion of this Paragraph 9 shall not invalidate or affect the remaining portions of this Paragraph 9 or this agreement. You acknowledge that in the event of a breach of any of Purchaser's obligations under this agreement, the damage (if any) caused to you thereby is not irreparable or otherwise sufficient to give rise to a right of injunctive or other equitable relief; and your rights and remedies in the event of a breach of this agreement by Purchaser shall be limited to the right, if any, to recover damages in an action at law.

PARAGRAPH 9: LIMITATION OF REMEDIES. Usually included and of major importance to the purchaser is the so-called "no rescission" clause, which provides that the rights granted irrevocably "vest" in (become the property of) the buyer, once he has exercised the purchase option and paid the purchase price, not including any deferments or participations payable out of profits from the picture. Provisions of this type typically limit the legal remedy of the party transferring the rights to money damages only in the event of a breach of the agreement (although the enforceability of such clauses has been questioned). This clause is crucial, since once large sums of money have been expended toward the production of a motion picture, the possibility that the seller of the rights can rescind the agreement, and thus terminate the entire project, is unacceptable to most financiers.

RECAPTURE AND TERMINATION UNDER THE COPYRIGHT ACT. The new Copyright Act of 1976 provides for certain rights of "recapture" of the copyright. The provisions are somewhat technical and beyond the scope of this article. Because of these provisions, agreements of this type will often include a specific clause giving the purchaser of the rights certain protection under the Copyright Act, i.e., a right of first refusal to re-acquire the rights granted in the event they are "recaptured" by the seller under terms of the Copyright Act.

> 10. Purchaser shall have the right to assign any or all of its rights under this agreement to any person or entity, but no such assignment shall relieve Purchaser of its obligations to you under this agreement. This agreement supersedes and replaces all agreements (oral or written) between you and Purchaser relating to the subject matter hereof and may be modified only pursuant to a written instrument executed by both parties hereto. This agreement shall be construed and enforced in accordance with the internal law of the State of California applicable to contracts negotiated, executed, and wholly performed within said State.

PARAGRAPH 10: ASSIGNMENT. Usually included is a clause providing for a right of assignment by either party of their respective rights under the agreement. This right of assignment is necessary to the purchaser in the event that he or she finds a production entity (i.e., a major) willing to take on financing and/or distribution of the production. However, the seller/owner will usually require the purchaser to remain obligated to make payments under the agreement, regardless of the party to whom an assignment is made. Thus, if the third party assignee fails to live up to the terms of the agreement the purchaser with whom the seller originally bargained will remain liable to make the payments due.

INTEGRATION, CONSTRUCTION AND MODIFICATION. Finally, a provision is usually included stating that the agreement is to be construed and enforced under the laws of the state in which it was negotiated. There is also usually a clause indicating that the agreement is fully "integrated," that is, that no other agreements or understandings regarding the subject matter of the agreement exist between the parties—previous deal memos or letter agreements become null and void. Finally, it is usually provided that any modification of the agreement will only be effective if it is undertaken by a written instrument signed by both of the parties—subsequent oral agreements will not change the terms of the contract.

11. All checks and notices from Purchaser to you shall be sent to you at the following address (checks shall be made payable to _____ as your agent):

All notices from you to Purchaser shall be sent to Purchaser at the following address:

Copies of all notices served on Purchaser by you shall be concurrently sent to:

Very truly yours,

By _____
        (Purchaser)

ACCEPTED AND AGREED TO:

_____
(Owner)

PARAGRAPH 11: This clause sets forth the address of the parties and manner in which notices and payments should be sent. Usually author's agent will be the party to whom payments and notices will be sent and the agent's receipt of same will be considered receipt on the part of the owner. Also, the notice provision may contain a clause indicating that the notice will be effective upon receipt or when mailed, depending on the standard form used.

WRITER'S SCREENPLAY AGREEMENTS

At some point in the development of a motion picture project, a producer will want to engage the services of a writer. The writer may be retained to write an original screenplay, an adaptation of a novel for which the producer has acquired motion picture rights, or to do a rewrite of an existing screenplay. Agreements regarding the services of a writer in the production of a screenplay for a motion picture will often contain many of the same provisions found in the literary/option purchase agreement, as discussed above, for example: rights granted and reserved; compensation (including initial compensation, deferments and profit participations); additional payments for sequel, remakes and TV productions (but generally only if the engaged writer has created the original story for the screenplay); warranties; and legal boilerplate. Those provisions have therefore been deleted from the screenwriter's agreement which is reproduced, in part, below. All agreements involving the services of a writer for a producer who is a signatory to the WGA are comprehensively governed by the terms of the WGA Basic Agreement, which is covered elsewhere in this book.

SCREENWRITER'S AGREEMENT

As of _____

Dear _____:

This will confirm the agreement between you [Writer's name] and _____ Productions, Inc. (hereinafter referred to as "we", "us" or the equivalent) with respect to your services as follows:

1. We hereby employ you to render your exclusive services for us as a writer in connection with our motion picture photoplay now entitled "_____" (the "Photoplay"), to write and deliver to us a first draft screenplay, and at our option, full and complete rewrite of said screenplay, and at our additional option, full and complete polish of said screenplay. The foregoing first draft screenplay, and rewrite and polish, if any, to be written by you hereunder, shall be based on an existing novel entitled _____, owned by us, and on such other material and ideas as we shall assign to you, and shall be written by you pursuant to our directions.

PARAGRAPH 1: A screenplay agreement will initially reference the parties involved and will also indicate specifically whether the author is undertaking a totally original screenplay (as opposed to one based on an idea provided by the owner), or an adaptation of a published or unpublished work, the rights in which are owned by the person retaining the writer's services.

2. The term of your employment hereunder shall consist of the following periods ("writing periods") during which you shall render your services hereunder in writing the literary material required of you hereunder and periods ("reading periods") during which we shall read and evaluate the literary material required of you hereunder, consult with you at such times and places we may reasonably designate, and notify you in writing or orally to make reasonable changes, revisions, deletions and/or additions in and to the literary material heretofore completed and delivered, which such changes, revisions, deletions and/or additions shall be made by you in the next succeeding writing period:

(a) The initial writing period, during which you shall complete and deliver to us the first draft screenplay shall commence upon a date to be designated by us, but in no event later than _____, 19xx, and shall continue thereafter for a period of ten (10) weeks.

(b) The initial reading period shall commence upon the completion and delivery to us of the first draft screenplay and shall continue thereafter for a period of three (3) weeks.

(c) If we exercise our option to require you to undertake a rewrite of the screenplay, the second writing period, during which you shall complete and deliver to us the rewrite, shall commence upon the conclusion of the initial reading period and shall continue thereafter for a period of four (4) weeks.

(d) The second reading period, if applicable, shall commence upon the completion and delivery to us of the rewrite and shall continue thereafter for a period of three (3) weeks.

(e) If we exercise our option to require you to undertake a polish of the screenplay, the third writing period, during which you shall complete and deliver to us, the polish shall commence at the conclusion of the second reading period and shall continue thereafter for a period of two (2) weeks.

It is agreed that time is of the essence hereof.

PARAGRAPH 2: A "start date" will be indicated and may be expressed as a specific date or as an outside date by which the purchaser of the services will have to notify the writer to begin rendition of the writing services required.

The development of a screenplay is usually undertaken in the following stages, which are specifically defined, and the minimum payments for which are established in the Basic Agreement:

(i) Initially, the writer will often produce a "treatment" which may be as short as ten or as long as forty pages and which sets forth in narrative form the basic plot, characters, milieu and major occurrences and locations to appear in the final screenplay. (In an adaptation, no treatment is called for since the novel will provide the foregoing elements.)

(ii) Next, the writer will produce a "first draft screenplay," fleshing out the treatment and creating dialogue, more specific characterizations and, to a certain extent, direction and blocking in terms of character movement, sequence of action and camera viewpoints.

(iii) The "final draft screenplay" is the culmination of the foregoing steps and usually represents, in the mind of the writer, the finished product.

(iv) If necessary, a "rewrite" of the screenplay may be undertaken by the writer, under the producer's direction, which would involve significant changes in the plot, story line or interrelationship of the characters in the screenplay.

(v) The final step is referred to as the "polish," which involves changes of less magnitude than those of the "rewrite" stage.

The period of the writer's services is usually expressed in terms of "writing periods" and "reading periods." The writer is usually given a specific period (say, twelve to sixteen weeks) within which to complete the first draft of the work (if the first stage is a treatment as opposed to a first draft screenplay this period may be shorter) for which he will receive a specific compensation. The compensation is usually paid one-half on commencement and one-half on completion of the specific component of the project involved. The employer/producer will then be given a reading period within which to evaluate the work and confer with the writer concerning its progress. The reading periods may be as short as two, but usually no more than four to six weeks.

The agreement may provide that, if the producer so chooses, the compensation agreed to be paid for that portion of the assignment will be deemed the total compensation, and the producer will not be required to utilize any additional services of the writer. Writers will normally attempt to bargain for a maximum compensation to be paid regardless of whether the employer exercises his option to require rewrites or polishes. In any event, however, the writer must receive the minimum Guild payment for each component he or she produces.

If, as here, the purchaser has retained the right to require a rewrite or a polish (or if the first stage was a treatment, an actual screenplay) based on the first draft submitted, then at the end of the first reading period, a second writing period will commence during which the writer, if the purchaser so requires, will complete the second step of the project. Thereafter, another reading period will commence, upon the expiration of which the producer may indeed have the right to require a second set of revisions or a polish on the project for additional compensation.

Agreements of this type usually include a specific provision requiring the writer to follow as closely as possible all of the directions of the producer, and to be available for consultations with the producer. Also usually included is a provision requiring the writer's exclusive services during the writing periods (although this provision is negotiable). Note that timely completion and delivery of the literary materials is deemed to be "of the essence" in this agreement. Thus, theoretically, if the writer fails to adhere strictly to the schedule, he will be in breach of the agreement.

4. All results and proceeds of your services hereunder shall be deemed a work-made-for-hire for us and we shall be deemed the author thereof, and we shall own all right, title and interest whatsoever therein including without limitation the entire copyright therein throughout the universe in perpetuity, with, among other things, the right to make any and all changes in the material written by you as we may desire.

PARAGRAPH 4: Employment agreements of this type invariably characterize the material to be written as a "work for hire" under the Copyright Act. Thus, the producer will be entitled to the copyright. (See the chapter on Copyright.)

The producer will usually require the writer to grant to the producer the right to change, revise and alter the work as the producer sees fit.

5. If it is determined pursuant to the Basic Agreement that you are entitled to credit, that credit shall be accorded as and to the extent required by the Basic Agreement. If you receive credit in connection with the Photoplay, we shall have the right to use your name, in a reasonable and customary manner, in connection with the promotion, advertising and exploitation of the Photoplay, including without limitation in connection with customary commercial tie-ups pertaining thereto.

PARAGRAPH 5: As with literary option/purchase agreements, the writer employed will be entitled to the credit prescribed by the Basic Agreement. With reference to credit, the producer will usually include a provision indicating that in the event the credit is not accorded as set forth in the agreement, the writer will be limited in his right to seek redress for this breach. The provision will usually preclude the writer from seeking injunctive relief, which could prevent distribution and exhibition of the picture if a court so ruled. The producer will usually agree to use its best efforts to cure any deficiency in the credit being accorded on the prints of the picture and will agree to require its distributors to be contractually bound to accord the required credit to the writer.

The production bonus and profit participations payable to the writer will often be expressed in terms of the credit he ultimately receives. Often, if the writer receives sole screenplay credit, he will receive a specific sum and perhaps a percentage of the net profits. If another writer participates in the project and thus screenplay credit is shared under the terms of the Basic Agreement, the first writer will typically get one-half of the original amount. If the first writer is rewritten to such an extent that he or she gets only "story by" credit, the first writer will receive an even smaller amount, or in some cases, no production bonus or profit participation at all.

Agreements of this type also will often grant to the producer the right to use the name of the writer in connection with the exploitation of the work produced, absent the bargained-for use of a pseudonym by the writer.

STANDARD FORM FREELANCE FILM TELEVISION WRITER'S EMPLOYMENT CONTRACT (UNIVERSAL)

STANDARD FORM FREELANCE FILM TELEVISION WRITER'S EMPLOYMENT CONTRACT

Agreement Dated _____ , Between **UNIVERSAL TELEVISION,** a division of Universal City Studios, Inc.,

hereinafter called "Producer" and _____ ,

hereinafter called "Writer" of _____ .

1. EMPLOYMENT: Producer employs the Writer to render services in the writing, composition, preparation and revision of the literary material described in Paragraph 2 hereof, hereinafter for convenience referred to as the "work." The Writer accepts such employment and agrees to render services hereunder and devote Writer's best talents, efforts and abilities in accordance with the instructions, control and directions of the Producer.

2. FORM OF WORK:

( ) Narrative synopsis; option for story and teleplay.
( ) Story   ( ) Rewrite.
( ) Story and teleplay   ( ) Polish.
( ) Teleplay   ( ) Format.
( ) Story; option for teleplay.
( ) Other material (described as _____).

The work is entitled _____

_____ (# _____)

and shall be suitable for motion picture intended primarily for television exhibition with a playing time of approximately _____ minutes. The work is based on, or, in the case of a rewrite or polish, is a rewrite or polish of: _____

Any option granted may be exercised by written notice to Writer within the maximum time permitted by the WGA Agreement.

3. DELIVERY: If the Writer has agreed to complete and deliver the work, any changes and revisions, or both, within a certain period or periods of time, then such agreement will be expressed in this paragraph as follows:

_____
_____

4. COMPENSATION: As full compensation for all services rendered and rights granted, and for all Writer's obligations, and conditioned upon Writer's full performance, Producer will pay Writer as follows:

(A) For writing the following forms of the work:

    (a) Format: $ _____
    (b) Narrative synopsis: $ _____
    (c) Story (less narrative synopsis
        payment, if any): $ _____
    (d) Teleplay: $ _____
    (e) Other: $ _____

If Writer's employment for one or more of the above forms of the work is optional, payment for that form of the work shall be made only if the applicable option is exercised.

(B) Advances for:

    (a) Television reruns: $ _____
    (b) Foreign telecasting: $ _____
    (c) Theatrical use: $ _____

No amount may be inserted in (a), (b) or (c) above unless the amount for story and teleplay in (A) above is at least twice the applicable minimum compensation under the WGA Agreement. Advances shall be paid concurrently with the last installment due under Subparagraph (C) below.

(C) Payment: All compensation for services shall be paid in accordance with the requirements of Article 13B of the WGA Agreement. If Writer is employed for a teleplay or story and teleplay, payment shall be made in the installments specified below upon delivery of each of the following forms of the work:

    (a) Story: $ _____
    (b) First draft teleplay: $ _____
    (c) Second draft teleplay: $ _____

If Producer has an option for teleplay, payments under subclauses (b) and (c) will be made only if Producer exercises that option.

(D) Reruns and foreign telecasts: If a photoplay based on the work is rerun on television in the United States or Canada, or is exhibited on foreign television, Producer shall pay Writer the minimum compensation prescribed therefor by the WGA Agreement, less any advance paid under Subparagraph (B) (a), or B(b).

(E) Theatrical Exhibition: If a photoplay based on the work is exhibited in theaters, as defined in the WGA Agreement, Producer shall pay Writer the additional sum of $_____ , less any advance paid under Subparagraph (B) (c).

(F) Separation of Rights: If Writer is entitled to Separation of Rights in the work under Article 16B of the WGA Agreement, Producer shall pay Writer for sequel photoplays the minimum amounts required therefor by the WGA Agreement.

(G) Minimum Payments: Payments under Subparagraphs 4 (D), (E) and (F) above shall be made only if, when and to the minimum extent required under the WGA Agreement. If story and/or teleplay credit is shared by Writer with one or more writers, then all the writers sharing such credit shall be considered a unit and shall participate equally and receive in the aggregate the applicable payments.

5. REPRESENTATIONS AND WARRANTIES: INDEMNITIES: Writer represents and warrants that the work shall be wholly original with Writer, except as to matters within the public domain, and shall not infringe upon or violate the rights of privacy of, or constitute a libel or slander against, or violate any common law or any other rights of, any person, firm or corporation. Writer shall hold Producer, and Producer's licensees and assigns and their officers, agents and employees, harmless from all liabilities, actions, suits or other claims arising out of the use by Producer of the work, and from reasonable attorney's fees and costs in defending against the same. The foregoing shall apply only to material furnished by Writer, and shall not extend to changes or additions made therein by Producer, or to claims of invasion of the privacy of any person unless the Writer knowingly uses the name or personality of such person or should have known, in the exercise of reasonable prudence, that such person would or might claim that his personality was used in the work.

Producer shall indemnify Writer to the same extent that Writer indemnifies Producer hereunder, as to any material supplied by Producer to Writer for incorporation into the work. The party receiving notice of any claim or action subject to indemnity hereunder shall promptly notify the other party. The pendency of any such claim or action shall not relieve Producer of its obligation to pay Writer any monies due hereunder and Producer shall not withhold such monies unless Producer has sustained a loss or suffered an adverse judgment or decree by reason of such claim or action.

6. MINIMUM BASIC AGREEMENT: This contract is subject to the Producer-Writers Guild of America 1981 Theatrical and Television Basic Agreement ("the WGA Agreement") and to the extent that the WGA Agreement is more advantageous to Writer, the terms of the WGA Agreement shall supersede and replace the less advantageous terms of this Agreement. Writer is an employee as defined by the WGA Agreement and Producer has the right to control and direct the services to be performed.

7. GUILD MEMBERSHIP: To the extent that such requirement may be lawful, Writer shall be a member of Writers Guild of America in good standing as required by the provisions of the WGA Agreement, and if Writer fails or refuses to meet such requirement, Producer shall have the right at any time thereafter to terminate this agreement.

8. RIGHTS: As Writer's employer, Producer shall own all rights in the work, except for rights that Producer is not permitted to acquire under the WGA Agreement. If Writer is entitled to Separation of Rights under the WGA Agreement, Producer shall have the right to acquire from Writer theatrical motion picture rights, merchandising rights and publication rights in the work, either separately or all together, for the minimum compensation and subject to the conditions prescribed in the WGA Agreement. Producer shall have the right to obtain copyright and renewals of copyright and other protection of the work. In Producer's sole discretion, Producer may use or not use the work and may make any changes in, deletions from or additions to the work. Producer shall have the right to assign this agreement or all or any part of the rights granted to Producer herein.

9. JOINT AND SEVERAL: If two or more persons are employed under this agreement, their obligations shall be joint and several, and their compensation shall be paid by separate checks payable in equal amounts and delivered to each of them.

10. FCA: Writer understands that, as to a television photoplay based on the work, it is a Federal offense, unless disclosed prior to broadcast to Producer or to the station or network which broadcasts the photoplay, to:

(A) Give or agree to give any member of the production staff, anyone associated in any manner with the photoplay, or any representative of the Producer, the station or network, any portion of Writer's compensation or anything else of value for arranging Writer's employment in connection with the photoplay.

(B) Accept or agree to accept anything of value, other than Writer's compensation under this agreement, to promote any product, service or venture on the air, or to incorporate any material containing such a promotion in the photoplay.

Writer is aware that Producer prohibits such conduct with or without disclosure, and any violation shall be a material breach and cause for dismissal.

11. NOTICES: A notice to Writer shall be given by delivery in person, or by mailing or telegraphing it, to Writer at Writer's above address or such other address as Writer may hereafter designate in writing; the date of such personal delivery, mailing or telegraphing shall be deemed the date of receipt.

12. STORY REVISION OPTION: If the work includes a story, Producer may require Writer, for minimum compensation under the WGA Agreement, to write a revision thereof in addition to those to which Producer is otherwise entitled under the WGA Agreement.

13. NAME AND LIKENESS: Producer shall have the right to use and permit others to use Writer's name and likeness for the purpose of advertising and publicizing the work, any photoplay based on the work, and, in connection therewith, any exhibitor or sponsor thereof, and any of said exhibitor's or sponsor's products and services, but not as an endorsement or testimonial.

14. QUALIFIED WRITER: Writer represents that he (is) (is not) a "qualified writer" as defined in Article 13B of the WGA Agreement.

Executed by the undersigned as of the above date.

UNIVERSAL TELEVISION,
a division of Universal City Studios, Inc.   (Producer)

By _____

_____

_____
                                    Writer

Social Security No. _____

TV-8(5)-A
Sing. Pict. Writer

Form 3128

YOUR HARDCOVER PUBLISHING AGREEMENT

Keith Korman

Your hardcover book agreement is in some ways the modern-day equivalent of Shylock's "pound of flesh": New York has become Shakespeare's Venice; authors have become the merchants and the goods. Instead of flesh, pages of prose are bartered for money. Essentially, a hardcover book contract is a grant of rights and a promise. As a writer you produce a book and own all rights to it; the minute it emerges from the typewriter the book is yours, unless it has been written after a contract has been negotiated and signed. When a publishing company takes over the responsibility of publishing your book, it does so only after you have granted it certain rights. In consideration for allowing it to publish your book, the publisher gives you money upon the conditions it sets forth. In addition you make a number of promises. Once you sign the contract and accept the money, you are bound by these promises.

Enter the flesh: Even the best endeavors coupled with the best intentions can crack under the heavy waves of the market place. Few institutions deal effectively with the individual, publishing included. Sometimes a writer is not able to fulfill his promises, and sometimes publishing companies are not able to live up to what they have promised. But ulti-

Keith Korman is a novelist and a literary agent at Raines & Raines Authors' Representatives in New York City. In June, 1980 Random House published his first novel, Swan Dive. Random House, Inc. is gratefully acknowledged for its permission to reprint their publishing agreement. In addition, Raines & Raines thanks Ellis Levine, Senior Counsel to Random House, Inc. for his objective and gentle consultation, the help free from motive.

mately the manuscript, the product, the book, has come from one head, one set of hands, one person's hopes and dreams, and the fortunes of marketplace war cascade bloodily around the contenders. I have chosen the Random House, Inc. contract because it is consistently better than average and because as a company, Random House is fairly representative of the publishing industry. Not on all counts, for each company has its own idiosyncracies. Publishing is a small business and, at most levels, is very personal. However, the book product lives or dies at the retail level. Therefore, we are talking about business and businessmen, not simply art and artisans.

Random House was owned by a conglomerate (RCA) and then, reversing the trend, was sold to an independent company (Newhouse Newspapers, a publishing empire). Both RCA and the Newhouse chain seem to realize that publishing, like all entertainment, is a gambling business, a risk business—accordingly they have taken the most sensible approach to their parental responsibilities by keeping a distance from the buying end of the industry, the editors' choices. Editors' choices are made basically on instinct; try to control the instinct, tamper with the unfathomable, and you can watch a publishing company self-destruct. Pleasure, pain, entertainment, and boredom live far away from an accountant's bottom-line columns. There is nothing clear-cut about the writing business; the production of shoes or toilet paper is more rational. People can argue forever about what makes a book good or bad. Few will do the same for toilet paper, deodorant, or toothpaste.

Like Milton's Lucifer, the writer may find that glory precedes a fall: The results of a signed contract may have no resemblance to what you expect.

It is best, therefore, to understand the contract. Each writer has his or her own clout in the marketplace, whether it be with the critics, the book-buying public or a handful of the faithful in Des Moines. Everyone thus gets a different deal—there are no unions, no guarantees—but not much censorship either, unless you work for the CIA.

In many cases an author never negotiates for himself. Those who do, without the assistance of an objective representative of some sort, generally are so thankful for the opportunity to get into print that it slips their mind who indeed *created* the product. Compliant authors hurt mostly themselves. So the more you know about your contract the better off you will be. Since I am not a lawyer, in no way do my comments imply or constitute legal counsel of any nature; this article is informational and my own opinion of the industry *only*.

ANALYSIS OF A CONTRACT

Below is the Grant of Rights (1.[a.] [i.—ix.]). Here the author grants to the Publisher the rights in certain geographic territories (usually the United States, its dependencies and Canada) *exclusively*. The publisher is also granted *non-exclusive* rights in the rest of the world, commonly known as an Open Market, where he can sell his own hardcover edition (but only in English) on a competitive basis with other world publishers. Rights in the British Commonwealth, the Republic of South Africa and the Irish Republic, are dealt with below in 1(b).

 RANDOM HOUSE, INC.

AGREEMENT made this   day of   , 19   between RANDOM HOUSE, INC. of 201 East 50th Street, New York, 10022 (referred to as the Publisher), and

whose address is

who is a citizen of   and resident of (state) (referred to as the Author and designated by the masculine singular pronoun)

WHEREAS the parties wish respectively to publish and have published a work (referred to as the work) of   provisionally titled

NOW, THEREFORE, they mutually agree as follows:

1. The author grants to the Publisher during the term of copyright, including renewals and extensions thereof:

Grants of Rights

a. Exclusive right in the English language, in the United States of America, the Philippine Republic, and Canada, and non-exclusive right in all other countries except the British Commonwealth (other than Canada), the Republic of South Africa, and the Irish Republic, to:

Sometimes an author will grant world rights to the publisher; a grant of world rights entitles the publisher to make any book deal in any form of license or sale throughout the world. Publishers generally ask for these rights when an author is not represented, knowing full well that few authors alone can dispose of foreign or translation rights without the necessary contacts and connections in the international publishing industry. Most agents have these contacts and almost always will reserve these world rights one hundred percent to the author.

i. Print, publish and sell the work in book form;

ii. License publication of the work (in complete, condensed or abridged versions) by book clubs, including subsidiaries of the Publisher;

In *i.* and *ii.* the author has granted the publisher the right to print and sell the work in book form; he has also allowed the publisher to license the work to book clubs, which if the author is lucky enough to get will be marvelous for the life of the book. Sometimes the book clubs want abridged or cut versions of an author's work. The author may not want anyone cutting or altering his or her work, so he or she may desire a provision giving the author approval rights, not to be unreasonably withheld, either over the granting of book club rights, or over any alteration to the book.

iii. License publication of a reprint edition by another publisher with the consent of the Author. The Author shall be deemed to have given consent if within twenty (20) days after the forwarding of written request he fails to notify the Publisher in writing of his refusal to consent;

This concerns the rights to license reprint rights to mass market paperback houses. Under this agreement, the consent of the author is required. Many publishers will grant the author this consent requirement, but few have it printed on their contract, as this one does.

iv. License publication of the work (in complete, condensed, adapted or abridged versions) or selections from the work in anthologies and other publications, in mail-order and schoolbook editions, as premiums and other special editions and through microfilm and with the Author's consent Xerox or other forms of copying;

This is standard. If an author is lucky enough to get into an Anthology, that's good. In the case of poetry, however, this should be reserved solely to the author. Many poets reap the most money from anthologies, not initial book sales.

v. License periodical publication including magazines, newspapers and digests prior to book publication;

This is also known as first periodical sale, or "first serial," such as a *prepublication* excerpt in *Playboy.* Custom has it that this is reserved one hundred percent to the author, but you have to ask to have the provision deleted.

vi. License periodical publication after book publication to the extent that any such right is available;

After book publication or "second serial": Good exposure, but there is not always that much money involved. Many publishers keep this right. Most agents and authors don't argue.

vii. License, subject to the approval of the Author, adaptation of the work for filmstrips, printed cartoon versions and mechanical reproduction;

Filmstrips and cartoons in children's books or coffee table books can be very valuable.

viii. License, without charge, transcription or publication of the work in Braille or in other forms, for the physically handicapped;

Obvious.

ix. For publicity purposes, publish or permit others to publish or broadcast (but not dramatize) by radio or television, without charge, such selections from the work as in the opinion of the Publisher may benefit its sale.

Sometimes you can limit selections for publicity to a certain number of words (e.g., 7,500). Grant of rights is now continued.

> b. Exclusive right to license in the English language throughout the British Commonwealth (other than Canada), the Republic of South Africa, and the Irish Republic, the rights granted in subdivision a. above, revocable by the Author with respect to any country for which no license or option has been given within eighteen (18) months after first publication in the United States.

> c. Exclusive right to license in all foreign languages and all countries, the rights granted in subdivision a. above, revocable by the Author with respect to each language or country for which no license or option has been given within three (3) years after first publication in the United States.

The publisher here has only eighteen months after the first publication in the United States to license or option publishing rights in these territories. If he has been sitting on these rights without exploiting them, they revert back to the author, so that the author may try to exploit these rights. The publisher has three years to set up deals for foreign language versions before the author can revoke foreign language rights. The author may wish to retain these rights from the outset.

> d. Exclusive right to use or license others to use, subject to the approval of the Author, the name and likeness of the Author, the work and the title of the work, in whole or in part, or any adaptation thereof as the basis for trademark or trade name for other products or for any other commercial use in connection with such other products.

This provision gives the publisher the right to use the author's name or likeness (e.g., photograph) or the title of the book or any portion of the book to help sell other products (this would give the publisher the right to license, for example, a Jim Fixx's *Complete Book of Running*-brand running shoe, a *World According to Garp* board game or a *Tale of Two Cities* T-shirt). Note that the provision says subject to the approval of the author. This is your minimum protection. Better yet, have the provision deleted.

Delivery of Satisfactory Copy

> 2. The Author agrees to deliver two complete copies (original and clean copy) of the manuscript of the work in the English language of approximately   words in length, satisfactory to the Publisher, together with any permission required pursuant to Paragraph 3, and all photographs, illustrations, drawings, charts, maps and indexes suitable for reproduction and necessary to the completion of the manuscript not later than

> If he fails to do so the Publisher shall have the right to supply them and charge the cost against any sums accruing to the Author. The complete manuscript shall include the following additional items

> If the Author fails to deliver the manuscript within ninety (90) days after the above date, or if any manuscript that is delivered is not, in the Publisher's judgment, satisfactory, the Publisher may terminate this agreement by giving written notice, whereupon the Author agrees to repay forthwith all amounts which may have been advanced hereunder.

Do yourself a big favor. Write the book you promised to write. Deliver it on time.

Very often the publisher is willing to wait through an artist's harder moments. They bought a book and they want it. Writing isn't always natural, and many publishers understand this. They can be very cooperative. If you need an extension on your deadline, ask for it. . . just don't let your contract run out.

Say you deliver your book on time, but the publisher then finds your work unsatisfactory. He turns down your book, terminates the agreement and demands his money back. A specification can be negotiated and added to this clause amending it to read: "If in the Publisher's judgment the manuscript is not satisfactory, the Publisher may terminate this agreement by giving written notice, whereupon the Author agrees to repay forthwith all amounts which may have been advanced hereunder *from the first proceeds upon sale of the work to another publisher.*" With this provision, the author does not have to repay the publisher out of his own funds. The second publisher pays the first publisher.

Caution: Publishers take this "satisfactory manuscript" clause very, very seriously. Many authors are not able to limit their obligations hereunder at all. In other cases, authors with sufficient clout can delete this provision altogether.

But if the clause remains and you don't deliver— WATCH OUT. Publishers have been known to hire collection agencies.

3. If the Author incorporates in the work any copyrighted material, he shall procure, at his expense, written permission to reprint it.

If you need permission to use excerpts from other writers' work, get them by all means. Sometimes this costs, sometimes it doesn't.

Publishers can supply permission forms. They can also be found in contract form books (go to the library). If the copyright holder wants you to pay a permission fee, you've got two choices: either forget about the material and don't use it, OR pay the fee. Sometimes you can negotiate downwards, but not often. Except in extraordinary cases, publishers expect you to pay for your permissions out of your advance. Budget yourself. In the case of an anthology or a book where a number of permissions are required, the author should attempt to secure an advance that takes into account the permission funds necessary. Or if possible, specify separately the amount of money needed for permissions.

4. a. The Author warrants that he is the sole author of the work; that he is the sole owner of all the rights granted to the Publisher; that he has not previously assigned, pledged or otherwise encumbered the same; that he has full power to enter into this agreement; that except for the material obtained pursuant to Paragraph 3 the work is original, has not been published before, and is not in the public domain; that it does not violate any right of privacy; that it is not libelous or obscene; that it does not infringe upon any statutory or common law copyright; and that any recipe, formula or instruction contained in the work is not injurious to the user.

A lot of promises are being made in this little paragraph. The author promises that he has not used a ghost writer; that no one else can lay claim to any rights granted to the publisher (he has not entered into a previous agreement with another publisher for any of the rights granted hereunder nor has he used the book as collateral on a loan, etc., or optioned the book to anyone else) and that it is an unpublished, original work. If the author has invaded anyone's privacy, or defamed anyone, or infringed a copyright, not only will the author be liable to those people, but he will be in breach of the agreement, giving the publisher the right to terminate the agreement and have the author pay for any damages suffered by the publisher due to this breach.

b. In the event of any claim, action or proceeding based upon an alleged violation of any of these warranties (i) the Publisher shall have the right to defend the same through counsel of its own choosing, and (ii) no settlement shall be effected without the prior written consent of the Author, which consent shall not unreasonably be withheld, and (iii) the Author shall hold harmless the Publisher, any seller of the work, and any licensee of a subsidiary right in the work, against any damages finally sustained. If such claim, action or proceeding is successfully defended or settled, the Author's indemnity hereunder shall be limited to fifty per cent (50%) of the expense (including reasonable counsel fees) attributable to such defense or settlement; however, such limitation of liability shall not apply if the claim, action or proceeding is based on copyright infringement.

If someone "claims" that your book has defamed him or invaded his privacy, or infringed his copyright, etc., it is most likely he will sue both you and the publisher. But it is you, not the publisher, who will have to pay the costs of defending against such claim, including court costs, attorneys' fees, the amount of any settlement, or, in the event you lose, the amount of any award from a judge or jury. And this is true even if the claim is just a nuisance suit. However, there are many protections you can try to get in this clause, and this particular printed form has some of them. Note that in (i) the publisher has the right to choose the lawyer. You may want a right of consultation. Note that in (ii) publisher can't agree to a settlement without the author's consent. This is good. Note that in (iii) the author is only responsible if the damages are "finally sustained." This means that the author is not liable until the judgment is final and there are no more courtroom appeals. This is good for the author. In the event you win, note that the publisher here has been nice enough to agree to pay half the expenses (except if the lawsuit was based on copyright infringement). This is nice, but you can try to get the publisher to pay for half the expenses even if the claim was based on copyright infringement. There are some more substantial protections you can try to get, such as: in no event will you be liable for more than the amount of money you have received pursuant to this deal; that you will only be liable for *knowing* breaches of your warranties. These warranties and indemnifications extend to the publisher's licensees: the book clubs, mass market reprinters, etc. These companies could also come after the author.

c. If any such claim, action or proceeding is instituted, the Publisher shall promptly notify the Author, who shall fully cooperate in the defense thereof, and the Publisher may withhold payments of reasonable amounts due him under this or any other agreement between the parties.

The publisher may withhold your money as long as a suit, or even the threat of one, hangs over your head. He should withhold *only* that money pertaining to the book that offends. He *should not* be allowed to withhold money on other books contracted with the same company; these other works may be perfectly harmless and be making loads of money. A provision could be added to this effect. Also, the amount withheld could be limited to, say, twenty-five percent of the royalties due. Better yet, have this provision deleted altogether.

d. These warranties and indemnities shall survive the termination of this agreement.

If the book is out of print and someone starts a copyright suit, these warranties and indemnities still apply.

Conflicting Publication

5. The Author agrees that during the term of this agreement he will not, without the written permission of the Publisher, publish or permit to be published any material, in book or pamphlet form, based on material in the work.

If the author publishes a book with another company, a book which resembles the book contracted herein or which uses characters from this book, the author may be in breach of this contract even if there has been no copyright infringement. The Random House version of this clause is in my opinion fairer than most in that it does not attempt to restrict the author's reserved rights, nor his movement in the publishing marketplace. Some publishers keep an author from writing *anything*. The clauses can be modified to refer to specific content, material or subject matter from the book under contract.

Date, Style and Price of Publication

6. Within one year after the Author has delivered the manuscript in conformity with Paragraph 2, the Publisher shall publish the work at its own expense, in such style and manner, under such imprint and at such price as it deems suitable. The Publisher shall not be responsible for delays caused by any circumstance beyond its control. No changes in the manuscript or the provisional title shall be made without the consent of the Author. However, in no event shall the Publisher be obligated to publish a work which in its opinion violates the common law or statutory copyright or the right of privacy of any person or contains libelous or obscene matter.

The publisher shall publish. Very good. But he prices the book, he gets it on the bookshelves in a year and he doesn't have to publish your work if in *his* opinion you have not lived up to your warranties. Some publishers take two years to publish. Other publishers make no commitment at all to publish. Most publishers *want* to publish: that's what they're in the business for. But don't take this for granted. Get a time limit on the life of the rights granted; if a publisher hasn't published in one to two years, all the rights granted the publisher should revert to the author so that he or she can find another publisher who may be more enthusiastic about the book.

Proofreading and Author's Corrections

7. The Author agrees to read, revise, correct and return promptly all proofs of the work and to pay in cash or, at the option of the Publisher, to have charged against him, the cost of alterations, in type or in plates, required by the Author, other than those due to printer's errors, in excess of ten per cent (10%) of the cost of setting type, provided a statement of these charges is sent to the Author within thirty (30) days of the receipt of the printer's bills and the corrected proofs are presented upon request for his inspection.

Note that the author has approval over changes. Try to get this in your contract. You should try to get your book in final form prior to it being typeset. Once it's in galleys, any changes you make (beyond ten percent of the printer's original cost of setting type) will be borne by you. Note that this agreement gives the publisher the right to actually bill you for these costs. You can try to change this provision so that these costs are only payable out of royalties that may ultimately be due you.

8. The Publisher shall copyright the work in the name of the Author, in the United States, in compliance with the Universal Copyright Convention, and apply for renewals of such copyright. If copyright should be in the name of the Publisher, it shall assign such copyright upon request of the Author. The Publisher agrees to arrange for the sale of the work in Canada. If the Publisher adds illustrations or other material, and if copyright is in the Author's name, he agrees, upon request, to assign the copyright of such material. If the Author retains the right to periodical or foreign publication before publication by the Publisher, he shall notify the Publisher promptly of any arrangement of such publication or any postponement thereof. In the event of a periodical publication, if the copyright shall be in the name of any person other than the Author, he shall promptly deliver to the Publisher a legally recordable assignment of such copyright or of the rights granted. In the event of a publication outside the United States, promptly thereafter, he shall furnish to the Publisher three copies of the first published work and the date of such publication.

The copyright will generally be in the author's name. Although Random House still runs this clause, it is apparently obsolete. Most likely, many publishers have yet to find the language to incorporate the changes in the new copyright law in their copyright clauses. Copyright automatically vests in the work as it is written. The publisher therefore does not "copyright the work." Also, the process of renewing the copyright has been eliminated under the new law. See the chapter on Copyright.

Random House has recently been including this additional provision and it is now #23 in the Random House Contract:

"It is a condition of the rights granted hereby that the Publisher agrees that all copies of the Work that are distributed to the public shall bear the copyright notice prescribed by the applicable copyright laws of the United States of America. The Author hereby appoints the Publisher as his attorney-in-fact in his name and in his stead to execute all documents for recording in the Copyright Office evidencing transfer of ownership in the exclusive right granted to the Publisher hereunder."

There are two reasons for this clause. Under the new law, copyright cannot be invalidated if the copyright notice is omitted in violation of the express requirement that all copies of the work printed shall bear such notice. This leaves the publisher an out, if he or she makes an error, or if the printer makes an error. But the author is in no way threatened. The first sentence in this clause sets forth the condition that all copies distributed to the public will bear a copyright notice. It would be wise to specify further, that the copyright notice should bear the author's name and that all other publishers licensed by this publisher shall conform to the condition set forth above. Moreover, the clause should state that the author is the "author of the work" and that copyright is vested in him under the U.S. Copyright Act.

The ostensible reason for this provision is to allow the publisher the swift action necessary to expedite a copyright assignment (in whatever manner the author chooses) should the author be unavailable. Moreover, there is an added purpose here allowing the publisher to file the memorandum of conveyance required by the copyright act as evidence of a transference of ownership and the power to dispose of the exclusive rights granted the publisher by the author.

In any event, the copyright of the work belongs to the author. If you sell your work to a magazine for first serial, the magazine can run a copyright line in your name and a provision for this must be made in the deal letter agreement between you and the magazine. If a magazine does not wish to use a second copyright notice other than the one usually run on the magazine's masthead, the copyright would still be in the author's name. The law does not require an assignment of copyright for the magazine to print a prepublication excerpt. If you sell the work in a foreign market, furnish the publisher with copies of the foreign edition.

Advance Payments

9. The Publisher shall pay to the Author as an advance against and on account of all moneys accruing to him under this agreement, the sum of
dollars ($), payable

Any such advance shall not be repayable, provided that the Author has delivered the manuscript in conformity with Paragraph 2 and is not otherwise in default under this agreement.

MONEY!! And hopefully lots of it. Generally an author gets half of his advance on signing the contract and half after the author has delivered and the publisher has accepted the work. If possible, the author should specify that the advance is non-returnable, if he delivers a complete work. Sometimes publishers want to pay in thirds: a third on signing, a third on delivery and acceptance and the final third on publication. Discourage this.

All advances are paid against all royalties. When your book has earned back the advance on sales, you will start accruing royalties. Not before. Writing may be a gift, but publishing is a business.

Royalty Payments

10. The Publisher shall pay to the Author a royalty on the retail price of every copy sold by the Publisher, less actual returns and a reasonable reserve for returns (except as set forth below):

a.　　　　per cent (　　%) up to and including　　　　copies;
　　　　per cent (　　%) in excess of　　　　copies up to and including
　　　　copies; and　　　　per cent (　　%) in excess of　　　　copies.

Where the discount in the United States is forty-eight per cent (48%) or more from the retail price, the rate provided in this subdivision a. shall be reduced by one-half the difference between forty-four per cent (44%) and the discount granted. In no event, however, shall such royalty be less than one-half of the rate provided herein. If the semi-annual sales aggregate fewer than 400 copies, the royalty shall be two-thirds ($\frac{2}{3}$) of the rate provided in this subdivision a. if such copies are sold from a second or subsequent printing. Copies covered by any other subdivision of this Paragraph shall not be included in such computation.

MORE MONEY!! Aaah, but "less returns." Publishers send their books out to the retailers via distributors, jobbers and other middlemen. Sometimes the publishers have their own distributing companies. In any case, the book retailers take books on a returnable basis: if the bookstore can't sell the books, they return them to the publishers. If they print and distribute 50,000 copies, and sell only 5,000, the publisher will get back 45,000. You don't get a penny on any books returned, unless they are shipped again and actually change hands at the retail level. If possible, specify a limit on the reserve: fifteen percent, twenty percent, thirty percent.

Your royalty is calculated on the publisher's price that he prints on the book jacket. This practice varies. It all depends on your track record. The book store may mark the prices up or down, but this normally doesn't affect the royalty.

Royalty rates vary depending upon the type of book an author is writing. Ten percent to the first 5,000 copies sold, twelve and one-half percent on the next 5,000, and fifteen percent thereafter is becoming a standard measure for many books, though rates vary. Some authors commence their royalty rate at fifteen percent on all copies.

The second part of this 10 (a.) is the discount clause. The infamous discount clause. When anyone reads this subdivision in a contract, their eyes roll around in their sockets and their brains heat up. But the clause works out to a simple calculation, and applies to a book sold to jobbers (small distributors filling orders for retail stores, one book at a time).

FIRST, the discount has got to be greater than 48%. Let's take a discount of 50%: Your book is priced at $10. At a 50% discount the over-the-counter price is $5.

But the retail price is $10; the author's discount royalty rate is calculated against the $10 figure. The clause states that the royalty rate shall be adjusted at half the difference between 44% and the discount granted.

50% MINUS 44% = 6%
One Half of 6% = 3%
ANSWER: At a 50% discount, a royalty rate of 10% would be reduced 3%.
10% MINUS 3% = 7%.
A 7% royalty on a $10 book equals $.70.

Not all discount clauses work this way; some are adjusted downwards on a different scale and with different criteria. Publishers created this formula so that they could achieve maximum over-the-counter sales with mixed titles. On the one hand, they want to give the retailer the ability to reduce prices drastically, but on the other hand the publisher himself can't get caught paying a royalty rate that is unprofitable. In order to get the books over the counter, he reduces what he owes the author on every copy sold at a drastically reduced price.

As it turns out, even using the discount clause to its fullest, publishers are often caught with books they can't sell over the counter. If this happens to your book, your royalties don't simply shrink . . . they evaporate.

As the end of this 10 (a.) makes clear, your royalty will never be less than half the rate provided. But don't smile yet. If you don't sell more than 400 copies every six months your royalty rate drops to two thirds of the overall. This applies to a second or subsequent printing. Copies sold in any subdivision of this are not computed in this statement; they are computed on a separate statement.

Some publishers' discount clauses reduce the royalty much further and much faster. Figure out the formula; know how your royalties drop. Sometimes it is possible to specify a limit of reduction to discounts and base it solely on the number of copies sold. When the discount clauses are applied the publisher winds up gaining.

Mail Order Sales

> b. Five percent (5%) of the amount received for copies sold directly to the consumer through the medium of mail-order or coupon advertising, or radio or television advertising.

If the publishers want to go straight to the consumer, circumvent the distributors and middlemen, and ship straight from his warehouse on orders placed directly with the publishing company, *let them*. Publishers don't regularly sell direct to consumers because it's expensive to literally get the word out: coupon advertising, radio advertising and television advertising are very expensive. My guess is that if the publisher begins to implement this clause, your book is already a big hit.

Premiums and Subscriptions

> c. Five per cent (5%) of the amount received for copies sold by the Publisher's Premium or Subscription Books Wholesale Department.

Five percent for wholesale isn't bad. Three percent is bad. Seven percent would be great.

College Sales

> d. Ten per cent (10%) for hard-cover copies and five per cent (5%) for soft-cover copies sold with a lower retail price as college textbooks.

School Editions

> e. For a School edition the royalty provided in subdivision a. of this Paragraph but no more than:
>> i. Ten per cent (10%) of the amount received for a Senior High School edition;
>> ii. Eight per cent (8%) of the amount received for a Junior High School edition;
>> iii. Six per cent (6%) of the amount received for an Elementary School edition.

College sales and school editions: On most books this never comes into play, but if it does happen to your book it just expands your market, since college and school sales are not strictly "trade." Regular college text royalties can run as low as three percent. But then again, the textbook publishers have print runs of 50,000 to 100,000 copies and up. No mean numbers. If your book gets into the schools, that's nice.

Lower-price Editions

> f. Five per cent (5%) for an edition published at a lower retail price or for an edition in the Modern Library (regular or giant size) or in Vintage Books; and two per cent (2%) or two cents (2¢) per copy, whichever is greater, for an edition in the Modern Library College Editions.

Modern Library and Vintage Books are imprints of Random House, Inc. They print both versions of "classics" and trade paperback editions. James M. Cain's *Double Indemnity* is published in softcover, through book store orders. Bruno Bettelheim's *Surviving and Other Essays* was reprinted by Vintage in a trade paperback version. Slightly smaller than the large hardcover, the trade paper version is priced more moderately and has a larger print run. In the Random House contract the author gets a seven and one-half percent royalty for a Vintage Book edition, less returns. Not bad. Some trade paperback editions can be larger than hardcover books; it depends a lot on the production cost and the desired production effect.

Export Sales

> g. Ten per cent (10%) of the amount received for the original edition and five per cent (5%) of the amount received for any lower-price edition for copies sold for export.

Who knows . . . maybe the bookstore in the French West Indies International airport can get a copy out of Random House for less than the French publisher you've just sold the French rights to. Maybe. Not often.

Special Sales

> h. For copies sold outside normal wholesale and retail trade channels, ten per cent (10%) of the amount received for the original edition and five per cent (5%) of the amount received for any lower-price edition for copies sold at a discount between fifty per cent (50%) and sixty per cent (60%) from the retail price and five per cent (5%) of the amount received for copies sold at a discount of sixty per cent (60%) or more from the retail price, or for the use of the plates by any governmental agency.

Most sales outside of "normal" wholesale and retail trade channels are a godsend. Be happy.

| *No Royalty*
Copies | i. **No** royalty shall be paid on copies sold below or at cost including expenses incurred, or furnished gratis to the Author, or for review, advertising, sample or like purposes. |

The publisher will not let you be greedy. He also wants a lot of influential literati to have a prepublication peek at your opus. This is a good thing.

| *Receipts*
From Other
Rights | j. Fifty per cent (50%) of the amount received from the disposition of licenses granted pursuant to Paragraph 1, subdivision a., ii, iii, iv, vi and vii. At the Author's request his share from book club and reprint licensing, less any unearned advances, shall be paid to him within two weeks after the receipt thereof by the Publisher. If the Publisher rebates to booksellers for unsold copies due to the publication of a lower-price or reprint edition, the royalty on such copies shall be the same as for such lower-price edition. |

The author receives fifty percent of all monies on paperback sales, bookclubs and second serial. Those are about all the highly lucrative rights the publisher has been left with., Sometimes you can get an escalation tacked onto this clause. For instance: the publisher sells for mass market reprint the same way the author sells to him. He sells your book for an advance against the paperback royalty and royalty on each copy sold. As this (j.) states, you get fifty percent of the take. Sometimes you can do better. Say, sixty percent of all paperback royalties if the hardcover publisher's reprint advance is more than $100,000—the numbers vary depending on the property.

If the publisher makes a mass market reprint sale, request payment. The publisher will deduct the money he originally paid you as a advance. Example: $100,000 paperback sale. Author's share: $50,000. If the author's advance was $10,000, the author will get a $40,000 check within two weeks.

Some publishers are slow to pay authors. The Random House contract specifies that the author must "request" payment. An author may want to stipulate the terms of payment on any reprint or book club sale, so that the author gets his money as soon as the publisher picks up the check from the licensee. I am told Random House likes to pay fast.

If your book is still in print in hardcover when the paperback version is published a year or two later, your hardcover publisher will have many hardbacks returned to him. He may remainder your hardcover books and the royalties from the hardcover will stop. You may urge him to keep the hardcover in print, but he is not obligated to do so.

First Serial	k. Ninety per cent (90%) of the amount received from the disposition of licenses in the United States and Canada granted pursuant to Paragraph 1, subdivision a., v.
British	l. Eighty per cent (80%) of the amount received from the disposition of licenses granted pursuant to Paragraph 1, subdivision b.
Translation	m. Seventy-five per cent (75%) of the amount received from the disposition of licenses granted pursuant to Paragraph 1, subdivision c.
Commercial	n. Fifty per cent (50%) of the amount received from the disposition of licenses granted pursuant to Paragraph 1, subdivision d., provided that all expenses in connection therewith shall be borne by the Publisher.

DELETE! These should be yours. An agent can help you dispose of them.

| *Share to*
Other Authors | o. If any license granted by the Publisher pursuant to Paragraph 1 shall include material of others, the amount payable to the Author shall be inclusive of royalty to other authors. |

If by some strange chance you have promised the owner of copyrighted material you want to use in your book not just a flat permission fee, but a cut of your proceeds, that comes out of your own pocket. The publisher doesn't get involved.

| *Performance*
Rights | 11. The Author appoints the Publisher as his exclusive agent to dispose of the performance rights including dramatic, musical, radio, television, motion picture and allied rights, subject to the Author's consent, and the Publisher shall receive a commission of ten per cent (10%) of the amount received.

In the event of the disposition of performance rights, the Publisher may grant to the purchaser the privilege to publish excerpts and summaries of the work in the aggregate not to exceed 7,500 words, for advertising and exploiting such rights, provided, however, that such grant shall require the purchaser to take all steps which may be necessary to protect the copyright of the work. |

DELETE! This is a whole new ball game. An agent or a lawyer will always help you keep and market your performance rights. As we know, a lot of money can be made in the movies, in TV or on the stage. There's money to be made in entertainment media not even yet developed for consumers. Re-

serve these rights to yourself one hundred percent.

If you are lucky enough to make good in Hollywood, the publisher should let the movie company use selections from your book in advertisements and publicity. This is natural. An author may want to change the word "may" to "shall" in the first line.

Rights Retained by Author

12. The Author agrees to notify the Publisher promptly of the disposition of any right which the Author has retained for himself.

In most contracts (including this one), there is no explicit statement to the effect that "all rights not herein granted to the publisher are reserved to the author for his use at any time." Make it explicit.

When you do dispose of a reserved right (e.g., sale of the movie rights), make sure you notify the publisher.

Reports and Payments

13. The Publisher shall render semi-annual statements of account to the first day of April and the first day of October, and shall mail such statements during the July and January following, together with checks in payment of the amounts due thereon.

Should the Author receive an overpayment of royalty arising from copies reported sold but subsequently returned, the Publisher may deduct such overpayment from any further sums due the Author.

Upon his written request, the Author may examine or cause to be examined through certified public accountants the books of account of the Publisher in so far as they relate to the sale or licensing of the work.

Notwithstanding anything to the contrary in this or any prior agreement between the parties, the Author shall in no event be entitled to receive under this and all prior agreements with the Publisher more than $ during any one calendar year. If in any one calendar year the total of the sums accruing to the Author under this and all prior agreements with the Publisher shall exceed such amount, he shall be entitled to receive the excess amount in any succeeding calendar year in which the sums accruing to him under this and all prior agreements with the Publisher do not exceed the maximum herein stated, provided that the total amount to which the Author may be entitled under this and all prior agreements with the Publisher in any succeeding calendar year shall not exceed the maximum herein stated.

The publisher calculates the book's earnings on a semi-annual basis for the periods ending on the first day of April and the first day of October. The actual royalty checks are then not mailed until three to four months later, during July and January respectively. Along with the checks come the royalty reports and sub-rights earnings statements. Publishers may have different accounting and payment schedules, coming in different months of the year, but generally they all run on a semi-annual basis. Notice that in the Random House contract there is no exact date by when the publisher is obligated to mail the check—the check will come sometime during July and January. Random House generally pays when money is due. Some publishers are notorious for withholding money due for weeks on end. Their royalty departments are then inundated with irate telephone calls from livid agents, lawyers and authors.

I can't let the urge to tell royalty hunting stories overcome me, but as an aside, I know of a case where an author actually came within a hair's breadth of calling the New York City Marshall into action. He was fully prepared for the good Marshall to post notice on the publisher's offices stating a

"lien" on the property. The author (a large man with big fists) chose a second alternative: he strode into the publisher's office and closed the door. The publisher, less physically endowed, got up to leave.

Things don't necessarily have to get to that point. Ninety-nine percent of the time, they don't. In the second paragraph of this clause, the words "reported sold" might raise an eyebrow. It is my understanding that the best-seller lists are compiled on the retail booksellers' *orders,* not final sales. The publisher's accounts reflect this, so they don't know exactly how well a given book is selling until the returns come back. It is conceivable that a publisher might keep an inadequate reserve and then pay an author without taking into account the possible return, but not very likely. Money is very tight and cash flow a publisher's loving lubricant. Any publishing company, like any company, wants as much cash leeway as possible. Everyone hates paying bills.

The third paragraph in this clause discusses the author's right to have his accountant audit the publisher's books to insure the author has been properly paid. Even in the computer age, royalty statements as presented by the publisher will sometimes contain errors and discrepancies. It is possible that your accountant can get enough information to correct the errors without leaving his desk, without going through a full-scale audit. To my knowledge, author's audits are much less frequent than audits of profit participation statements in the movie business.

The fourth and last paragraph is the Limitation Clause. If filled in with a money figure, this allows the publisher to dispense money to the author in lit-

tle dribs and drabs. There have been incidents where authors let this clause be used to the tune of say $10,000 per year while their books accrued many hundreds of thousands of dollars. If a dollar figure is inserted in the Limitation Clause, the publisher is generally reluctant to amend the agreement. Your best bet is to delete this clause.

As a final word on royalty statements: READ THEM CAREFULLY! CHECK THEM!

Option for Next Work

14. The Author agrees to submit to the Publisher his next book-length work before submitting the same to any other publisher. The Publisher shall be entitled to a period of six weeks after the submission of the completed manuscript, which period shall not commence to run prior to one month after the publication of the work covered by this agreement, within which to notify the Author of its decision. If within that time the Publisher shall notify the Author of its desire to publish the manuscript, it shall thereupon negotiate with him with respect to the terms of such publication. If within thirty (30) days thereafter the parties are unable in good faith to arrive at a mutually satisfactory agreement for such publication, the Author shall be free to submit his manuscript elsewhere, provided, however, that he shall not enter into a contract for the publication of such manuscript with any other publisher upon terms less favorable than those offered by the Publisher.

It is not uncommon to hear an author gleefully say that he has an option for his next book with Publisher X. In reality, however, the publisher has an option on *him*. Options have become a grisly bone of contention in the publishing industry. Publishers often say they want assurances and guarantees that an author will return to them: "What if his next book *really* sells??" Agents argue that an option restricts an author's freedom in the marketplace; that it is a form of artistic servitude. How about the Random House option?

If this option is included (as it stands) in your book deal, you, the writer, must submit your next *completed* work to the publisher. No proposals, no outlines, you must send in the next book-length work. The publisher considers your new book one month after the book covered in this agreement is published. This allows the publisher time to review your old book's earnings. Are you a winner or a loser?

So they start considering your new book a month after you have been published and *then* they have six weeks to make a decision. They take six weeks while you sweat bullets.

If the publisher decided they want to publish your next book, you start negotiating. That's normal. But what if the author and the publisher can't come to an agreement? What if the author needs more money to write, to revise or to rework the next book? Well, the author has thirty days to work it out with the publisher. Then, if no agreement can be reached, the publisher allows the author to go back out in the marketplace. You take your book to an-

other publisher and lo!, that new publisher goes wild over your newest endeavor. You're a hit.

But wait! You're not through yet. The last sentence in this option is the killer. That new publisher you've found had better be offering you a "more favorable" deal than the old publisher.

More favorable? What in God's name is *more favorable?* Money? Any issue in the contract? That, unfortunately, is subject to interpretation. There is very little clear-cut about the words. That last sentence in the option implies that the publisher is allowed to examine your new contract, a private document between the author and his new publisher in order to determine whether or not your new deal *is* more favorable. For how, pray tell, would your old publisher know the private terms of your new arrangement if he didn't see them.

Don't like it. Don't like it at all. But in reality editors and publishers sometimes will tell an author, "Oh, you can get out of this option."

At their discretion. Not yours. If a publisher is adamant about requiring an option on your next book (and they almost always are when a writer is without representation), sometimes you can alter the option terms. You amend the option so that it allows you to turn in a proposal, not a completed work, so that it makes the publisher consider your next proposal thirty days after the book covered in this agreement has been accepted for publication. Strike the sentence dealing with "more favorable terms." Some options restrict writers from writing anything at all. As written, the Random House option precludes the author from obtaining an advance before he or she completes the second work. Options can be tailored to suit. But nothing suits better than no option at all.

If a publisher has done well by your book, you will go back to him, gladly. And in a sense, performance is the key to any publishing enterprise. If the publisher meets the author a little more than halfway, and the author meets the publisher a little more than halfway, the next thing you know, the two of them will be dancing a fox-trot down the bookstore aisles.

Copies to
Author

15. On publication the Publisher shall give ten (10) free copies to the Author, who may purchase further copies for personal use at a discount of forty percent (40%) from the retail price.

For your friends, for the lovers that left you hanging (who now come back in droves) for your mother (God bless her!) and don't forget that third grade teacher who wouldn't let you go to the bathroom.

You can ask for more copies than the printed figure. Sometimes you get them, sometimes you don't. The forty percent discount off the retail price is standard.

Discontinuance
of
Publication

16. If the Publisher fails to keep the work in print and the Author makes written demand to reprint it, the Publisher shall, within sixty (60) days after the receipt of such demand, notify the Author in writing if it intends to comply. Within six (6) months thereafter, the Publisher shall reprint the work unless prevented from doing so by circumstances beyond its control. If the Publisher fails to notify the Author within sixty (60) days that it intends to comply, or, within six (6) months after such notification, the Publisher declines or neglects to reprint the work, then this agreement shall terminate and all rights granted hereunder except those deriving from the option in Paragraph 14 shall revert to the Author, subject to licenses previously granted, provided the Author is not indebted to the Publisher for any sum owing to it under this agreement. After such reversion, the Publisher shall continue to participate to the extent set forth in this agreement in moneys received from any license previously granted by it. Upon such termination, the Author shall have the right for thirty (30) days thereafter to purchase the plates, if any, at one-fourth of the cost (including type setting).

If the work is under contract for publication or on sale in any edition in the United States, it shall be considered to be in print. A work shall not be deemed in print by reason of a license granted by the Publisher for the reproduction of single copies of the work. If the Publisher should determine that there is not sufficient sale for the work to enable it to continue its publication and sale profitably, the Publisher may dispose of the copies remaining on hand as it deems best, subject to the royalty provisions of Paragraph 10. In such event, the Author shall have the right, within two (2) weeks of the forwarding of a written notice from the Publisher, to a single purchase of copies at the "remainder" price.

So how do you know whether your book is in print or not? You write a letter asking whether the book is in print, and if not, demanding they put it back in print. The publisher gets the letter, scraps around for sixty days while they check inventory at their warehouse, and if the book is somewhere in the warehouse (cut-off point is about fifty copies in the warehouse), they'll prove it to you: "See here, fifty copies in our warehouse in New Jersey." You're in print. The ultimate test for the publisher, to decide if you're in print, is whether he can fill orders for the book. If he can't, you're not in print. If no copies can be found in the warehouse or if no paperback edition is in print, you're not *in print,* and if the publisher feels like doing the dance all over again, they'll let you know within sixty days. Six

months later, you're back on the shelves.

But! If the publisher fails to return your letter in the sixty-day period, and you don't hear anything at all in the six-month period, all rights granted by the author to the publisher revert to the author.

A single-copy reprint license granted by the publisher, for reasons of say, a special non-profit group or organization, does not constitute being in print. If the publisher doesn't want to keep your work in print, you can buy whatever copies they've got lying around at "remainder price"—very, very, cheaply. That'll keep you warm in body and chill in spirit throughout the winter. An author should specify that the publisher *shall* notify him of its intention to "remainder" his work.

Author's
Property

17. Except for loss or damage due to its own negligence, the Publisher shall not be responsible for loss of or damage to any property of the Author.

If the publisher loses the only copy of your manuscript, he will not be held responsible—unless of course he was negligent.

| *Return of* | 18. In the absence of written request from the Author prior to publication for their return, the Publisher, after publication of the work, may dispose of the original manuscript and proofs. |
| *Manuscript* | |

Specify that you want your manuscripts and proofs returned in good condition.

Suits for	19. If the copyright of the work is infringed, and if the parties proceed jointly, the expenses and recoveries, if any, shall be shared equally, and if they do not proceed jointly, either party shall have the right to prosecute such action, and such party shall bear the expenses thereof, and any recoveries shall belong to such party; and if such party shall not hold the record title of the copyright, the other party hereby consents that the action be brought in his or its name.
Infringement	
of Copyright	

Infringements of copyright are serious business. However, there have been occasions when a publisher has declined to take legal action. In a case of possible infringement, consult an independent lawyer. Don't rely on the publisher's lawyer. If the publisher is joining you in a suit, remember, *you* have paid for your own counsel, *you* control the actions of your counsel, no one else does. In some contracts, publishers attempt to control the author's independent counsel. This quasi-independence is unacceptable.

Bankruptcy	20. If (a) a petition in bankruptcy is filed by the Publisher, or (b) a petition in bankruptcy is filed against the Publisher and such petition is finally sustained, or (c) a petition for arrangement is filed by the Publisher or a petition for reorganization is filed by or against the Publisher, and an order is entered directing the liquidation of the Publisher as in bankruptcy, or (d) the Publisher makes an assignment for the benefit of creditors, or (e) the Publisher liquidates its business for any cause whatever, the Author may terminate this agreement by written notice and thereupon all rights granted by him hereunder shall revert to him. Upon such termination, the Author, at his option, may purchase the plates as provided in Paragraph 16 and the remaining copies at one-half of the manufacturing cost, exclusive of overhead. If he fails to exercise such option within sixty (60) days after the happening of any one of the events above referred to, the Trustee, Receiver, or Assignee may destroy the plates and sell the copies remaining on hand, subject to the royalty provisions of Paragraph 10.
and	
Liquidation	

Specify that if the publisher goes bankrupt, that all the rights granted to him revert to the author. Many contracts avoid this issue.

| *Sums Due* | 21. Any sums due and owing from the Author to the Publisher, whether or not arising out of this agreement, may be deducted from any sum due or to become due from the Publisher to the Author pursuant to this agreement. For the purposes of this Paragraph a non-repayable unearned advance made to the Author pursuant to another agreement shall not be construed as being a sum due and owing, unless the Author is in default under such other agreement. |
| *and Owing* | |

Any money the author owes the publisher can be deducted by the publisher from royalties due. Make sure your agreement provides (as this one does) that if you have more than one book with the same publisher, he cannot offset royalties due on one book against advances from a different book.

Law Applicable	22. This agreement shall be interpreted according to the law of the State of New York.
	23. It is a condition of the rights granted hereby that the Publisher agrees that all copies of the work that are distributed to the public shall bear the copyright notice prescribed by the applicable copyright laws of the United States of America. The Author hereby appoints the Publisher as his attorney-in-fact in his name and in his stead to execute all documents for recording in the Copyright Office evidencing transfer of ownership in the exclusive rights granted to the Publisher hereunder.
Assignment	24. This agreement shall be binding upon the heirs, executors, administrators and assigns of the Author, and upon the successors and assigns of the Publisher, but no assignment except to an affiliate of the Publisher, shall be binding on either of the parties without the written consent of the other.

If you make a deal with one publisher because of his or her reputation and expertise in a certain area, you would not want that publisher to assign this deal to some less attractive publishing company. Your consent should be required. On the other hand, in this industry of merges and corporate reorganizations, the publisher wants the right to assign the contract to one of its affiliates (such as a subsidiary).

25. This agreement constitutes the complete understanding of the parties. No modification or waiver of any provision shall be valid unless in writing and signed by both parties.

The only modification to this agreement or waiver of any of its clauses that a judge will listen to are those that are in writing and signed by both you and the publisher. Don't let anyone tell you differently.

And below.... you sign.

IN WITNESS WHEREOF the parties have duly executed this agreement the day and year first above written.

RANDOM HOUSE, Inc.

In the presence of

.... By ....

The Publisher

In the presence of

....

The Author

1208 4-79 ....

Social Security Number

This chapter cannot cover every issue in a publishing experience and some contracts are stitched together like a handmade set of clothes. As in the music industry, the "chicken-salad-sandwich-waiting-in-the-dressing-room-clause" can also be applied to publishing agreements. But there are many contractual specifications which though slightly unusual, are not gratuitous. Clauses specifying the author's approval over jacket design and copy can be inserted, and clauses restricting advertising in a book, unwanted advertising, or if advertising is proposed, a sharing of the advertising revenue. The right to rewrite in the galley stage is a favorite of some authors. Sometimes an author can get the publisher to explicitly prohibit changes in the text in any down-the-line license deal.

There are cracks and loopholes in even the tightest contracts. Some people declare that the more complicated the contract, the more strictly defined it becomes, the more likely the parties will lose sight of their obligations and fall into a dogfight. In my heart of hearts I find a certain logic to that notion. Openhanded compromise can give birth to trust. An experience in the entertainment industry or publishing can be a richly rewarding enterprise. But no one can guarantee that even the best-advised artists will always get what they want. Oddly enough, even the most poorly advised artists sometimes come away unscathed. It seems today that more than ever luck and talent, experience and the willingness to learn conspire toward a beautiful marriage. But once in a while, even with the best of everything, the luck, the talent, the experience and the learning fly off to Reno and sue for a divorce. No one is immune.

COLLABORATION

Alexander Lindey

In his Souvenirs Dramatiques, Dumas wrote: "Of two collaborators one is generally the dupe, and that one is the man of talent. For your collaborator is like a passenger who has embarked on the same ship with you and who gradually reveals to you that he cannot swim. When shipwreck comes you have to keep him afloat at the risk of drowning yourself; and when you reach land, he goes around telling everybody that without him you would have perished."

"I've always believed in writing without a collaborator," said Agatha Christie, whose detective stories have found favor all over the world, "because where two people are writing the same book, each believes he gets all the worries and only half the royalties." "I don't understand how two men can write a book together," said Evelyn Waugh. "To me that's like three people getting together to have a baby."

"The symbiosis between the specialist, who knows something but can't write it for a general audience, and the popularizer, who can write to engage a wide readership, is an uneasy one. The specialist accuses the popularizer of glibness; the popularizer disdains the hermetic world of experts. Not to mention ego-conflicts and crass money matters revolving around how much the popularizer

should profit from the specialist's research; or the specialist from the specialist's research; or the specialist from the popularizer's writing flair." Book Review, *The New York Times*, May 30, 1976, p. 17.

Collaboration may be of various kinds. Two persons may develop an idea for, say, a novel, and contribute more or less equally to its execution. In such a case both of them get authorship credit; both have equal voice in the disposition of all rights; and the proceeds are usually divided equally between them. One person may complete a work by himself, and another may be engaged to rewrite it. There may be a ghost-writing arrangement. One person may get an idea, and arrange with another to develop it.

Whatever the arrangement, questions are bound to arise. What will be the rights of the collaborators in the work if they quarrel and part company before it is completed? What will happen with respect to authorship credit, sharing of proceeds and so on if one of them dies or becomes incapacitated before the work is finished? What will happen if they cannot agree on the choice of a publisher, or on the disposition of any of the subsidiary rights?

Ghost-writing is, of necessity, a form of cooperative venture, but it should be clearly distinguished from a true collaboration. In the latter case, the collaborators are usually co-owners of the work and all rights in it, and obtain a copyright in the names of both. They have equal rights in negotiating a publication contract. Both get authorship credit, and as a rule share equally in book royalties and other proceeds. In the case of a ghost-written book, the copyright is customarily obtained in the name of the

161

nominal author, and not that of the ghost-writer, and special arrangements may obtain as to the disposition of rights and the division (if any) of the proceeds.

As to practical and legal considerations, see Irwin Karp, "Collaboration Agreements" *Authors Guild Bulletin,* Nov.–Dec. 1966, p. 9, and Jan.–Feb. 1967, p. 9.

Collaboration Agreement

The following is a general form of collaboration agreement which could be adapted to fit most specific situations.

General Form; Parties to Collaborate on Non-Fiction Book; Method of Collaboration Defined; Joint Control of All Rights in Book; Copyright; Authorship Credit; Division of Proceeds; Appointment of Agent; Changes in Manuscript; Disposition of Either Party's Share; Expenses; Provisions as to Completion; Duration; Arbitration

This Agreement between [Richard Johnson], residing at _____, City of _____, State of _____ (herein called Johnson), and [Robert Goodman], residing at _____, City of _____, State of _____, (herein called Goodman).

WITNESSETH:

The parties desire to collaborate in the writing of a book, on the terms hereinafter set forth.

NOW THEREFORE, in consideration of the premises, and of the mutual undertakings herein contained, and for other good and valuable considerations, the parties agree as follows:

1. The parties hereby undertake to collaborate in the writing of a certain non-fiction book (herein called the Book), dealing with _____, and provisionally entitled _____

2. They have agreed on a tentative outline, a copy of which is hereto annexed. [In the outline, the name of [Johnson] has been placed opposite the titles of certain proposed chapters; and the name of [Goodman] has been placed opposite the titles of certain other chapters. It is the intention of the parties that the first draft of each chapter shall be prepared by the party whose name it bears, and shall be submitted to the other party for comments and suggestions. The final drafts shall be worked out by the parties together.]

3. The parties contemplate that they will complete the manuscript of the Book by _____. If they fail to do so, they may by mutual agreement extend the time for completion. In the absence of any such extension, they shall endeavor to fix by negotiation their respective rights in the material theretofore gathered and written, and in the project itself, i.e., whether one or the other of them shall have the right to complete the Book alone or in collaboration with someone else, and on what terms. Their understanding as to these matters shall thereupon be embodied in a settlement agreement. If they are unable to agree, their respective rights and the terms pertaining thereto shall be fixed by arbitration. In either event, this agreement shall cease when the rights of the parties have been fixed as aforesaid; and thereafter they shall have only such rights and obligations as will be set forth in the settlement agreement on the arbitration award, as the case may be.

4. If the manuscript of the Book is completed, the parties shall endeavor to secure a publisher. Each shall have the right to negotiate for this purpose, but they shall keep each other fully informed with reference thereto. No agreement for the publication of the Book or for the disposition of any of the subsidiary rights therein shall be valid without the signature of both parties. However, either party may grant a written power of attorney to the other setting forth the specific conditions under which the power may be exercised. For services rendered under such power of attorney, no agency fee or extra compensation shall be paid to the attorney-in-fact.

5. The copyright in the Book shall be obtained in the names of both parties, and shall be held jointly by them.

6. The parties shall receive equal authorship credit on the same line and in type of equal size, except that the name of [Johnson] shall precede that of [Goodman].

7. All receipts and returns from the publication of the Book and from the disposition of any subsidiary rights therein shall be divided equally between the parties. All agreements for publication and for the sale of subsidiary rights shall provide that each party's one-half share shall be paid directly to him.

8. If the parties by mutual agreement select an agent to handle the publication rights in the Book or the disposition of the subsidiary rights therein, and if the agent is authorized to make collection for the parties' account, such agent shall remit each party's one-half share direct to him.

9. After the completion of the manuscript of the Book, no change or alteration shall be made therein by either party without the other's consent. However, such consent shall not be unreasonably withheld. No written consent to make a particular revision shall be deemed authority for a general revision.

10. If either party (herein called the First Party) desires to transfer his one-half share in the Book or in the subsidiary rights thereof to a third person, he shall give written notice by registered mail to the other party (herein called the Second Party) of his intention to do so.

(a) In such case the Second Party shall have an option for a period of [ten] days to purchase the First Party's share at a price and upon such terms indicated in the written notice.

(b) If the Second Party fails to exercise his option in writing within the aforesaid period of [ten] days, or if, having exercised it, he fails to complete the purchase upon the terms stated in the notice, the First Party may transfer his rights to the third person at the price and upon the identical terms stated in the notice; and he shall forthwith send to the Second Party a copy of the contract of sale of such rights, with a statement that the transfer has been made.

(c) If the First Party fails for any reason to make such transfer to the third person, and if he desires to make a subsequent transfer to someone else, the Second Party's option shall apply to such proposed subsequent transfer.

11. All expenses which may reasonably be incurred in connection with the Book shall be subject to mutual agreement in advance, and shall be shared equally by the parties.

12. Nothing herein contained shall be construed to create a partnership between the parties. Their relation shall be one of collaboration on a single work.

13. If the Book is published, this agreement shall continue for the life of the copyright therein. Otherwise the duration hereof shall be governed by the provisions of clause 3.

14. If either party dies before the completion of the manuscript, the survivor shall have the right to complete the same, to make changes in the text previously prepared, to negotiate and contract for publication and for the disposition of any of the subsidiary rights, and generally to act with regard thereto as though he were the sole author, except that (a) the name of the decedent shall always appear as co-author; and (b) the survivor shall cause the decedent's one-half share of the proceeds to be paid to his estate, and shall furnish to the estate true copies of all contracts made by the survivor pertaining to the Book.

15. If either party dies after the completion of the manuscript, the survivor shall have the right to negotiate and contract for publication (if not theretofore published) and for the disposition of any of the subsidiary rights, to make revisions in any subsequent editions, and generally to act with regard thereto as if he were the sole author, subject only to the conditions set forth in subdivisions (a) and (b) of clause 14.

16. Any controversy or claim arising out of or relating to this agreement or any breach thereof shall be settled by arbitration in accordance with the Rules of the American Arbitration Association; and judgment upon the award rendered by the arbitrators may be entered in any court having jurisdiction thereof.

17. This agreement shall enure to the benefit of, and shall be binding upon, the executors, administrators and assigns of the parties.

18. This agreement constitutes the entire understanding of the parties.

IN WITNESS WHEREOF the parties hereunto set their respective hand and seal this _____ day of _____, 19__.

_____(L.S.)
[Richard Johnson]

_____(L.S.)
[Robert Goodman]

[ACKNOWLEDGMENTS]

[Annex tentative outline]

WRITER-AGENCY AGREEMENTS

David E. Goldman

After the writer and his or her newly acquired agent have solidified their relationship with a handshake, they will undoubtedly commit themselves to one another with one or more written agreements. Although oral agreements pertaining to the employment of a writer or the sale of literary material are generally valid and enforceable, most states have enacted statutes that specifically require agency agreements to be in writing in order to be enforceable. Typically, the writer will be asked to sign an agreement covering his services as a writer (often referred to as a "services agreement") and one covering representation of individual literary properties (often referred to as a "materials agreement"). Samples of both of these agreements appear at the end of this article.

It's been my experience that the writer generally has three concerns when entering into agency agreements. Naturally, there is the concern that the agent will faithfully carry out his part of the bargain in representing the writer competently and diligently. Secondly, the writer is concerned that the agent will deal fairly with him; i.e., that the agent will charge reasonable commissions, make timely payment of monies, render proper accountings, etc. Lastly, the writer wants to be sure that if his first two concerns are not met he can get himself a new agent without any contractual obligation to his former agent.

The Writers Guild of America, through its Artists' Managers Basic Agreement of 1976, goes a long way in allaying the basic fears of writers working in the motion picture and television industries. Although these protections are not as readily avail-

able to authors of books or playwrights, an examination of these protections by all writers is helpful in knowing what to ask for in negotiating an agency agreement. Writers should also note that state labor codes provide certain protections. This chapter is intended to provide the writer with a brief summary of what these guild and statutory protections are.

WGA ARTISTS' MANAGERS BASIC AGREEMENT

Before getting into the heart of the WGA Artists' Managers Basic Agreement (referred to hereafter as the "Basic Agreement"), a few words of caution are necessary.

The Basic Agreement affords protection only to WGA members. Moreover, it binds only those agencies that are signatories to it; however, all reputable agencies representing writers in the radio, television and motion picture areas are signatories to the Guild (the status of a particular agency can be easily verified by contacting the Guild). Lastly, the Basic Agreement only affords protection to members rendering services in the radio, television and motion picture areas. Therefore, the publishing and dramatic stage areas are not covered.

Notwithstanding the limits of Guild protection, agency contracts are generally negotiable, and the writer who is not a member of the Guild can still ask to have Rider "W" (described in detail below) incorporated into his agency contract. Writers rendering services in the book publishing or dramatic stage area can choose provisions of Rider "W" applicable to them and incorporate them in their agency contracts.

David Goldman is a business affairs executive with the William Morris Agency. He is a graduate of the University of California at Los Angeles School of Law and received an undergraduate degree from UCLA in political science.

RIDER "W"

The Basic Agreement provides that Rider "W" will be incorporated into the agency contracts of every WGA member. (Copies of Rider "W" may be obtained by contacting the WGA.) Rider "W" provides an exhaustive list of protections for the writer; the following is an outline of its most pertinent provisions.

Term

The maximum term of the writer's agency agreements is two years. If the writer has the right to and does terminate the services representation agreement, he will concurrently have the right to terminate the materials representation agreement.

If an agreement for the sale of a specific piece of literary property is not entered into within one year after the date of submission to the agent, either the writer or the agent may withdraw the literary property from further representation by the agent.

The writer has the right to terminate his initial representation agreement for services and/or materials at any time within eighteen months from the inception of the agreement, and such termination will be effective at the expiration of the eighteen-month period.

Commissions

Commissions are calculated on the basis of the writer's gross compensation. The agent may not collect a commission on minimum "backend" payments (e.g.,residuals, passive rights, supplemental market uses). The agent may collect a commission on backend payments in excess of WGA minimum, but such commissions cannot reduce the writer's compensation to a sum less than WGA minimum.

Agency commissions on any one deal may not exceed ten percent unless (i) the writer failed to disclose the existence of a prior relationship with an agent who may assert a claim against the writer; or (ii) after signing agency contracts, the writer incurs an obligation to pay a commission to others without the consent of the agent.

Where an agent represents both the writer and the packager (i.e., the owner or producer) of a particular television program that the writer renders services on or provides literary material for, the agent may not collect a commission from the writer for compensation received with respect to the television package program.

At the time the representation agreement begins, the writer must designate whether existing deals are or are not to be commissionable by the agent in the future. After the agency agreement terminates, the writer will be obligated to pay commission on contracts of employment procured by his former agent and options picked up thereon; however, the former agent will not be entitled to commissions on increased compensation or improvements in the employment agreement negotiated after the termination of the representation agreement.

Upon the expiration of the agency agreements, the writer may request within thirty days after expiration a list of all engagements entered into during the term or which are in negotiation at the time of expiration. If the writer objects to his former agent commissioning such engagements he must make his objection within thirty days.

Continuity of Management

In order to assure that those agents responsible for causing the writer to sign with a particular agency will continue to service the writer at the agency, the writer may designate up to two persons who will be active in the operation of the agency and who will be available generally to render services for the writer at the writer's request. The agency may designate one such additional person if it has more than 150 employees. If *all* persons designated cease to be active in the agency, the agent must notify the writer and the writer will have the election to terminate his agency agreements.

Conflict of Interest

Where the agent represents the purchaser of the writer's services or materials and the writer, the agent must inform the writer of the agent's commission, profit participation on other financial interest in the production, project, sale, literary material, show, package or services involved and must obtain the writer's consent prior to making a commitment for the writer. After the writer learns of the agent's interest, he may represent himself or obtain representation by another agent or attorney.

Legal Expenses

If it becomes necessary for the writer to engage an attorney to collect monies due from an employer or purchaser, commissions on sums received by the writer shall be based on the net sum received after deducting attorney fees and costs.

Ninety-Day Clause

The writer may terminate his services agreement if during any ninety-day period the writer has not been employed under, or received offers for, contracts in which he would receive compensation of at least $10,000 in fields in which his agent is authorized to represent him. Periods during which the writer is unavailable to perform services are excluded from the ninety-day period.

Miscellaneous Termination Provisions

In addition to the ninety-day clause, the writer may terminate his agency agreements for any of the following reasons:

- If the agent materially breaches any of his fiduciary obligations to the writer.
- If the agent during a WGA strike obtains employment or makes the sale of any literary material for any writer with a producer or other person with whom the WGA is on strike.
- If the agent represents a writer who has been denied membership in the WGA or whose membership in the WGA has been revoked by reason of acts prejudicial to the WGA's welfare.
- If the agent is no longer listed as subscribing to the WGA Basic Agreement.
- If a six-month period expires during which the agent has secured for the writer assignments on only WGA minimum terms; provided, however, that if the writer consents in advance to such assignments in the place indicated in Rider "W," he will have waived his right to so terminate.
- If the agent negotiates or approves on behalf of the writer any employment agreement or contract of sale of materials which violates the WGA collective bargaining agreement or a WGA working rule, unless the writer is aware of such violation and insists that the contract be negotiated.

Assignability

A writer's agency agreement may not be assigned without the writer's consent except in certain in-

stances where the assignee is the original agent doing business in a different form (e.g., the agent incorporates).

Accounting

The agent must obtain prior written authority to collect monies on behalf of the writer. If the agent does collect monies for the writer, he must render faithful accountings and make prompt payments to the writer of his compensation less agency commissions. Additionally, the agent is forbidden to commingle his client's monies with agency monies.

Package Representation

Rider "W" does not in any way govern an agent's representation of television or radio package programs, as distinguished from the representation of writer's services or literary materials.

CALIFORNIA LABOR CODE

Agencies representing writers in the entertainment industry will generally be doing business in California and fall within the jurisdiction of the California Labor Code. The provisions of the code are somewhat general in that they are geared to all forms of talent, but the protection the code provides is substantial. The following is an outline of the pertinent provisions of the code.

- Agents (often referred to as "artists' managers" in the code) must be licensed by the California Labor Commissioner. The commissioner requires that the agent submit two character affidavits as part of his application.
- The Labor Commissioner must approve the form of an artist–agent agreement, which will not be approved if it is unfair, unjust and oppressive to the artist.
- The agent's fees must be filed with the Labor Commissioner for his scrutiny.
- The agent must maintain accurate records of transactions affecting the artist.
- In order to avoid conflicts of interest, the agent is prohibited from splitting his fee with an employer of the artist.

CONCLUSION

If the writer is a member of the WGA, his position with his agent (providing his agent is a signatory to the Basic Agreement) has been negotiated to a point where there is little room for improvement. If the writer is not a member of the WGA, or is not rendering services in an area covered by the WGA, he may champion his cause by seeking the protections of Rider "W" that are pertinent to him. If the writer's agent is doing business in California, the writer will have the additional protection of the California Labor Code.

The following forms are part of the package of contracts that need to be signed with an agency. The "General Services" agreement is representative of agreements used for writers, whether they are active in publishing, screenwriting, or both. The Rider to the General Services Agreement (Rider W) and the Negotiator Letter are required by the Writers Guild for screenwriters who sign with agencies franchised by the Writers Guild.

NEW YORK   BEVERLY HILLS   NASHVILLE   LONDON   ROME   SYDNEY   MUNICH

TALENT AGENCY

ESTABLISHED 1898

WILLIAM MORRIS AGENCY
INC.

GENERAL SERVICES

William Morris Agency, Inc.
151 El Camino
Beverly Hills, California

Beverly Hills, California

Date_____, 19 _____

Gentlemen:

This will confirm the following agreement between us:

1. I hereby engage you for a term of   years, commencing
as my sole and exclusive agent, adviser, artists' manager, and representative with respect to my services, activity and participation in all branches of the entertainment, publication, and related fields throughout the world, including but not limited to merchandising, testimonials and commercial tie-ups, whether or not using my name, voice or likeness.

This agreement also applies to agreements to refrain from any service or activity.

2. All contracts shall be subject to my prior approval.

3. You accept this engagement, and will advise and consult with me during normal business hours at your office with respect to the matters covered thereby for the purposes of developing, advancing and directing my professional career, and in connection therewith, you agree to use all reasonable efforts to procure employment for me, subject to the following:

(a) You may render similar services to others, including persons of the same general qualifications and eligibility for the same or similar employment, and including owners of package programs or other productions in which my services are used. Such representation shall not constitute a violation of your fiduciary or other obligations hereunder.

(b) You may appoint others to aid you, including your subsidiary and/or affiliated corporations and your associated persons, firms and corporations, but I shall have no obligation to pay any sums beyond those specified herein for the services of anyone you so appoint.

4. I warrant and represent that I have the right to enter into this agreement and that I do not have, nor will I enter into any contract, or incur any obligation in conflict herewith.

5. I agree to pay you, as and when received by me or by any person, firm or corporation on my behalf, directly or indirectly, or by any person, firm or corporation owned or controlled by me, directly or indirectly, or in which I now have or hereafter during the term hereof acquire any right, title or interest, directly or indirectly, and you agree to accept, as and for your compensation, a sum equal to ten (10%) percent of the gross compensation paid and/or payable, during or after the term hereof, under or by reason of every engagement, employment or contract covered by this agreement, now in existence or made or negotiated during the term hereof, and whether procured by you, me or any third party. In lieu however of said 10%, your compensation shall be with respect to: (i) concerts, readings, recitals, and any other engagements presented in places where concerts, readings and recitals are given, and tours; constituting or similar to any of the foregoing: 15%; (ii) merchandising, testimonial and commercial tie-up rights and licensing of such rights: 20%; and (iii) lectures and/or appearances of a similar nature: 20%. You shall be entitled to your said compensation (ten 10%), fifteen (15%) or twenty (20%) percent, as the case may be) with respect to any specific aforesaid engagement, employment or contract, for so long as I may continue to be entitled to receive compensation pursuant thereto, including all modifications, additions, options, extensions, renewals, substitutions for, and replacements of such engagements, employment or contracts, directly or indirectly. For this purpose, any engagement, employment or contract with the same employer or any person, firm, corporation or other entity, owned and/or controlled by such employer, directly or indirectly, including but not limited to any affiliate or subsidiary of such employer, made, entered into or resumed within the four months immediately following the termination of any prior engagement, employment or contract with such employer, shall be deemed a substitution or replacement of such engagement, employment or contract. "Gross compensation", as used herein, means one hundred (100%) percent of all moneys, properties, and considerations of any kind or character, including but not limited to salaries, earnings, fees, royalties, rents, bonuses, gifts, proceeds, shares of stock or profit and stock options, without deductions of any kind.

6. (a) If, within 6 months after the end of the term hereof, I accept any offer on terms similar or reasonably comparable to any offer made to me during the term hereof, from or through the same offerer or any person, firm or corporation directly or indirectly connected with such offerer, the contract resulting therefrom (oral or written), shall be subject to all the terms hereof, including the payment provisions of paragraph 5 above.

(b) As to the proceeds of any motion picture, film, tape, wire, transcription, recording or other reproduction or result of my services covered by this agreement, your right to payment under paragraph 5 shall continue so long as any of these are used, sold, leased, or otherwise disposed of, whether during or after the term hereof.

(c) As to every engagement, employment or contract, including all modifications, additions, options, extensions, renewals, substitutions for and replacements of such engagement, employment, or contract, requiring my services, in connection with which you are entitled to compensation as provided in Paragraph 5 hereof after the termination of this agreement, you agree that, notwithstanding such termination, you shall remain obligated to continue to render agency services with respect thereto.

7. In the event I am presently under contract to, or hereafter enter into a contract with, any person, firm, corporation or other entity owned or controlled in whole or in part by me, either directly or indirectly (hereinafter referred to as "third party") pursuant to which such third party has or hereafter obtains the right to furnish my services in any of the fields covered by this agreement, I agree to cause such third party forthwith to enter into a written exclusive agency agreement with you with respect to such services

upon all the same terms and conditions as herein contained, specifically including such third party's agreement to pay compensation to you as herein provided in paragraph 5, based on the gross compensation paid and/or payable to such third party, directly or indirectly, for furnishing my services. Notwithstanding that such third party may enter into any such written exclusive agency agreement with you, I shall remain primarily liable, jointly and severally, with such third party, to pay compensation to you as provided in Paragraph 5 above, based on the gross compensation paid and/or payable to such third party, directly or indirectly, for furnishing my services. For the purposes of Paragraph 5 above, the term "gross compensation" shall be deemed to include such gross compensation paid and/or payable to such third party. If such third party fails, for whatever reason, to execute such written exclusive agency agreement with you, you shall nevertheless remain my exclusive agent to represent me in connection with my services on the terms and conditions as herein contained and I shall remain liable to pay compensation to you as provided in this contract and in the preceding sentence hereof.

8.   No breach of this agreement by you shall be deemed material unless within 30 days after I learn of such breach, I serve written notice thereof on you by registered mail and you do not remedy such breach within 15 days, exclusive of Saturdays, Sundays, and holidays, after receipt of such notice.

9.   (a) Notwithstanding anything elsewhere contained in this agreement, should I not obtain a bona fide offer, from a responsible source, for my employment in any field in which you are authorized to represent me, pursuant to this or any other contract, of any nature in any field in which you are authorized to represent me therefor, pursuant to this or any other contract, during a period in excess of 4 consecutive months in the term hereof, throughout which time I am unemployed and ready, willing and able to accept employment and to render the services required in connection therewith, either party shall have the right to terminate your engagement hereunder by notice in writing to such effect sent to the other party by Registered or Certified Mail to the last known address of such party; provided, however, that such right shall be ineffective if, after the expiration of 4 months but prior to the time I exercise such right, I have received from a responsible source a bona fide offer of employment. No termination hereunder shall affect your rights under Paragraph 5 and 6 hereof to receive compensation after such termination and/or the expiration of the term hereof upon the terms and conditions therein stated.

   (b) Controversies arising between us under the Labor Code of the State of California, and the rules and regulations for the enforcement thereof, shall be referred to the Labor Commissioner of the State of California as provided in Section 1700.44 of said Labor Code, save and except to the extent that the Laws of the State of California now or hereafter in force, may permit the reference of any such controversy to any other person or group of persons.

10. This agreement shall not apply with respect to:

   (a) my activity covered by any other exclusive agency contract between you and me, so long as such other agreement remains in effect.

   (b) my activity within the jurisdiction of any union with which you have an agreement prohibiting your entering into an exclusive agency agreement with me on this form, so long as such union agreement remains in effect.

11. You may assign this agreement and all rights herein granted to a corporation controlling, controlled by or under common control with you or to any corporation affiliated with you or to a subsidiary wholly owned by you, but any such assignment shall not relieve you of your obligation hereunder.

12. In the event this agreement is signed by more than one person, firm, corporation or other entity, it shall apply to the undersigned jointly and severally, and to the activities, interests and contracts of each of the undersigned individually. If any of the undersigned is a corporation or other entity, the pronouns "I", "me" or "my" as used in this agreement shall refer to the undersigned corporation or other entity, and the undersigned corporation or other entity agrees that it will be bound by the provisions hereof in the same manner and to the same extent as it would, had its name been inserted in the place of such pronouns.

13. This instrument sets forth the entire agreement between us. No promise, representation or inducement, except as herein set forth, has been made by you or on your behalf. Should any provision of this agreement be void or unenforceable, the rest of this agreement shall remain in full force. It may not be cancelled, altered or amended except in writing and no termination of any other agency agreement between us shall have the effect of terminating this agreement.

AGREED TO AND ACCEPTED: Yours very truly,
WILLIAM MORRIS AGENCY, INC.

By _____   _____

THIS TALENT AGENCY IS LICENSED BY THE LABOR COMMISSIONER OF THE STATE OF CALIFORNIA.
This form of contract has been approved by the State Labor Commissioner of California on September 29, 1979.

3M 12 80

NEW YORK
BEVERLY HILLS
NASHVILLE
LONDON
ROME
SYDNEY
MUNICH

WILLIAM MORRIS AGENCY, INC.
151 EL CAMINO DRIVE ● BEVERLY HILLS, CALIFORNIA 90212 ● 274-7451

TALENT AGENCY XXXX EST. 1898

Cable Address:
"WILLMORRIS"

GENERAL MATERIALS AND PACKAGES

William Morris Agency, Inc.
151 El Camino
Beverly Hills, California

Date _____ , 19 _____

Gentlemen:

This will confirm the following agreement between us:

1. I hereby engage you for a term of   years, commencing as my sole and exclusive agent and representative in all fields and media, throughout the world, to negotiate for, and with respect to, the disposition, sale, transfer, assignment, rental, lease, use, exploitation, furnishing or otherwise turning to profit (herein collectively referred to as the "disposition") of all and/or any part of the following:

(a) (i) All creative properties and package shows now or at any time during the term hereof created in whole or in part by me or in which I own or hereafter during the term hereof acquire any right, title or interest, directly or indirectly, and

(ii) All creative properties and package shows in which any person or firm owned or controlled by me, directly or indirectly, has any interest or in which any corporation, partnership, joint venture or other entity in which I, directly or indirectly, have any right, title or interest, has any interest.

(b) The creative properties and/or package shows presently called or identified as:

2. I have the right to enter into this agreement and I will not hereafter enter into any agreement which will conflict with the terms and provisions hereof.

3. You accept this engagement and agree to advise and consult with me at my request at your office in any locality in which you may then maintain an office with respect to the matters covered thereby, subject to the following:

(a) You may render similar services to others, including owners of creative properties or package shows in which my creative properties or package shows are used, and owners of other creative properties or package shows, and whether or not similar to or competitive with the creative properties or package shows covered by this agreement.

(b) I may from time to time desire to acquire certain rights, properties or materials from or employ other clients of yours for or in connection with my creative properties or package shows. I agree that you may represent such other clients in their negotiations with me and such negotiations you will be acting solely as the agents or representative of such other clients and not as my agent or representative. Your representation of or your receipt of compensation from such other clients therefor shall not be construed as a breach of your obligations hereunder, or of any fiduciary or other relationship between you and me, and you shall nevertheless be entitled to your compensation hereunder.

(c) You may appoint others to assist you, including your subsidiary and/or affiliated corporations and your associated persons, firms and corporations, but I shall have no obligations to pay you or such appointees any sums except as specified herein.

(d) With respect to syndication, merchandising, advertising, testimonials and commercial tie-ups and stock and amateur stage rights in and to the creative properties or package shows hereunder, you shall have the exclusive right to represent me in negotiations with any person, firm or corporation specializing therein to act on my behalf in connection with such activity, and you shall cooperate with such person, firm or corporation. The compensation to be paid by me to any such person, firm or corporation shall not diminish any sums payable by me hereunder, except as specified in paragraph 4 (b) hereof with respect to syndication.

(e) (i) You will make your services available to assist me in bringing together key elements of said package shows, for the purpose of creating a product for sale, and to assist in negotiating agreements in connection therewith.

(ii) You will make your services available to consult with me as to the creation and/or development and/or production of said package shows, as such matters relate to the licensing or sale thereof.

(iii) You will make your services available in connection with soliciting and negotiating agreements for the sale or exploitation of said package shows, and shall render advice with respect thereto.

4. (a) I agree to pay to you, as when received, during and after the term hereof, and I hereby assign to you 10% of the "gross compensation" paid and/or payable to me or any person, firm or corporation on my behalf, directly or indirectly, or to any person, firm or corporation owned or controlled by me, either directly or indirectly, or in which I now have or hereafter during the term hereof acquire any right, title or interest, pursuant to or as a result of any contract covered by this agreement, whether procured by you, me or any third party. In lieu however of said 10%, your compensation shall be with respect to: (i) printed publications in other countries of the world other than the United States: 20%; (ii) concerts, recitals, readings and/or appearances of similar nature, including engagements and/or tours for dramatic and/or musical shows: 15%; (iii) amateur stage rights: 20%; (iv) lectures and/or appearances of a similar nature: 20%; and (v) merchandising, testimonial and commercial tie-up rights and licensing of such rights: 20%.

(b) If I am engaged in the business of syndicating television programs generally, and I undertake or a third party undertakes the syndication of any package show hereunder or the reproducions thereof made primarily for television, then the distribution fee in connection therewith and the actual cost of exhibition prints and direct advertising shall be deducted from the gross compensation derived from such syndication, in computing the compensation to be paid by me to you hereunder. If I undertake such syndication, the distribution fee shall not exceed the rates normally and generally charged. If a third party undertakes such syndication, the distribution fee shall be the amount paid by me or deducted by the distributor.

(c) You agree at my request (provided I have retained such rights) to negotiate, or to assist me in negotiating for the disposition of television reproductions hereunder for distribution in syndication: (i) to a distributor or syndicator, and (ii) in the major foreign markets with which you have contact.

(d) If you negotiate, or your affiliate, subsidiary or correspondent agent assists you in negotiations for and with respect to the disposition of any television reproductions covered by this agreement for usage outside of the Continental United States, I agree to pay to you 15% of the gross compensation payable to me or on my behalf in connection with such disposition. If such disposition is made by me in accordance with the provisions of paragraph 4 (b) hereof, or by a syndicator, then your compensation shall be 10%, which shall be computed in the manner provided in paragraph 4 (b).

5. (a) The term hereof shall be automatically extended, re-extended or renewed from time to time with respect to any specific creative property or package show or any rights therein whenever and so long as any contract or contracts covered by this agreement, relating to such specific creative property or package show, or any rights therein, shall be or continue in effect; and for one (1) year thereafter, or the stated term referred to in paragraph 1 above, whichever is the longer.

(b) If any disposition is made of any reproduction of any creative property or package show covered by this agreement, in whole or in part, during or after the term hereof, my obligation hereunder to pay compensation with respect thereto shall continue, during and after the term hereof, whenever any disposition thereof is made.

6. No breach of this agreement by you shall be deemed material unless within 30 days after I learn of such breach, I serve written notice thereof to you by registered or certified mail and you do not remedy such breach within 15 days, exclusive of Saturdays, Sundays and holidays, after receipt of such written notice.

7. (a) Except as set forth in subdivisions (b) and (c) of paragraph 7 hereof, any disposition of any creative property or package show or reproduction thereof (including stock or other ownership thereof) covered by this agreement, or any disposition effected by merger, consolidation, dissolution or by operation of law, shall be subject to all of your rights hereunder and to my first obtaining and delivering to you an assumption agreement in writing, of my obligations hereunder, by the party to whom any such disposition is made, or if such disposition is made by operation of law, then said assignee shall either assume this agreement in writing, or take such rights subject to the provisions and obligations of this agreement. No such disposition or assumption shall relieve me of my obligations hereunder. The aforesaid provisions shall likewise be applicable to any subsequent disposition of the type set forth in this subdivision, of any such interest or any part thereof.

(b) The provisions of subdivision (a) of paragraph 7, shall not be applicable to a disposition of a creative property or package show or reproduction thereof, or any rights therein, in an arms' length transaction for full and adequate consideration. With respect to such disposition, the provisions of paragraph 4 hereof shall apply, except that if the disposition is an outright disposition, then the provisions of paragraph 7 (c) hereof shall apply.

(c) In the event of a contemplated outright disposition by me of all, or a part of, my right, title and interest in and to a creative property or package show, or of any reproduction thereof (including stock or other ownership thereof) covered by this agreement, then I agree to give you not less than fifteen (15) days prior written notice thereof, by registered or certified mail, setting forth the proposed terms and conditions thereof and pertinent information respecting the proposed purchaser. You shall then have fifteen (15) days from the receipt of such notice (or amended notice, if any) within which to elect one of the following (such election shall be made by registered mail or certified mail): "A" — to take your compensation for and in connection with such disposition, or "B" — to waive your compensation on such disposition. If you elect to waive your compensation on such disposition pursuant to "B" above, then concurrently with such outright disposition, the purchaser shall execute and deliver to you a written assumption agreement, in form acceptable to you, assuming with respect to any and all subsequent dispositions of said creative property(s) and package show(s), including all reproductions thereof, and rights therein, all of my obligations to you pursuant to this agreement (as it may have been theretofore amended). In the event I fail to obtain and deliver to you such assumption agreement, then I shall remain obligated to pay to you such amount of compensation, as would have been payable by the purchaser, had such assumption agreement been obtained and delivered to you. If you elect to take your compensation, for and in connection with such disposition pursuant to "A" above, then the following shall be applicable:

(i) I shall pay to you ten percent (10%) of the gross compensation paid or payable to me, or on my behalf in connection with said outright disposition, without any deductions whatsoever, and in addition thereto,

(ii) I shall require the purchaser to pay to you a sum equal to one-ninth of the residual payments (including but not limited to: salaries, fees, royalties and deferred payments) paid or payable to any person, firm or corporation, for the repeat and residual uses of such reproductions in the television and theatrical fields (including payroll taxes and payroll insurance, pension funds and similar costs directly allocated to such residual payments), and I shall require the purchaser to deliver to you a written assumption agreement, in form acceptable to you, with respect to such residual payments as would have been payable by the purchaser, had such assumption agreement been obtained and delivered to you.

If you fail to advise me of your election with respect to such contemplated outright disposition, then you shall be deemed to have elected the compensation referred to in "B" of paragraph 7 (c) hereof.

8. When used in this agreement, the following terms are defined as follows:

(a) "Creative properties" shall mean and include all rights, interests, properties and material of a literary, entertainment, advertising and promotional nature, including, but not limited to, art, characters, characterizations, compositions, copyrights, designs, dramatic and/or musical works, drawings, formats, formulaes, ideas, outlines, literary works, music, lyrics, musical arrangements, bits of business, action, incidents, plots, treatments, scripts, sketches, themes (literary and musical), titles, trade marks, trade names, patents, slogans, catchwords, and writings or any part or combination of any of the foregoing and any reproduction of any of the foregoing, or any other rights, interests, properties or materials which may heretofore have been or may hereafter be acquired, written, composed or utilized for, on or in connection therewith, or developed therefrom, including, but not limited to, any creative property or package show based upon or produced as part of, or developed from any element of, any creative property or package show covered by this agreement.

(b) "Package shows" means any and all manner of exploitation of creative property, by any present or future means or process, and whether transitory or permanent in character, including but not limited to any show, production, presentation, program or recording and any series thereof, and any reproduction of any of the foregoing; and any person, unit, group, organization or combination of elements or other creative property or package show which may heretofore have been or may hereafter be acquired, written, composed, utilized, presented, produced, or exploited for, on or in connection therewith or developed therefrom, including, but not limited to, any creative property or package show based upon or produced as part of, or developed from any element of, any creative property or package show covered by this agreement; and any and all forms of merchandising, advertising, testimonials, and commercial tie-ups in connection with or relating to any creative properties or package shows.

(c) "Reproduction" means the incorporation or embodiment of any creative properties or package shows, or any part thereof, in any motion picture, kinescope, film, recording, transcription, tape, wire, cassette or other form of production or reproduction by any process now known or hereafter devised.

(d) "Gross compensation" means all moneys, properties and considerations of any kind or character, including but not limited to earnings, fees, royalties, rents, bonuses, gifts, proceeds, allowances or deductions to cover rerun fees, shares of stock or profit and stock options without deduction of any kind. Without limiting the generality of the foregoing, there will be no deduction of any of the following: any share of the proceeds received by a theatrical producing manager; distribution fees (except as provided in paragraph 4 (b) hereof); deferred or postponed payments or rerun fees of residual fees or any other costs and expenses whether paid or payable by me or by any other person, firm or corporation; profit participations or ownership interest of any other person, firm or corporation, including those of any person, firm or corporation to whom any disposition hereunder is made. With respect to any sale or assignment of a package show or creative property or any part thereof or any right or interest therein covered by this agreement to a person, firm or corporation having a profit participation or ownership interest therein, a fair and reasonable value for such participation or ownership interest shall be added to and included as part of gross compensation in connection with such disposition.

(e) "Contracts covered by this agreement" means any and every agreement, oral or written, directly or indirectly relating to or connected with the disposition or the refraining or withholding from or limitation upon the disposition of any creative property or package show or any part thereof or any right or interest therein, covered by this agreement, whether procured or negotiated by you, me or any third party, whether any such agreement is now in existence or is made or negotiated or to become effective during the term hereof (or within 6 months after the term hereof, if any such agreement is on terms similar or reasonably comparable to any offer made to me during the term hereof and is with the same offeror thereof or any person, firm or corporation directly or indirectly connected with such offeror); and all agreements, oral or written, substituted for or replacing any such agreement, directly or indirectly, and all modifications, supplements, extensions, additions and renewals of any such agreement or substitutions or replacements thereof, whether made, negotiated or to become effective during or after the term hereof and whether procured or negotiated by you, me or any third party.

(f) "Term hereof" or words of like reference means the period specified in paragraph 1 hereof and any and all extensions or renewals thereof pursuant to the provisions of paragraph 5 (a) hereof.

(g) "Syndication" means any disposition of the television and/or radio rights in a package show anywhere in the world, other than a disposition for national network broadcasts and repeat national network broadcasts in the United States.

(h) "Print costs" referred to in paragraph 4 (b) hereof, shall mean the actual cost of printing 35mm and 16mm prints (or making a new dub of a tape in connection with a live/tape program), and specifically shall not include such costs as cans, reels, shipping, insurance, dubbing or redubbing, editing storage, customs, duties, tariffs, taxes or any similar charges or costs.

9. In the event, I, acting alone or as a party of a partnership, joint venture, corporation or other entity, shall at any time hereafter enter into an exclusive General Materials and Packages agency agreement with you, relating to a specific creative property or package show covered by this agreement, then during the term of such subsequent agency agreement, said specific creative property and package show shall be deemed excluded from the scope of this agreement, but it shall not otherwise be so excluded.

10. This instrument sets forth the entire agreement between us. No promise, representation or inducement, except as herein set forth, has been made by you on your behalf. Should any provision of this agreement be void or unenforceable, the rest of this agreement shall remain in full force. This agreement may not be cancelled, altered or amended except in writing, and no termination of any other agency agreement between us shall have the effect of terminating this agreement. This agreement shall bind my heirs, executors, administrators, successors and assigns; and the pronouns "I", "me" or "my" where used in this agreement shall likewise refer to said heirs, executors, administrators, successors and assigns. You may assign this agreement and all of your rights hereunder to a firm or corporation controlling, controlled by or under common control with you or to any firm or corporation affiliated with you or a subsidiary wholly owned by you, but no such assignment will relieve you of your obligations hereunder.

11. In the event this agreement is signed by more than one person, firm or corporation, it shall apply to the undersigned, jointly and severally, and to the activities, interests and contracts of each and all of the undersigned. If any of the undersigned is a corporation or other entity, the pronouns "I", "me" or "my" where used in this agreement shall likewise refer to such corporation or other entity.

Yours very truly,

AGREED TO AND ACCEPTED:
WILLIAM MORRIS AGENCY, INC.

By _____

_____

This Talent Agency is licensed by the Labor Commissioner of the State of California. The Labor Commissioner of the State of California has ruled that this form of contract does not require the approval of the Labor Commissioner.

RIDER TO GENERAL SERVICES AGREEMENT (WRITER)

1. Rider 'W' as amended by the 1976 WGA Basic Agreement dated as of September 22, 1976 with the Writers Guild of America, West, Inc., is deemed incorporated herein. For the purposes set forth in Paragraph 4 of Rider 'W' entitled CONTINUITY OF MANAGEMENT, the following names are hereby inserted.

At least one and not more than two persons active in the business of Talent Agency shall be inserted.

_____

_____

_____
(WGA may insert a third name of its choice)

2. If there are any existing deals in effect on the date hereof I agree that the same will be commissionable by you under this agreement. ☐ NO ☐ YES

3. I am willing to accept minimum assignments.

☐ YES ☐ NO

4. I am entitled to call upon and use the services of the Negotiator in connection with any or all proposed agreements where you represent the owners of a package program and I am offered employment (or an offer is made to purchase or license my literary material) in connection with said package program. The Negotiator may be called in to assist and advise me and, if requested by me, to negotiate said employment agreement and/or material agreement on my behalf at no cost to me. However, I may give you in advance a blanket authorization to negotiate agreements with such package programs on my behalf without the participation of the Negotiator by checking the box below and affixing my signature in the space provided. Said blanket authorization may be rescinded by me with respect to any particular negotiation by my simply contacting the Negotiator at the time.

☐ I do not desire the services of the Negotiator in the circumstances referred to above.

The name and address of the Negotiator is available at WGA.

_____

NEW YORK
BEVERLY HILLS
NASHVILLE
LONDON
ROME
SYDNEY
MUNICH

WILLIAM MORRIS AGENCY, INC.
151 EL CAMINO DRIVE ● BEVERLY HILLS, CALIFORNIA 90212 ● 274-7451

TALENT AGENCY
XXX
EST. 1898

Cable Address:
"WILLMORRIS"

Dated:

Dear

You have the right to have the Negotiator consult
with you and if you so request, to negotiate on your
behalf with respect to the terms of any package representation agreement covering your writing services
or materials which agency asks you to sign. If you do
not desire the services of the Negotiator please check
the box below. In any event, please sign this letter
before signing the package representation agreement
offered to you for signature and return same to us.

                    Very truly yours,

                    WILLIAM MORRIS AGENCY, INC.

                    By:_____

☐   I do not desire the services of the Negotiator.

        _____

The name and address of the Negotiator is available at WGA.

Money and the Writer

An Introduction to Tax Planning for the Writer

Gary J. Freedman and Dale S. Miller of Diller & Freedman, A Professional Corporation

Many writers and other taxpayers seek advice regarding the preparation of their annual income tax returns, but too few seek guidance with respect to minimizing income taxes through appropriate planning. Tax planning is a complex subject which must take into account the particular facts and circumstances of each taxpayer. The literature, judicial decisions, statutes and regulations concerning taxation are voluminous. This chapter was not undertaken with the view of making the writer an expert on tax planning but rather to impart a basic understanding and awareness of certain tax issues and concepts that may prove useful to the beginning writer as well as the author who has achieved a level of financial success.

We suggest that the beginning writer initially consult with a tax adviser for information with respect to estimated income taxes, bookkeeping systems and bank accounts. The tax adviser can answer questions concerning state or city income taxes as well as determining whether other local taxes must be paid in the writer's place of business.

We hope that this brief summary of certain tax concepts will act as a catalyst for the writer to seek competent counsel.

PRIZES, AWARDS, SCHOLARSHIPS, AND FELLOWSHIPS

Although prizes and awards received by the writer are generally taxable income, there are exceptions. For the most part, prizes and awards given to a writer in recognition of educational, artistic or literary achievements such as the Nobel or Pulitzer prizes are not includable in gross income, provided that the writer was selected without any action on his or her part to enter the contest and is not required to perform future services in connection

Gary J. Freedman graduated from University of Illinois in 1964 and Hastings College of Law, University of California in 1967. Mr. Freedman practices in Los Angeles with the firm of Diller & Freedman, A Professional Corporation, principally in the areas of entertainment, corporation and tax law.

Dale S. Miller graduated from University of California at Los Angeles in 1972, Pepperdine University in 1976 and received an LL.M from New York University School of Law in 1977. Mr. Miller was formerly an attorney for the California Corporation Commissioner and currently is an adjunct instructor of finance. Mr. Miller practices in Los Angeles with the firm of Diller & Freedman, A Professional Corporation, principally in the areas of securities, entertainment and tax law.

with the award. If a writer is a candidate for a degree from an educational institution, then scholarships and fellowship grants are also excluded from gross income unless a portion of the grant is in consideration for the performance of services not required of all candidates for the degree. Those writers who are not candidates for degrees may only exclude grants from gross income if such grants are received from certain charitable, governmental or international organizations and only to the extent that such grants do not exceed $300 times the number of months for which the grant is received, provided that the writer must also have not received such grants for more than thirty-six months in his lifetime.

BUSINESS EXPENSES

The writer's gross income is reduced by business expenses, the deductibility of which generally depends upon two tests. First, the expense must be connected to the business of writing. Second, it must be shown that the expense arose from a transaction which is ordinary and necessary to the writer's business. The burden is on the taxpayer to prove that the expenditure was in fact made as well as the nature and circumstances that give rise to the deductibility of the expense. The importance of detailed and accurate business records setting forth the amount, date, place and business purpose of all business expenses cannot be overstated in order to substantiate expense claims. Travel and entertainment expenses require especially detailed substantiation.

The expense of acquiring a business asset with a useful life of more than one year may not be deducted as a business expense. The cost of a capital asset less its salvage value may instead be deducted from the writer's gross income by annual depreciation deductions over the useful life of the asset.

The professional writer may claim as deductible expenses the reasonable cost of supplies, dues for professional organizations, subscriptions to professional journals and amounts expended for telephone, postage and books, as well as entertainment and travel expenses. Travel expenses may also include the cost of meals and lodging incurred while the writer is away from home on business overnight, or if sleep or rest is required during such travel. The travel expenses incurred between the

writer's residence and place of business are personal expenses and therefore are not deductible.

The expenses of the writer in operating or maintaining an office, including the usual expenses of rent and salaries, are deductible. Many writers as well as other professionals use part of their residence as an office. In this regard, Congress has established very strict requirements for the deductibility of expenses incurred in connection with the use of an office-residence. Generally, the office must be used exclusively and on a regular basis by the writer as the writer's principal place of business, but if the office is contained in a separate structure detached from the writer's residence or is used in the normal course of business to meet clients, then the home office need not be the writer's principal place of business. A writer who is not self-employed must also establish that the exclusive use of the home-office is for the convenience of his employer. The deductions that a taxpayer may take for the business use of home-office may not exceed the income derived from its use, less the allocable share of home deductions such as interest and taxes which are otherwise allowable.

Business expenses for the services of employees, attorneys, accountants, agents or business managers may also be deducted from the gross income of the writer.

The deduction of business expenses from the writer's gross business income may be limited where the writer's activities are determined to be a hobby rather than an activity engaged in for profit. If the writing activities are treated as a hobby, the business expenses related to writing are only deductible to the extent of writing income or otherwise allowable deductions such as interest and taxes, whichever is larger. The writer who receives significant non-writing income which is sheltered by writing expenses is most susceptible to attack by the IRS for hobby losses.

The IRS may look at many factors in order to determine whether the taxpayer's writing-related activities were undertaken to make a profit. Importance may be given to whether the writer's activities were carried on in a businesslike manner, whether the writer maintains complete books and records, whether the writer consulted experts such as agents, attorneys or accountants, whether the writer has obtained a certain level of financial success from writing activities. There is a rebuttable presumption that a taxpayer is engaged in an activity for profit if profits resulted in two or more of the last five consecutive taxable years. It may prove beneficial to maintain a record of all correspondence and agreements with publishers, producer, agents and others which would indicate a profit motive.

INCOME AVERAGING AND DEFERRED COMPENSATION

Although a writer may take many years to create a single work, the entire compensation may be received in a single tax year. This might be disadvantageous to the writer because of the progressive nature of federal income taxation. For example, a writer with net income of $30,000 in each of two successive tax years should pay less income tax than a writer who during the same period had no income the first tax year but who reccived income of $60,000 during the second tax year. It may have been possible for the writer with earnings in only one year to contractually defer a portion of such earnings to subsequent tax years where the income may be taxed at a lower rate. Additionally, the writer may receive beneficial tax treatment through averaging the current taxable income with the taxable income of the previous four years. The use of income averaging and deferred compensation should be explored with a tax adviser prior to entering into any contractual agreements where the writer's income will substantially rise above previous years.

RETIREMENT PLANS

The writer who has surplus earnings available for savings or investment should consider the benefits of an Individual Retirement Account (IRA). A writer who is under age 70½ and not a participant in another qualified plan may contribute annually to an IRA a maximum sum of $1,500 ($1,750 for a writer with an unemployed spouse) or fifteen percent of compensation, whichever is less, on or before the due date (with extensions) of the writer's federal tax return. Contributions to an IRA are tax deductible to the writer, and the contributed funds may accumulate earnings tax-free until withdrawal, usually at a time when the taxpayer is in a lower tax bracket. Contributions to an IRA are discretionary and are made at the election of the taxpayer. But

penalties are assessed against the taxpayer for withdrawals before age 59½, death or disability.

For the writer with high income who is desirous of saving a greater portion of earnings, the IRA is of little advantage since contributions are very limited. Writers who desire to defer a greater amount of annual earnings should explore the benefits of the Simplified Employee Pension (SEP) and Keogh plans, which offer the taxpayer a greater potential deferral of earnings through contributions than that offered by the IRA. The maximum yearly contribution in both defined contribution Keogh and SEP plans is $7,500 or fifteen percent of the taxpayer's annual compensation. Even larger contributions can be made to a defined-benefit Keogh plan.

INVESTMENT TAX CREDIT

The writer may be eligible for an investment tax credit if he purchases or leases certain tangible depreciable property such as an automobile, typewriter or office furniture. The credit for property with a useful life of seven years or more is ten percent of the cost of the property. The writer's tax liability is reduced by the amount of the credit.

LOAN-OUT CORPORATIONS

Writers sometimes form what has become known as a "loan-out" corporation in which the writer's services are performed through a corporate entity. The writer, through a contractual agreement, becomes an employee of the corporation, and the corporation, in turn, contracts for the performance of the writer's services on an independent contractor basis with those desiring to retain the services of the writer. A corporation is a separate legal entity from the individual taxpayer and therefore, must file separate income tax returns as well as maintain separate books and records. The employee-writer receives compensation in the form of a salary from the corporation. Although operating in a corporate form may make the writer's income subject to double taxation, one tax at the corporate level and another tax at the level of the employee receiving a salary, generally, loan-out corporations pay out most of the corporation's earnings as deductible expenses in the form of salaries, bonuses and contributions to retirement plans to avoid corporate income taxes.

REASONS FOR INCORPORATING

The primary reason for a writer to incorporate and thereby become an employee of a loan-out corporation is to gain substantial tax advantages. The corporation has the ability to adopt what are called "qualified" retirement plans such as defined-benefit or defined-contribution plans that are not subject to the same limitations on the deductibility of contributions as the IRA, Keogh or SEP plans.

The most common types of defined-contribution plans are profit-sharing plans and money purchase pension plans. Profit-sharing plans allow employer contributions of up to fifteen percent of the employee annual compensation or $36,875, in 1980, as adjusted for cost-of-living increases, whichever is less. The funding of such contribution may be subject to the employer's discretion. Money purchase pension plans allow deductible contributions of up to twenty-five percent of employee annual compensation or $36,875, in 1980, as adjusted for cost-of-living increases, whichever is less. Contributions to this plan are not discretionary but are made an obligation of the employer.

In the defined-benefit pension plan, the employer's contributions are actuarially determined based on the amount needed to fund the retirement benefit the employee desires to receive. Generally, the employee's annual retirement benefit is subject to limitations based on one hundred percent of the average of the employee's three highest consecutive years of compensation or a sum in the amount of $110,625, in 1980, as adjusted for cost-of-living increases, whichever is less. In addition, corporations may form combinations of defined-contribution and defined-benefit plans to achieve greater flexibility.

Contributions to qualified retirement plans are deductible to the corporation, and the benefits are not taxed to the writer-employee until distributions are made. In addition, the earnings from contributions subject to certain exceptions accumulate free of tax. The subject of qualified retirement plans is highly complex and requires careful analysis by the writer's attorney and accountant in order to tailor such plan to the individual needs and requirements of the writer.

In addition to the primary advantages of incorporating there are tax advantages that are not generally available to the self-employed taxpayer. The corporation may deduct, subject to certain limitations, expenses for group-term life insurance, medical and dental expenses, and disability insurance without a corresponding tax placed on the benefitted employee. Other advantages of incorporation include using a taxable year other than the calendar year for the corporation. Most individual taxpayers are on a calendar year for purposes of reporting income tax. The corporation can establish its tax year in another twelve-month period. The imposition of taxes can be deferred from one tax year to another by establishing a corporation with a non-calendar fiscal year even though taxes will, ultimately, be paid on such income. For example, if the writer-employee is on a calendar tax year and the corporation has a fiscal year ending in April, a portion of the writer's compensation can be paid by the corporation after December thereby deferring the writer's taxes on such income. The corporation may avoid the imposition of corporate tax on such sum by paying the compensation to the writer prior to its fiscal year end.

ASSIGNMENT OF INCOME

It may be advisable for the writer to consult with a tax adviser with respect to the advantages of incorporation before executing an agreement for a substantial sum of money. Once the contract is executed and work commences a transfer of the taxpayer's income for tax purposes to a corporation may be attacked by the IRS as a prohibited assignment of income and thereby disregarded.

CERTAIN PROBLEMS OF THE LOAN-OUT CONCEPT

The advantages of incorporating must be weighed against the disadvantages caused by increased operating costs, increased tax complexities, initial expenses of incorporation, including legal and accounting fees and administration expenses for retirement plans and to the extent that contributions are made to qualified retirement plans, the taxpayer will have less spendable cash. Generally, the economic benefit of incorporation must exceed the tax benefits that can be obtained through the Keogh or SEP plans sufficiently to justify the increased expenditures connected with incorporation.

Loan-out corporations pose potential problems that may result in detrimental economic consequences to the writer such as the imposition of tax penalties for accumulating income in excess of the reasonable needs of the corporation or for failing to distribute corporate income. Alternatively, the compensation of the writer-employee, once distributed, may be attacked as unreasonable and disallowed, in whole or part, as a deduction to the corporation thereby resulting in an additional tax at the corporate level. Additionally, if the business affairs of the corporation and the writer-employee have the same identity through commingling of records, operations and conduct, corporate income may be reallocated to the employee taxpayer resulting in the loss of the advantages of incorporation.

Loan-out corporations offer a significant tax planning tool for entertainment figures such as writers with high incomes who have substantial surplus earnings available for investment, but careful tax planning by attorneys and accountants must be provided in order to avail the benefits of operating in the corporate form.

IRS Recordkeeping Requirements and a List of Tax Publications

Department of the Treasury
Internal Revenue Service

Publication 552
(Rev. Nov. 82)

You can get the tax forms and publications mentioned in this publication by following the directions in the back of this pamphlet.

Introduction

You must maintain records that will enable you to prepare a correct tax return. These records will help you prepare your income tax return so that you will pay only your proper tax. If you keep a record of your expenses during the year, you may find that you can reduce your income tax by itemizing your deductions. Your deductible expenses may include a part of your medical and dental bills, interest payments, contributions, taxes, and certain other expenses. You must have a record of the amounts spent to take these deductions.

Good records will help you if the Internal Revenue Service selects your tax return for examination. Usually, an examination occurs one to three years after a return is filed. If you have kept good records, you should be able to clear up questionable items and arrive at the correct tax with a minimum of effort. If you have not kept good records, you may have to spend time getting statements and receipts from various sources. Also, you may have to pay more tax because you cannot prove your deductions or because you cannot prove the basis you used in figuring your gain or loss on the sale of property.

Use this publication to help you decide what records should be kept and how long to keep them. Publication 583, *Information for Business Taxpayers*, has a discussion of business records.

If you have questions about the tax treatment of income, expenses, or other items, see the list of publications at the end of this publication. Most questions that come up in filing a tax return or a claim for refund are answered in these publications.

Read the instructions that come with your tax forms each year to see if changes in the law affect you.

Records You Should Keep

The law does not require that you keep any particular kind of records. However, you should keep all sales slips, invoices, receipts, cancelled checks, stock brokerage statements, Forms W-2, W-2P, and 1099, and other documents that prove the amounts you show on your return as income, deductions, and credits. Your records must be kept available for inspection by the Internal Revenue Service in a manner that will enable the Service to determine your proper tax.

Copies of tax returns. You should keep copies of your tax returns as part of your tax records. They may help you prepare future tax returns, and they are necessary if you file an amended return. Copies of your returns, and your other records, may be helpful to either your survivor, or the executor or administrator of your estate, or both.

If necessary, you may request a copy of a return by sending a Form 4506, *Request for Copy of Tax Return*, to the Internal Revenue Service Center where you filed the return. Prepare a separate Form 4506 for each return you request, and allow a minimum of several months for receipt of the copy or copies. You should be able to get copies of your returns for at least 6 years. You must pay a small fee for the copy or copies.

Employee expenses. If you have travel, entertainment, and gift expenses related to your job, see Publication 463, *Travel, Entertainment, and Gift Expenses*, for a discussion of the records you need to keep.

Reporting earnings for self-employment social security tax. The social security benefits paid to you for disability or retirement, or to your family if you die, depend on your reporting accurately your earnings from self-employment. Therefore, keep accurate records of your business income and expenses (see Publication 583).

Capital gains and losses. You may be able to report the sale of an asset as a capital gain or loss. To do this, your records must show when and how an asset was acquired, how the asset was used, and when and how it was disposed of. Records must also show your cost or other basis, the gross selling price, and the expenses of sale. You also may be allowed to postpone paying tax on certain gains.

For more information on capital gains and losses, see Publications 544, *Sales and Other Dispositions of Assets*, and 550, *Investment Income and Expenses*.

Basis of property. You should keep records that show the basis of property you own.

Your home. If you own a home, you must keep records on the property to show your purchase price, your purchase expenses, your cost of improvements, and any other adjustments to basis, such as for depreciation and casualty losses.

The records you keep on your home should include information on a house you sold and replaced with your current house if you postponed tax on the gain on the sale of the former house. The basis of your current house is affected by the postponed gain. See Publication 523, *Tax Information on Selling Your Home.*

Reinvested dividends. If dividends on stock you own are reinvested, that is, the company buys additional whole or fractional shares for you with the dividends, you should keep records to show the amount of all the reinvested dividends.

Basis of property received as a gift. Sometimes you can increase the basis of property received as a gift if your records show your basis, the donor's basis, the fair market value of the property on the date of the gift, and any gift tax paid. This is explained in Publication 551, *Basis of Assets.*

Performing services for a charitable organization. If you perform services without pay for a charitable organization, you should keep records of the out-of-pocket expenses you pay to perform the services. For information about these expenses, see Publication 526, *Charitable Contributions.*

Pay statements. If you receive pay statements, each pay day or less often, keep them together for a record of deductible expenses that are withheld from your paycheck.

Divorce decree. If you take a deduction for alimony payments, keep your cancelled checks as well as a copy of the divorce, separate maintenance, or support decree, or written separation agreement. See Publication 504, *Tax Information for Divorced or Separated Individuals.*

The following are suggested types of receipts you should keep for specific expenses—

Medical and dental expenses. Keep bills along with the cancelled check to show when the expense was paid. If you pay by cash, most providers of medical and dental services will give you a signed receipt. You can keep a log to record mileage, taxi, or bus fares for medical transportation. If your employer withholds from your wages for medical insurance, keep your payroll statements to establish the premiums you paid through withholding.

Taxes. Form W–2 shows the state income tax withheld from your wages. If you made estimated state income tax payments, keep your cancelled checks and a copy of the state estimated tax return. Your prior year state return

shows any additional state tax paid in the current year. Keep cancelled checks and statements or other documents for your real estate and personal property taxes paid.

Interest. Keep statements, notes, and cancelled checks to prove your interest payments on loans, a mortgage, and credit cards.

Contributions. Many churches use an envelope system and send a statement of contributions to each parishioner using the envelopes for donations. If you make a gift of property, most organizations will give you a letter or receipt acknowledging the gift. If you make cash contributions, keep any receipts and an up-to-date listing of amounts and the organizations to which paid.

Union dues. If union dues are withheld from your wages, keep your pay statements to show the amount. If you pay by cash or check, keep the receipts and cancelled checks.

How To Keep Records

It may be helpful to write down your ordinary expenses that may be deductible. How often you record these expenses is up to you. A sample record is shown below.

Income statements. You should also keep your income statements. These include Form W–2 for your wages and Form 1099 for interest and dividends.

Your checkbook. Your checkbook can be a basic source for keeping a record of your deductible expenses. If your checkbook has enough space, record sufficient information at the time you write a check so you can determine, when preparing your return, whether the amount is a deductible or nondeductible expense. Cancelled checks, alone, are not always adequate evidence that an amount is deductible. You should keep receipts, sales slips, and any other documents that establish the deductibility of an amount.

You may keep receipts in any manner that best suits you as long as you can adequately

document each deduction you take. One method is to use an envelope for each type of deductible expense. You may use the list below as a guide to write on each envelope. For example, you may keep all medical and dental receipts in one envelope and all tax receipts in another envelope.

If you pay a lot of expenses with cash, make it a habit to ask for a dated and, if appropriate, signed receipt if the expense may be deductible.

Accounting Methods and Periods

All income tax returns are prepared using an accounting method and period. You establish your accounting method and period when you file your first federal income tax return.

Accounting method. An accounting method is a set of rules that you use to report income and deduct expenses. The two most common accounting methods are the cash method and the accrual method.

The cash method. Most taxpayers who are employees use this method because Form W–2 is prepared on the cash basis.

With this method, you report all items of income in the year they are received or credited to your account, or made available to you on demand. You deduct most expenses in the year you pay them. Expenses paid in advance can be deducted only in the year to which they apply.

The accrual method. With this method, you account for income when it is earned, whether or not you receive it. You deduct expenses when they are incurred rather than when they are paid.

You must use the same method from year to year. If you want to change your method of accounting, you must first get the consent of the Internal Revenue Service. See Publication 538, *Accounting Periods and Methods.*

Accounting period. Every taxpayer must figure

Expense Record

Date 19__	Payee	Medical Expenses	Taxes	Interest	Charitable Contributions	Miscellaneous Expenses	
						Explanation	Amount

Medical and Dental Expenses	Medicines and drugs, fees for doctors, dentists, nurses, hospital care, insurance premiums for medical care, hearing aids, dentures, eyeglasses, transportation for medical purposes, etc.
Taxes	Real estate taxes, personal property taxes, general sales taxes, etc.
Interest Expense	Home mortgage, bank loans, credit card finance charges, etc.
Contributions	Cash contributions or gifts of property to community chest, church or synagogue, colleges and universities, etc.
Miscellaneous Expenses	Union dues, subscriptions to professional journals, uniforms, political contributions, tax assistance fees, child care, etc.

taxable income and file a federal income tax return on the basis of an annual accounting period called a *tax year*. A tax year is usually 12 months long. It may be a calendar year or a fiscal year. A calendar year is January 1 through December 31. A fiscal year is 12 months in a row ending on the last day of any month but December.

Your tax year is established when you file your first federal income tax return. Most individual taxpayers who do not operate a business use the calendar year as their tax year. Forms W–2 and 1099 are prepared on the basis of the calendar year.

If you file your first return as a wage earner using the calendar year and later begin a business as a sole proprietor, your business books must be kept on a calendar year basis. You cannot change your accounting period without permission from the Internal Revenue Service.

A *newly married wife or husband* may adopt the accounting period of the other spouse without getting permission of the Service, if certain conditions are met. See Publication 538 for more information on accounting periods and how to change your tax year.

How Long You Should Keep Records

Generally, your records must be kept as long as they are important for any federal tax law. Records that support an item of income or a deduction on your return should be kept at least until the period of limitation expires for that return. Usually this is 3 years from the date the return was due or filed, or 2 years from the date the tax was paid, whichever is later. If an amount of income that should have been reported was not reported, and it is more than 25% of the income shown on the return, the period of limitation does not expire until 6 years after the return was filed. There is no period of limitation when a return is false or fraudulent, or when no return is filed.

Sometimes you should keep your records longer than the period of limitation. For example, if you want to use income averaging to figure your tax, you must show your taxable income for the 4 previous years. The taxable income figures can be obtained from copies of your tax returns.

Sometimes new laws give tax benefits to taxpayers who can prove from their records from previous years that they are entitled to such benefits.

Tax Publications

This list gives the titles and publication numbers for IRS publications. To order any of these free publications write the Forms Distribution Center for your area and say which publication number you want.

How to Get IRS Forms and Publications

You can order federal tax forms and publications from the IRS Forms Distribution Center for your state at the address below. You can also photocopy tax forms from reproducible copies kept at many public libraries.

Alabama—Caller No. 848, Atlanta, GA 30370

Alaska—P.O. Box 12626, Fresno, CA 93778

Arizona—P.O. Box 12626, Fresno, CA 93778

Arkansas—P.O. Box 2924, Austin, TX 78769

California—P.O. Box 12626, Fresno, CA 93778

Colorado—P.O. Box 2924, Austin, TX 78769

Connecticut—P.O. Box 1040, Methuen, MA 01844

Delaware—P.O. Box 25866, Richmond, VA 23260

District of Columbia—P.O. Box 25866, Richmond, VA 23260

Florida—Caller No. 848, Atlanta, GA 30370

Georgia—Caller No. 848, Atlanta, GA 30370

Hawaii—P.O. Box 12626, Fresno, CA 93778

Idaho—P.O. Box 12626, Fresno, CA 93778

Illinois—6000 Manchester Trafficway Terrace, Kansas City, MO 64130

Indiana—P.O. Box 636, Florence, KY 41042

Iowa—6000 Manchester Trafficway Terrace, Kansas City, MO 64130

Kansas—P.O. Box 2924, Austin, TX 78769

Kentucky—P.O. Box 636, Florence, KY 41042

Louisiana—P.O. Box 2924, Austin, TX 78769

Maine—P.O. Box 1040, Methuen, MA 01844

Maryland—P.O. Box 25866, Richmond, VA 23260

Massachusetts—P.O. Box 1040, Methuen, MA 01844

Michigan—P.O. Box 636, Florence, KY 41042

Minnesota—6000 Manchester Trafficway Terrace, Kansas City, MO 64130

Mississippi—Caller No. 848, Atlanta, GA 30370

Missouri—6000 Manchester Trafficway Terrace, Kansas City, MO 64130

Montana—P.O. Box 12626, Fresno, CA 93778

Nebraska—6000 Manchester Trafficway Terrace, Kansas City, MO 64130

Nevada—P.O. Box 12626, Fresno, CA 93778

New Hampshire—P.O. Box 1040, Methuen, MA 01844

New Jersey—P.O. Box 25866, Richmond, VA 23260

New Mexico—P.O. Box 2924, Austin, TX 78769

New York—

Western New York: P.O. Box 240, Buffalo, NY 14201

Eastern New York (including NY City): P.O. Box 1040, Methuen, MA 01844

North Carolina—Caller No. 848, Atlanta, GA 30370

North Dakota—6000 Manchester Trafficway Terrace, Kansas City, MO 64130

Ohio—P.O. Box 636, Florence, KY 41042

Oklahoma—P.O. Box 2924, Austin, TX 78769

Oregon—P.O. Box 12626, Fresno, CA 93778

Pennsylvania—P.O. Box 25866, Richmond, VA 23260

Rhode Island—P.O. Box 1040, Methuen, MA 01844

South Carolina—Caller No. 848, Atlanta, GA 30370

South Dakota—6000 Manchester Trafficway Terrace, Kansas City, MO 64130

Tennessee—Caller No. 848, Atlanta, GA 30370

Texas—P.O. Box 2924, Austin, TX 78769

Utah—P.O. Box 12626, Fresno, CA 93778

Vermont—P.O. Box 1040, Methuen, MA 01844

Virginia—P.O. Box 25866, Richmond, VA 23260

Washington—P.O. Box 12626, Fresno, CA 93778

West Virginia—P.O. Box 636, Florence, KY 41042

Wisconsin—6000 Manchester Trafficway Terrace, Kansas City, MO 64130

Wyoming—P.O. Box 2924, Austin, TX 78769

Foreign Addresses—Taxpayers with mailing addresses in foreign countries should send their requests for forms and publications to:
Director, Foreign Operations District,

Internal Revenue Service, Washington, DC 20225.

Puerto Rico—Director's Representative, U.S. Internal Revenue Service, Federal Office

Building, Chardon Street, Hato Rey, PR 00918

Virgin Islands—Department of Finance, Tax Division, Charlotte Amalie, St. Thomas, VI 00801

☆ U.S. GOVERNMENT PRINTING OFFICE: 1982—381-543/720

UNEMPLOYMENT INSURANCE AND THE WRITER

Alan Abrams

Since the employment opportunities in the entertainment industry tend to be, for many writers, sporadic in nature and generally offer only short-term employment, unemployment insurance benefits can prove to be very important to the writer.

The purpose of the California unemployment insurance program is to lessen a person's hardship when he becomes unemployed through no fault of his own. Unemployment insurance programs are beneficial not only to those who are unemployed but to society in general since they tend to stabilize, somewhat, the purchasing power of the unemployed. Unemployment insurance benefits, however, are not available to all those who are out of work involuntarily: persons who are performing services as "independent contractors" are deemed to be not covered under the benefit program. Unfortunately, many writers fall within this category. Writers working outside the motion picture and television industries may have difficulties establishing that they are eligible to receive unemployment insurance benefits. Writers who write novels or magazine articles are oftentimes considered to be independent contractors rather than employees and are therefore likely to be denied benefits when they are in between books or assignments. However, it should be remembered that it is impossible to state categorically that persons engaging in activities in these sectors of the writing profession are ineligible to receive benefits since the determination must be made on a case-by-case basis. The single most important factor in determining whether an employment relationship exists is the presence

of the right of the employer to control or direct the means by which work is accomplished. There have been times, however, when writers in fields other than the motion picture and television industries have been able to establish a right to unemployment insurance benefits. For example, a writer of freelance magazine articles in the San Francisco area, reportedly, was able to establish that the requisite "control" existed by showing that his publisher had the right to order changes in the literary manuscripts he prepared and had exercised this right. This particular case, however, does not set a precedent for all other freelance magazine writers.

Motion picture and television writers have for some time enjoyed the right to receive unemployment benefits by virtue of relevant case law and legislative enactments. Under the collective bargaining agreement currently in existence between the Writers Guild of America and the vast majority of television and motion picture producers, writers who are employed by these producers are deemed to be employees, and the minimum compensation payable to writers performing those writing services constitutes wages or salaries. This compensation is, therefore, subject to all state, federal and local laws relating to withholding. The only exception to this rule would be in the case of a writer who writes a screenplay on speculation and later sells it to a producer. He is not an employee and therefore the money received in payment for an option or purchase of literary material is not subject to withholding.

In the motion picture and television industries, unemployment insurance benefits may sustain the writer while he is between assignments, supplementing the incomes of even very well-established writers. Unemployment insurance can also provide weekly payments to writers who are actively seeking work but who are using their time in between

Alan Abrams, formerly Associate Resident Counsel to the Writers Guild of America, West, Inc., is now practicing law with the firm of Russell and Glickman in Century City specializing in the area of entertainment law.

assignments to prepare a script "on speculation." The following represent some of the special problems which these writers may face in the entertainment industry.

FREELANCE EMPLOYMENT

Writers in the entertainment industry, and especially the television industry, are oftentimes employed on a freelance or "flat deal" basis to prepare scripts. The writing of the particular script is done in stages. Commonly, a writer writes a story which is then delivered to the producer. The producer, who may have an option to employ the writer to prepare a teleplay based upon the story, has a certain limited period in which to review and to approve the story. Assuming that the story is approved, the writer will then be asked to prepare a first-draft teleplay. After delivery of the first-draft teleplay, the producer will review the teleplay and make certain requests for revisions or modifications of the teleplay which the writer will then incorporate into the finished final-draft teleplay. The actual periods of time between delivery of the story and commencement of the first-draft teleplay and delivery of the first draft and of the need for the writer's services to revise the teleplay will often vary depending upon the nature of the employment and sometimes the producer's schedule. The latter waiting period may last up to one month or longer in certain cases. This type of freelance employment, unlike week-to-week or term employment, poses special problems to the writer who wishes to receive unemployment insurance benefits.

Generally where the writer is engaged to write a story with option for teleplay, the producer has up to fourteen days after delivery of the story and in special types of employment sometimes longer, to decide whether or not to exercise his option and to engage the services of the writer in preparing a teleplay based upon the submitted story. During this waiting period, many writers make the mistake of assuming that because they are not working and receiving compensation while waiting for their options to be exercised, they are unemployed. That is clearly not the law. Writers are considered to be employed and hence ineligible for unemployment insurance benefits from the date the assignment is accepted until such time as the producer has no fur-

ther right to call upon the writer to perform services. Thus, when the writer turns in his story, if the producer has a fourteen-day period in which to exercise a teleplay option, the writer will be deemed to be employed and ineligible for benefits until that fourteen-day period expires and the producer has no further contractual right to the writer's services. This is also true of the idle periods between stages of the work when engagement consists of guaranteed employment in writing both story and two drafts of a teleplay.

Some writers learn this rule the hard way. If a benefit claim is made, and benefits are paid to the writer in error, the Department has the right to seek to recover from the writer the amount of any such overpayment. If the claimant can prove that the overpayment was not due to fraud, misrepresentation or willful nondisclosure on the part of the recipient, and that the overpayment was received without fault on his part and that its recovery would be against equity and good conscience, he is not responsible to repay the benefits. If the writer makes this mistake for more than one week, the amount for which he may be liable may constitute a considerable sum by the time the Department learns of the overpayments.

RESIDUALS OR "REUSE PAY"

Writers, like actors, may receive residuals for reuses of their literary materials. Receipt of these residuals will have a bearing upon a writer's eligibility to receive unemployment insurance benefits.

Residuals, or rerun or reuse pay, as they are sometimes called, are considered to be wages for past services performed and are thus reportable to the Department as wages earned during any weeks in which benefits would otherwise be payable. Thus, if you receive a residual in a given week which is in excess of the unemployment insurance benefits otherwise payable to you, you cannot receive unemployment insurance benefits for any week in which that residual was allocated.

The Writers Guild of America, generally speaking, administers the residuals payable to writers under the collective bargaining agreements it has negotiated. The practice is that the employer pays to the Guild the residual due the writer, and then that check is forwarded to either the writer or his designated agent. The Department will consider the residual to be wages payable with respect to the week in which either the check is mailed to the writer by the employer or the union or the week in which notice is mailed to the writer by the employer or union that the check is available, or the week in which notice is mailed to the writer by the employer or union that the check is available, or the week in which the check is actually given to the claimant without a prior notice being mailed. For purposes of unemployment insurance benefits, payment of the residual to the writer's agent or business manager will have the same effect as payment to the writer.

Again, a writer may become liable for any overpayment of benefits made because of an unreported residual payment received by the writer.

SELF-EMPLOYMENT

Many times writers will seek unemployment insurance benefits during the period in which they are preparing literary materials for future sale or use in the production of a motion picture or television film. These benefits can help finance the preparation of the work by providing to the writer a steady weekly check in between writing assignments.

In Benefit Decision 5650, it was held by the Unemployment Insurance Appeals Board that a writer who is engaged in the writing of literary materials for future sale is self-employed, and that these activities do not constitute the performance of "services" within the meaning of the Unemployment Insurance Code, and that accordingly, as the writer received no remuneration for this activity, he was unemployed and therefore eligible to receive unemployment insurance benefits.

OTHER PROBLEMS

Many times writers are confronted with special problems concerning their unemployment insurance benefits which the Department itself may not adequately be prepared to handle or to advise the writer-claimant about. Sometimes, the Legal Department of the Writers Guild of America, West, Inc. can help a writer who is having trouble receiving benefits. The phone number of the Writers Guild is included in this book in the Appendix. Other sources of helpful advice other than the Department itself would include the writer's agent or the writer's neighborhood legal aid society.

A NOTE ON BENEFITS

Under the California system, weekly benefits can be as high as $120 per week depending upon the claimant's prior wages. These benefits may continue for up to twenty-six weeks in the twelve-month period immediately following filing of the claim. This twenty-six-week limitation may from time to time be extended in periods of relatively high unemployment. For other particulars, such as eligibility requirements, the amount of the individual benefit award, filing procedures and appeal rights, the writer should consult the California Employment Development Department.

Appendix

Writers' Service Organizations

Ellen Binder

Throughout the United States, a multitude of literary service organizations exist to serve writers of every ilk. Some administer a variety of programs, ranging from loans and grants to business and legal advice. Others have a narrower scope. Although a majority are membership organizations serving their own limited constituencies, many have programs directed toward non-members as well. For the most part, membership organizations keep their annual dues relatively low. A few ask for initiation fees. Information on services and publications, as well as guidelines and applications for membership, when pertinent, can be obtained by writing an organization directly.

Following are brief descriptions of some of the more prominent national organizations. This list is by no means exhaustive. The names and addresses of other organizations can often be obtained by calling those listed here or by referring to literary directories such as *Literary Market Place* and *Writer's Market*. Regional and state literary organizations, which have a more limited outreach, are usually listed with state councils of the arts. It is also worthy to note that many organizations not classified as literary nonetheless have services or publications useful to writers. One of these, Theatre Communications Group, is listed below.

The American Society of Journalists and Authors, Inc., is a national membership organization of more than 650 professional freelance writers of nonfiction. The programs and services offered by ASJA are directed toward the professional business interests of independent writers and are available solely to members. Among these are a monthly newsletter containing confidential market information and current listings of competitions and awards, an exclusive referral service, and craft sessions and conferences. ASJA will also investigate and mediate editor-writer disputes, but only upon request. All members receive the ASJA Directory of members and Guidelines Brochure which includes ASJA Code of Ethics and Fair Practices. Both publications can be purchased by anyone seeking professional writers. Membership is open to any writer who meets ASJA's publication requirements. American Society of Journalists and Authors, Inc., 1501 Broadway, Suite 1907, New York, NY 10036; (212) 996-0947.

The *Authors Guild*, a corporate member of the Authors League (see page 196), is a professional association consisting of 6,000 authors, predominantly of trade books. The Guild's principal functions are to promote and protect the professional and business concerns of its members, such as contract terms and protection of subsidiary rights, and to keep its members informed on market trends and practices through its newsletter and discussions. The Guild provides members with a Recommended Trade Book Contract and Guide and will advise them on undesirable clauses in publishers' standard contracts. It will also attempt to persuade publishers to adopt Guild recommendations in contracts and royalty statements. The Guild does not act as legal counsel or literary agent. Various reference guides on copyrights and contracts prepared by the Guild are free and available to members only. Authors Guild, 234 West 44th St., New York, NY 10036 (212) 398-0838.

Ellen Binder is Associate Coordinator of PEN American Center's Freedom to Write Committee.

The *Authors League of America, Inc.* is a separate corporation whose membership is the joint membership of both the Authors and Dramatists Guilds. Through the League, Guild members act on matters of mutual concern to both writers and playwrights, such as tax legislation, copyright protection, and freedom of expression. The League also administers interest-free loans to professional, published writers needing financial assistance due to health or temporary emergencies. Authors League, 234 W. 44th St., New York, NY 10036; (212) 391-9198.

The *Dramatists Guild*, like the Authors Guild, is a corporate member of the Authors League (see above). A professional association of more than 3,500 playwrights, composers and lyricists, the Guild serves its members exclusively, securing fair contracts for them and advising them on individual business and professional concerns. The Guild's Minimum Basic Contract is used by its members to insure against script alterations and unfair casting, royalties and copyrights. The Dramatists Guild is not a union and thus does not bargain collectively, strike or enter into contracts that require use of members. The Guild's staff counsels members on specific business matters concerning options, taxes and other technical questions. Up-to-date information on grants, contests, agents and conferences are provided by its information service. The Guild's two publications, *Dramatist Guild Quarterly* and the Guild *Newsletter* also offer current information on marketing and the theatre in general. Guild-sponsored symposia and weekend workshops address various aspects of theatre and playwriting. There are three categories of membership: active, associate and subscribing. Dramatists Guild, 234 W. 44th St., New York, NY 10036; (212) 398-9366.

The *National Writers Club, Inc.*, is a membership organization of predominantly American freelance writers of fiction and non-fiction books and articles, and of television, stage and movie scripts. Its programs and publications are directed toward informing, assisting and protecting the business concerns of its members. NWC provides a personal consultation service to which members can bring individual difficulties ranging from where to market specific ideas to questions on avoiding libel. Members can bring more specific business problems, such as in negotiating with a publisher, to NWC's complaint service. With the writer's consent, NWC will intercede and, if needed, help the member acquire legal aid. **Writer** Research reports prepared by NWC

highlight such subjects as income tax, reading contracts and market surveys. NWC also holds workshops in various areas of the United States and sponsors five contests for fiction and non-fiction. All members receive three publications: *Authorship*, with listings on market places, collaborators and NWC events; the NWC *Newsletter* with information on news services and non-NWC workshops; and *Freelance Market Newsletter*. NWC has both associate and professional members. Only those seeking professional membership are required to hold specific writing credentials. National Writers Club, Inc., 1450 S. Havana, Suite 620, Aurora, CO 80012; (303) 751-7844.

PEN American Center is one of 82 centers that compose International PEN (poets, playwrights, editors, novelists and translators), a worldwide association of literary writers. Although American PEN is a membership organization of international scope, its programs and committees serve the national literary community. Loans and grants of up to $500 are provided to published writers in extreme financial need. PEN also administers four translation prizes and two awards for fiction. Among PEN's free pamphlets and brochures are *The Rights of the Translator* and *PEN Standards for Magazine and Periodical Assignments*. Publications such as *Grants and Awards Available to American Writers* and the quarterly *PENewsletter* provide information of general concern to the writing community. PEN's staff will provide writers with names and/or addresses of other organizations and reference works. Public panel discussions and conferences on problems and trends in publishing, translation and playwriting, as well as PEN-sponsored readings, are free. PEN is also actively involved in promoting freedom of expression and the press and researches and publishes reports on restriction of the same. Candidates for membership must be nominated, either by a member or by themselves, and must meet specific publication requirements. PEN American Center, 47 5th Ave., New York, NY 10003; (212) 255-1977.

Poets & Writers, Inc., a non-profit, non-membership organization serves primarily as a clearinghouse for information concerning literary activity nationwide. While its focus is on literary writers, its services and publications are pertinent and available to other writers. Its Information Center contains files with up-to-date information (addresses, publications, minority affiliations, etc.) on nearly 5,000 American writers. Any writer who meets the organization's basic publishing requirements can apply to be listed. No fee is charged. From this listing, the organization compiles and publishes annually *A Directory of American Poets and Writers*. Among P&W's other publications: *CODA*, a subscription newsletter highlighting news on jobs, taxes and grants and awards; a *Writers Guide to Copyright*; a complete guide on literary agents; a pamphlet listing 606 national organizations that sponsor programs involving writers; and reprints from *CODA* with information pertinent to writers, such as those on income taxes and wills. While publications can be purchased by anyone, listed writers do receive discounts. P&W Readings/Workshops program matches funds for events sponsored by non-profit organizations and held in New York state, although expansion to a nationwide program is projected. Only writers listed with the organization are eligible to receive fee payments for readings. Poets & Writers, 201 W. 54th St., New York, NY 10019; (212) 757-1766.

The *Theatre Communications Group, Inc.*, is a national organization which services professional, non-profit theatre. While its constituency is made up of individual theatre groups, artists, technicians and administrators, TCG publishes a directory valuable to scriptwriters of every medium. *Information for Playwrights* describes membership and services organizations, publications and conferences of interest to playwrights, fellowships, grants, contests and loan sources. The directory also contains an extended list of non-profit, professional theatres nationwide seeking unsolicited manuscripts. An expansion of TCG's literary service department is projected. Theatre Communications Group, 355 Lexington Ave., New York, NY 10017; (212) 697-5230.

Directory of Writers' Service Organizations

compiled by
Gregory T. Victoroff, Esq.

GUILDS, UNIONS AND ASSOCIATIONS

Below is a list of writers' membership organizations nationwide.

American Guild of Authors
and Composers—AGAC
6430 Sunset Blvd., Suite 1113
Los Angeles, CA 90028
(213) 462-1108

American Society of
Journalists and Authors
1501 Broadway, Suite 1907
New York, NY 10036
(212) 997-0947

Authors Guild, Inc.
234 West 44th Street
New York, NY 10036
(212) 398-0838

Authors League of
America, Inc.
234 West 44th Street
New York, NY 10036
(212) 391-9198

Gregory T. Victoroff is an attorney practicing with the law firm of Johnson and Lang in Los Angeles with an emphasis in entertainment and copyright law. He received his B.A. and teaching certification in Theatre Arts from Beloit College in 1975 and his J.D. from the Cleveland-Marshall College of Law in 1979. He is the author of The Artists Resource Directory for Greater Los Angeles.

Canadian Authors Association
Box 3681, Station C
Ottawa, Ontario
Canada K1Y 4J8

Caucus for Producers,
Writers & Directors
760 North La Cienega Blvd.
Los Angeles, CA 90069
(213) 652-0222

Dramatists Guild, Inc.
234 West 44th Street
New York, NY 10036
(212) 398-9366

PEN American Center
47 5th Avenue
New York, NY 10003
(212) 255-1977

International Womens
Writing Guild
Box 810
Gracie Station
New York, NY 10028
(212) 737-7536

National League of American
Pen Women—Hawaii Branch
404 Piikoi, Room 218
Honolulu, HI 96814

National League of American
Pen Women—Santa Cruz Branch
100 North Rodeo Gulch Road #63
Soquel, CA 95073

National Writers Club
1450 South Havana
Suite 620
Aurora, CO 80012

Poets and Writers, Inc.
201 W. 54th Street
New York, NY 10019
(212) 757-1766

Society of Children's Book Writers
Box 296
Los Angeles, CA 90066

Society of Children's Book
Writers—Rocky Mountain Chapter
1901 Arapahoe Drive
Longmont, CO 80501

Southeastern Writers
Association, Inc.
3400 East Evans Mill Court
Lithonia, GA 30058

Story Analysts,
Local 854
7715 Sunset Blvd.
Los Angeles, CA 90046
(213) 876-1600

Theatre Communications Group, Inc.
355 Lexington Avenue
New York, NY 10017
(212) 697-5230

The Word Guild
119 Mount Auburn Street
Cambridge, MA 02138
(617) 492-4656

Writers Guild of
America, East
22 West 48th Street
New York, NY 10036
(212) 575-5060

Writers Guild of
America, West
8955 Beverly Blvd.
Los Angeles, CA 90048
(213) 550-1000

LEGAL ASSISTANCE AND INFORMATION

These organizations provide lawyer referrals, legal information and volunteer lawyers to writers and others in the arts. Publications are also available.

Bay Area Lawyers for the
Arts—BALA
Building B, Room 310
Fort Mason Center
San Francisco, CA 94123
(415) 775-7200

Committee for the Arts
Beverly Hills Bar
Association Barristers
300 South Beverly Drive
Beverly Hills, CA 90212
(213) 556-1598

Lawyers for the
Creative Arts
220 South State Street
Chicago, IL
(312) 987-0198

Volunteer Lawyers for
the Arts
36 West 44th Street
Suite 1110
New York, NY 10036
(212) 575-1150

RESEARCH AND REFERENCE

Here is a list of groups that are helpful in the informational and reference phases of the creative process. Additionally, many colleges and universities offer courses and workshops in TV and film writing. Contact schools in your area for specific details.

Academy of Motion Picture
Arts and Sciences (library)
8949 Wilshire Blvd.
Los Angeles, CA
(213) 278-4313

American Film Institute Center
for Advanced Film Study—AFI
2021 N. Western
Hollywood, CA 90027
(213) 856-7600

Drama Book Shop
150 W. 52nd Street
New York, NY
(212) 582-1037

Dramatists Play Service
440 Park Avenue
New York, NY 10016
(212) 683-8960

Larry Edmonds Bookstore
6658 Hollywood Blvd.
Los Angeles, CA
(213) 463-3273

Los Angeles Public Library
Art, Music & Recreation Dept.
630 West 5th Street
Los Angeles, CA 90071
(213) 626-7461

Media Alliance
Building D, Room 310
Fort Mason Center
San Francisco, CA 94123
(415) 397-4449

Poets and Writers, Inc.
201 West 54th Street
New York, NY 10019
(212) 757-1766

Samuel French, Inc.
7623 Sunset Blvd.
Los Angeles, CA 90046
(213) 876-0570

Sherwood Oaks Experimental College
1445 North Las Palmas
Los Angeles, CA 90028
(213) 462-0669

Society for the Preservation
of Variety Arts, Inc.
940 South Figueroa Street
Los Angeles, CA 90015
(213) 623-9100

Tams-Witmark Music Library, Inc.
757 3rd Avenue
New York, NY 10017
(212) 688-2525

University of California,
Los Angeles—UCLA
Extension Office
10995 Le Conte Blvd.
Los Angeles, CA 90024
(213) 825-8895

University of California
Extension Center
55 Laguna Street
San Francisco, CA 94102
(415) 552-3016

University of California,
Los Angeles—UCLA
Theatre Arts Library
University Research Library
405 Hilgard Avenue
Los Angeles, CA 90024
(213) 825-4880

Writers Digest Books
9933 Alliance Road
Cincinnati, OH 45242
(513) 984-0717

Selected Bibliography

compiled by
Gregory T. Victoroff, Esq.

Applebaum, Judith, and Evans, Nancy. *How to Get Happily Published*. New York: Harper & Row, 1978.

Ashley, Paul P., and Hall, Camden H. *Say It Safely: Legal Limits in Publishing, Radio and Television*. Seattle: University of Washington Press, 1976.

Balkin, Richard. *A Writer's Guide to Book Publishing*. New York: Hawthorn, 1977.

Baumgarten, Paul A., and Farber, Donald C. *Producing, Financing and Distributing Film*. New York: Drama Book Specialists, 1973. A provision by provision analysis of motion picture contracts.

Bluem, William, and Squire, Jason E. *The Movie Business*. New York: Hastings House, 1972. A collection of articles by prominent producers, directors, writers, agents, distributors, etc.

Blum, Richard A. *Television Writing from Concept to Contract*. New York: Hastings House, 1980.

Coopersmith, Jerome. *Professional Teleplay/Screenplay Format*. New York: The Writers Guild of America, East, 1970

Crawford, Tad. *The Writers Legal Guide*. New York: Hawthorn, 1977. Good background in various legal areas, mostly for writers of books.

Farber, Donald C. *From Option to Opening*. New York: Drama Book Specialists, 1977. Theatre, mostly from the producer's (and his lawyer's) perspective.

Field, Syd. *Screenplay*. New York: Dell, 1979. Useful information on the form and the art of screenwriting.

Lindey, Alexander. *Entertainment, Publishing, and the Arts*. New York: Clark Boardman Co. Ltd., 1963, Supp. 1975. A hefty lawyer's treatise, yet quite understandable. Available at law libraries.

Nimmer, Melville. *Nimmer on Copyright*. Albany: Bender, 1978. A four-volume treatise which is the recognized authority. Available at law libraries.

Register of Copyrights. *Copyright Information Kit*. Copyright Office, Library of Congress, Washington, D.C. 20559. Send for this kit for complete instructions on registering your copyright.

Schemenaur, Peggy, ed. *Writer's Market*. Cincinnati: Writer's Digest Books, perennial. A directory of where to send your work.

Shanks, Bob. *The Cool Fire—How to Make It in Television*. New York: Vintage Books, 1977. Excellent overview of the business from a producer's point of view.

What Is the Committee for the Arts?

This book, and the Third Annual Artists Symposium: For Writers in conjunction with which this book was conceived and published, are the products of merely one facet of the work of the Committee for the Arts (CFTA). CFTA is an ongoing project of the Barristers (young lawyers division) of the Beverly Hills Bar Association, a non-profit organization.

CFTA was formed early in 1978 when approximately 30 young lawyers and artists had a series of meetings to discuss how to satisfy the needs of struggling artists and entertainers in the Los Angeles area for affordable, first-rate legal counseling. As enthusiasm for undertaking this project spread among artists and lawyers and as ideas for starting the project began to take concrete form, the Beverly Hills Bar Association quickly embraced CFTA and threw its considerable support behind the project.

CFTA began with two broad objectives: first, to provide educational and informational services relating to the interface of arts and law to both lawyers and artists, and, second, to provide art-related legal services to individual artists, entertainers and arts organizations, whatever their financial means might be. CFTA's working membership grew rapidly, and it spawned several subcommittees, whose work is briefly outlined below, to take a more specific focus on those broad objectives.

The Symposium Subcommittee was formed to produce annual, all-day symposiums, each for a particular type of artist or entertainer (e.g., actors, painters, writers, and musicians), in which well-known professionals working in the subject area would present a series of lectures, panel discussions and workshops on the practical, legal and business aspects of working within that area. The Symposium Subcommittee is also responsible for publishing a reference work, such as this one, in conjunction with each such symposium.

The Legal Services Subcommittee worked for well over a year to establish a lawyer referral service which provides first-rate, free or affordable legal services specifically to artists and entertainers working in the Los Angeles area. Legal services are furnished on a free, low-cost or negotiated-fee basis, depending on the client's ability to pay, which is determined by a simple screening process. The problems handled include contract negotiation and drafting, copyright matters and any other arts- or entertainment-related problem, excluding litigation.

The Community Outreach Subcommittee was established to serve the same educational function as is being served by the Symposium Subcommittee, but on a smaller, more personal scale. It sends attorneys to meet with arts organizations at their headquarters in the Los Angeles area to present lectures and workshops on legal topics selected by those organizations and their members as being of interest to them. The topics are not limited to "arts law," but include any topic directly related to the artist's ability to engage in his profession, such as taxation, zoning ordinances and laws relating to non-profit organizations, to name just a few.

The Council for the Disabled in the Arts is a subcommittee composed of both disabled and able-bodied artists and attorneys. It is at the vanguard of a growing movement to foster awareness of and compliance with the legal rights of the disabled, to assure the accurate portrayal of disabled persons in motion pictures and television, and to integrate disabled artists into the mainstream of all facets of motion picture and television production. To this end, it has provided consulting services to the networks and the major studios on matters relative to the disabled and is encouraging the developing of programs to provide training and experience sufficient to develop employable skills among the disabled in the entertainment and arts industries. CODA has become a clearinghouse for a wide variety of information concerning the disabled and the entertainment industry.

The Finance Subcommittee works to provide necessary funds for the development and continuation of all substantive activities of CFTA. It seeks grants from foundations and governmental agencies that support the arts and/or public-interest legal programs, and organizes and promotes fund-raising events in the Los Angeles area such as motion picture premieres and "gala events."

The opportunity to experience works of art undeniably benefits every individual in our community. The majority of those in our community who enjoy the vast array of art forms available to them never realize how difficult the road is for a young artist/entertainer to have his or her creations displayed to the public in any medium or forum. Even when the artist/entertainer, after numerous trials and tribulations, has attained public exposure and, perhaps, public recognition, that does not mean that he or she has been fairly compensated for all of the time and effort which has gone into achieving that public exposure or recognition. The public interest, as seen by CFTA, will be well served by fostering in the artists/entertainers of the greater Los Angeles area an awareness of the legal fabric in which their artistic endeavors are intertwined and by providing them with the access to affordable legal services. Our hope is that an informed arts community will have the foresight and knowledge to command fair treatment from the businesses they help to create. We will all reap the rewards.

Index